Sofka Zinovieff trained as an anthropologist and has worked as a journalist. She lives in Athens. This is her first book.

'An account of an Englishwoman's first year in Athens and a beguiling picture of "becoming Greek"' *Traveller Magazine*

'As an anthropologist, the author observes the process with an objective eye; as a wife and mother, it's nothing less than total immersion ... here is the inside track on what it means to be Greek: a lovely book, full of poetry, history and insights. Aspiring Shirley Valentines ... shouldn't leave home without it' *Daily Mail*

'This is an insightful account of a chaotic and exhilarating city, where the writer had personal as well as cultural obstacles to overcome' *Daily Telegraph*

'A witty and engaging account of life in Athens ... at points the pitch of her narrative rises from that of personal memoir and catches something more elevated' *Economist*

EURYDICE STREET

A Place in Athens

Sofka Zinovieff

Granta Books
London

Granta Publications
2/3 Hanover Yard, Noel Road, London N1 8BE

First published in Great Britain by Granta Books 2004
This edition printed by Granta Books 2005

Typeset by M Rules

Printed and bound in Great Britain by
Bookmarque Limited, Croydon, Surrey

To Vassilis, Anna and Lara

Με αγάπη

ACKNOWLEDGEMENTS

So many people helped in different ways with this book, and I am grateful to them all.

My dear friend Adam Nicolson gave generously from the time when it was all still an idea.

I am indebted to all the people mentioned in the book (a few of whom have had their names changed), but especially to: Stelios Kouloglou, Christos Papadimitriou, Stella Papadimitriou, and Panayiotis Mavropoulos. My daughters, Anna and Lara, turned out to be magnificent research assistants. Many others gave their time to help me understand more about my adopted country. They are: Evthymios Papataxiarchis, Maria Kokkinou, Andreas Kourkoulas, Panos Samouris, Gregory Vallianatos, Eleni Miami, Hercules Millas, Rena Sourouni and Father Alexander Fostiropoulos. Ευχαριστώ.

I am eternally grateful to Mark Dragoumis, Rachel Howard and Yanis Varoufakis for their readings of the whole text, and their intelligent, questioning and illuminating comments. Kyril Zinovieff gave inspiration and good advice throughout. Huge thanks also to my agent, Caroline Dawnay, for her support.

I feel very lucky in having had George Miller as my wonderful, clever, encouraging editor.

To dearest Vassilis, thanks are not enough.

Greece and its neighbours

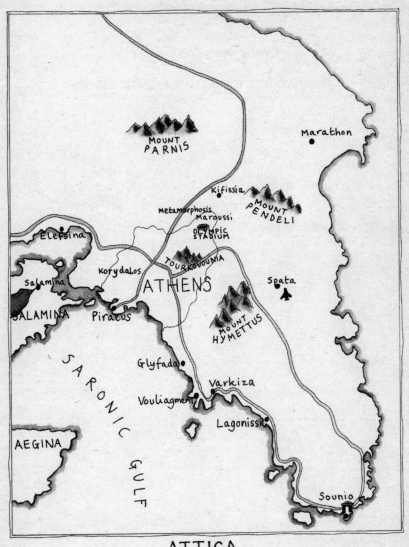

ATTICA

Come home to Greece!

CONTENTS

CHAPTER 1

SCORCHED EARTH

'Love has led me here, Love, a god all powerful with us who dwell on the earth ...'
Orpheus in the underworld, pleading with Hades and Persephone for his wife.

Thomas Bulfinch, *Bulfinch's Mythology: The Age of Fable*

The new highway to Athens was like a soft, steaming slick of black treacle. We had just driven off the ferry in Patras, and the air conditioning in the car was broken. It felt as though we were being roasted alive in a tin can. I wanted some sort of sign that we had arrived – a band at the port to mark the historic moment of starting a new life. Here we were, returning to the country we loved, and it all seemed wrong. I tried not to show my sense of anti-climax, but Vassilis, my husband, looked weary too.

1

'Well, we've just come to the country which invented tragedy,' he said drily, putting his hand over mine in a gesture of solidarity. We looked out at the stretches of charred, stinking hillside on either side of the road, where forest fires had been raging. Only the olive trees had survived the devastating scorching, their dense, twisted wood mysteriously blessed with the power to protect them from flames.

We turned on the radio. A strong, low, female voice was pouring out her torments in a song:

Torture, torture, every embrace . . . I grew up like Greece, in doubt and rags.

Anna and Lara, our daughters, were now too tired to even complain, and had flopped into a sweaty, lethargic heap with the dog on the back seat.

It was early evening by the time we arrived at our new home – a maisonette in Vouliagmeni, a suburb of Athens whose name means 'sunken'. Our removal lorry was due to arrive the next day, and we spent our first night on Lilos in the empty apartment. It was early July but it felt like deepest August. Police sirens, dogs and car alarms howled somewhere in the darkness. Outside the window an automatic watering system hissed on and off. It was spraying our neighbour's small manicured lawn, which he had fought against Greece's nature to create in his rocky patch of hillside garden. Suburbs, lawns, maisonettes. Was this the new Greece?

Ever since I met Vassilis, we'd dreamed about going to live in Greece. Now that it was actually happening, though, I was afraid it might turn out to be what it had always been: a fantasy. For Vassilis it was a homecoming to his fatherland and mother tongue after many years abroad. For me it was like a return to first love; the ground was less sure and the roots less deep. Greece had captured my imagination as a student, but no matter how much I embraced it, I'd always be an outsider.

Athenian friends had told us we were mad to want to bring up our children where they were bringing up theirs.

'Greece is good for holidays but not for living,' they said. 'It's impossible to work, and it's unbearably hot.' I recalled various British friends who just thought that Athens was hideous and polluted. They imagined it would be hard for me to continue working as a freelance journalist in a Balkan back of beyond. The dream had already begun to look more like a nightmare.

Before our move, we had gone to Athens on a house-hunting trip. Like increasing numbers of Athenian families, we'd decided to resist the pull of the centre and go for the suburbs; it was a chance to live near the sea, and to give our children some space and fresh air after years of urban existence. I risked sounding foolish, and told the estate agents that my ideal home would be something old. I didn't add that I was picturing a slightly dilapidated little neoclassical villa, with a garden full of lemon and fig trees, because I knew such a thing was practically non-existent. One agent replied most positively.

'Yes, we have something old. It's in a block that was built at least nine years ago.'

Athens may be an ancient city, but it is also uncompromisingly modern. And there's hardly anything else in between the two extremes. It's almost as though the Athenians went straight from carved marble to reinforced concrete, skipping the intervening centuries. Few people live in a building which is old, and out by the sea where we were looking, many homes were barely finished.

Searching for somewhere to rent quickly got depressing. We enjoyed the fireplaces disguised as the Parthenon and the plaster caryatids and classical columns that were scattered around brand new houses like icing sugar decorations on wedding cakes. And we laughed about the ubiquitous and horrible, dungeon-like room known euphemistically in Greek as the *playroom*. But we didn't want to live in these places. Friends from the more traditional, inland suburbs of Kifissia, Maroussi and Psychiko, in northern Athens, were sardonic. They told us pointedly that the seaside areas we were exploring were especially popular with ex-basketball players, the nouveaux riches, and Russian mafiosi. We'd never get through a winter there, they said.

Athens's new areas have frilled out around the edges like a skin disease. Aerial maps of even a decade ago show the coastline to the south of the city as including great expanses of open hillside on the tail-end of Mount Hymettus. Now the land was covered with the wound-like cuts of new roads and construction sites, and one built-up suburb followed another. There was an incongruous and bewildering collection of cheap, speculative developments mixed with the expensive 'dream houses' of people who didn't know whether their dream was a Swiss chalet, a Mexican hacienda or the White House.

Just as we were becoming despondent, an agent took us to Eurydice Street in Vouliagmeni – Athens's version of a Riviera, about eighteen kilometres to the south of the centre. *Evrydiki* (as the name is in Greek) led, predictably perhaps, to Orpheus – a street making a vertiginous descent to the sea, if not the underworld. We climbed up a long and steep flight of external steps past several interlocking apartments cut into the rocky hillside, until we arrived at the last one. On one side of the *mezonetta* (maisonette) was a gateway giving onto the open hill, which was covered in spring flowers. On the other, a spacious terrace surveyed what looked like half of Greece.

It didn't seem to matter that the flat was new, dull and badly laid out, with too many small rooms on too many levels. In fact we hardly bothered to look around. We just gazed transfixed, across the small, strangely tropical bay at the bottom of the hill, and the surrounding palm trees and sandy beaches. Beyond the bay was the wide expanse of the Saronic Gulf, with its distant traffic of boats leaving for the islands and returning to the port at Piraeus.

Over to the north we could see the sprawling lower end of the Athens basin, capped with a delicately lilac-tinged mist.

'Is that the *nephos*?' I asked Vassilis, referring to the horrible noxious cloud that had plagued the Athenian atmosphere for years. It sometimes combined with summer heat to produce air so heavily poisoned that you could wake up in the morning and feel as though you'd just smoked a packet of cigarettes in an engine room.

'No, the *nephos* has practically disappeared now,' replied Vassilis optimistically. 'That's just a haze. But look, come here.' He held on to my shoulder, and stretched his arm out in front, pointing at something in the massive, urban cluster.

'Can you see that little lump sticking up on the horizon?' he asked. 'It's the Acropolis.' Somehow it was ludicrously pleasing.

The sun was going down like a great blood orange slipping behind the mountains of the Peloponnese. If a film had shown these colours I'd have thought the cameraman was cheating with filters ('a bit more vermilion over there, and add some tangerine glow to the water'). Directly opposite this irresistible eagle's nest of a terrace I identified Aegina, the island where my mother became engaged to my father at the age of seventeen. Her mother was supposedly chaperoning her on the holiday, but was content to let her teenage daughter be swept up by a 'mad Russian' ten years her senior. A few months later my parents were married in London's Russian Orthodox Church. Crowns were placed over their heads, and the beautiful child-bride's veil caught fire from one of the tall candles. Like the sinister bird flying over at Orpheus and Eurydice's nuptials, this was thought to be an omen.

My parents did separate, but not before they had produced three children. I was the first, born the year after they were married. When I was three days old, a mysterious telegram arrived for me at the Royal Northern Hospital in Holloway. It read: 'Welcome Eurydice,' and was signed: 'Orpheus'. Later, when a Russian Orthodox priest submerged me in the baptismal font, I was named after my grandmother, with a second name in honour of Orpheus' tragic, snake-bitten wife.

As a child I learned of my father's fascination with the mystifying, shamanic bard. He even wrote an epic and wildly complex libretto for an opera called *The Mask of Orpheus*. I used to sit in his work room, painting characters and episodes out of the myth, still half-believing that my first telegram had come directly from Hades or Lesbos, or wherever Orpheus had ended up after he was torn apart by the Maenads, the crazed and promiscuous female followers of Dionysus. Later, I started to appreciate how the myth contains many of the most dramatic human emotions, which I saw lived out with an extra degree of intensity in Greece. It is no chance that Orpheus' tragedy has been dramatized so much, with its compelling, universal elements of erotic love, accidental death, desire, grief, the ruthlessness of the gods, and the power of music.

Vassilis and I agreed that the view and the address were both too good to miss. Eurydice Street was like another welcome for me; it was a return to the enormous, bright skies of a living Greece, which the elusive, original Eurydice never managed, after Orpheus made his fatal mistake of looking back to see if she was following him out of the underworld. But if I was getting romantic about mythological associations, the agent was quick to bring me down to earth. The realities of renting somewhere in Athens involve an annoyingly predictable degree of financial intrigue, and we had found that even the agents were playing games with us, trying out outrageously hiked-up prices to test the level of our gullibility. They all explained that we would 'of course' declare one amount on the contract and pay twice as much rent to the landlord. 'It's what everyone does.'

* * *

Our first weeks in Eurydice Street were spent in a sort of limbo. Vassilis's brother and three sisters turned up in the first days, heroically helping us unpack our stuff and put up shelves. They got annoyed when I thanked them. It goes without saying that family help you and that you would do the same; if you say thank you it cancels out the natural obligation and is almost insulting. After they left, we collapsed in a stupor. It was so hot we could hardly move.

Most of our Athenian friends were away on holiday, and we didn't even bother to look up the others. We didn't go exploring either, just managing to make the odd foray out for provisions or to buy a fridge. It was like being in quarantine, almost as though we hadn't arrived at all. We spent hours during the scalding middle part of the day shut in a darkened bedroom, lying naked on the bed, with the air conditioning blowing a cold, dry wind. Anna and Lara sprawled about watching daytime television. As nine- and six-year-olds they were just the right age to develop a taste for the outrageously melodramatic Mexican and Brazilian soap operas dubbed into Greek. Despondently, I recalled the fantasy that now looked pathetic – that my daughters would evolve into the wholesome-looking Greek teenagers you see on school outings, gathered happily around a guitar, singing nostalgic songs.

Every so often, there was a fire on the hills in our region, though fortunately none that spread too badly. Two chubby yellow planes would circle over our house, before swooping down to sea level. They looked like something Noddy might fly, as they skimmed the surface to scoop up water, and returned to the burning hill to drop their liquid cargo. But it wasn't funny. The media reports came far too frequently describing areas which had been burned by unscrupulous developers, who hoped that protected woodland would become available for building if it were treeless.

At the end of the day, when the air cooled, we'd mooch down to the sea for a swim. Lara and Anna were fascinated by the entwined couples who lay kissing on the beach, or wallowing a little way out to sea.

'Love spot,' they shrieked, pointing and giggling, each time they located one.

In the evenings we ate takeaway pizzas on our terrace, and then slept fitfully. Sometimes, I woke up to find Vassilis's feet near my face; he explained that he'd been trying to get as close as possible to the window for some air. I wasn't sure whether it was the heat or the move which was more overwhelming; either way, there's no disillusionment like having a dream come true.

It was in this state of dislocation that I started wondering what it was that attracted me to this country in the first place. As a young child I imagined Greece to be something like the scenes in my evocative story books by H. E. Bates, featuring Achilles the donkey, who escapes from his brutal owner and ends up with a loving, island family. The marvellous illustrations incorporated some Greek writing (in shop signs and graffiti), and I was attracted by the exotic, unintelligible letters, sensing that they somehow marked Greece as being different from other foreign places.

These images of a rural idyll were supplemented by my father who made various trips to Greece over the years. His travels were usually child- and wife-free as they tended to involve complicated romantic intrigues or strenuous walks around the male-only monasteries of Mount Athos. He'd come back laden with alien and intriguing objects: kitsch, tin-framed icons, aluminium pots, boxes of island-blue powder paint, rag rugs, and food that was still unfamiliar in the London of the early 1970s – bags of dark, purple olives and wedges of sweet, sticky halva.

I had certainly never thought of Greece as my destiny. In fact if I'd been a less wayward student, I suppose I might have ended up married to a Nepali and be writing a book about life in Kathmandu. In the mid-1980s, my tutor at Cambridge suggested that I follow in his footsteps and carry out my doctoral research in an isolated nunnery up a mountain in Nepal. He agreed that my boyfriend could go too and live in a monastery on another mountain. It sounded novel. I began to read books about Himalayan society, until, one day, I realized that I couldn't do it. I was sitting in a small Formica booth in the university 'language labs', headphones clamped to my ears, trying to reproduce the strange, nasal twangs and tone changes of Nepali. But my stomach was tied up in knots, and I felt sick.

In a wildly uninformed and instinctive volte-face, I decided that what I really wanted was to go and live by the sea in the Mediterranean. I scraped together a new plan, which didn't involve nuns, and with little justification (and feeling slightly fraudulent) plumped on an investigation of the ravages of tourism and social change on an unspecified but beautiful town in Greece. Thankfully, my tutor was sympathetic, and I ended up spending three years in Nafplio – an elegant, Italianate port in the Peloponnese. I arrived there with the English boyfriend who had considered coming to Nepal, but the relationship was doomed. The beginning of my joyful and intense love affair with

Greece eclipsed everything else, and especially anything to do with England, which I rejected with the ease of a rebellious teenager.

England came to represent constant grey skies, the oppression of background and class, dysfunctional families, and tense intro-spection. I colluded with Greek friends to create an image of my country as a sort of Dickensian, fog-bound place, and Greece as a land where the sunny skies reflected personal freedoms and passions, and where families loyally nurtured their old and their young. In spring, the air around Nafplio smelled overpoweringly of orange blossom from its legendary citrus groves, and it was entirely appropriate to my state of mind that I could watch the sun setting behind the mountains of Arcadia. These unrealistic stereotypes may have missed the point, but the sentiments were real. Each step I took deeper into the Greek language seemed not only to take me into a new world, but to make me into a new person. Now, rereading my 'field diaries' I am intrigued. Somewhere there, between the traipsing house visits, dutiful note-taking, the all-night partying, and a love affair, I was being transformed.

By the time I finished my Ph.D. I was confused; I knew I didn't want to be an academic, but I didn't know where I belonged any more. I decided to fulfil a lifelong desire, and travel to Russia to see where my paternal grandparents had lived in St Petersburg. I was also writing an article about the plight of the Pontian (Black Sea) Greeks. Like other persecuted minorities in what was still the Soviet Union, they were desperate to leave. Although many couldn't even speak their ancestral language, they were willing to try anything to get to what they imagined would be a welcoming motherland.

On a sunny June morning in 1990, I arrived at the Greek Embassy in Moscow. I had an appointment to interview the

Consul, and had to push my way through a sea of unhappy Pontians who were clinging to the railings, shouting and pleading for visas. I stood awkwardly in the courtyard, taking photographs of the scene and waiting. The Consul didn't arrive. It was at this point that the Press Attaché emerged from the little pastel-tinted palace that housed the Embassy. With hindsight it is annoying that I didn't realize instantly that my future stood in front of me. Fortunately, Vassilis did, and before I left, he managed to extract my phone number in England. Later that summer, Vassilis arrived in London, and it didn't take long to convince me. By the autumn, I had returned to Moscow, this time with my snow boots. The country of my ancestors had pulled me in through the back door, using someone from my adopted country as a lure.

After eleven years living together in Moscow, London and Rome, Vassilis and I were finally returning to Greece. It was not only a changed country; we were changed people. Vassilis had gone to study in Venice aged nineteen, and had only spent two of the last twenty-three years in the land of his birth. Anna and Lara had only come here on holiday. I'd often felt myself a kind of honorary Greek; Vassilis and I have usually spoken Greek together, and arriving in Greece I always feel a physical lurch of excitement – a sense of coming home. This time, though, I was out of kilter, floundering between the different versions of 'my' Greece, and looking suspiciously (and humiliatingly) like the foreign wives I used to pity with condescension in my student days.

CHAPTER 2

PLUNGING IN

I find it very moving to write sky, sea, moon as they were written by Sappho and Pindar, and as they continue to be said by the people today.

Odysseus Elytis

In August we did what most Athenians do; we left. The docks at Piraeus were heaving with people, and we pushed and jostled along with everyone else to get onto the boat to Patmos. Had it not been for the rubber dinghies and surfboards on the roof racks, one could almost have imagined that this was a swarming mass of refugees taking flight. Shops pulled down the shutters, businesses were closed, and even building work was halted. By mid-August only migrants, tourists, waiters and burglars were left in the capital. Everyone else was on holiday or had left for the festivities held on the days around 15 August, celebrating the *Panayia*, the 'All Holy' Mother of God.

The weeks spent on Patmos restored some equilibrium. The austerely beautiful landscape of bare, rocky hills and small, stony beaches was buffeted by the summer winds. The cool, dark Aegean water refreshed us, and our simple routines provided a return to the essentials. During the day, we read and swam and picked warm, plump figs from the trees. In the evenings, we met up with friends and ate at beach tavernas. The night skies were enormous and brilliantly clear; I had forgotten the joy of looking up into the deep darkness, unpolluted by any urban, orange glare. Sometimes, we would sleep outside on the terrace, watching the glittering galaxies as they were streaked by flitting, black bats and burning shooting stars.

We returned to Vouliagmeni on 1 September – the dog-end of the summer. It may have been the season of plenty and the time of the grape harvest, but the desiccated landscape looked exhausted. The hills were covered with spiky, skeletal bushes. In the past, this day was said to be the start of the New Year, the point when the Angel of Death wrote down the names of people who would die within the coming twelve months. The holidays were over, the days were shortening, and in spite of the heat, people were already wishing each other 'Good Winter!' As a child, I was told that September is a time of melancholy, when the year starts its annual death, but I'd seen that it is often the month for new beginnings. I hoped that this second arrival would prove more auspicious than the first.

Vassilis and I took Anna and Lara to their first day at the local primary school, walking there through the quiet roads of Vouliagmeni. The streets bear the names of ancient heroes, gods and nymphs: Jason, Aphrodite, Thalia, the Muses. There was a smell of salt, pine and jasmine. Smiling nervously at each other, absorbed in our unspoken fears, we hung around in the crowded school yard, our elongated shadows from the low morning sun stretching out on the tarmac. It emerged that there were not going to be any proper lessons for the first days; time is needed to get over the shock of going back to school. That morning there was just a blessing ceremony.

The headmaster greeted everyone by shouting at the parents to step away from their offspring, and a dour Orthodox priest arrived, wearing heavy ceremonial robes, a long headdress, and an impressive crucifix. He looked hot as he joined the teachers, the headmaster and the mayor, on a raised walkway. The 250 children below began crossing themselves mechanically, and reciting some prayers.

'I am going to tell you the worst sin of all,' the priest announced somewhat dramatically. It sounded promising, until he revealed that rather than murder, stealing or adultery, it was in fact 'wasting your time'. Then, taking a bunch of basil dipped in holy water, he flopped it on each teacher's head (to the delight of their pupils), and flicked it nonchalantly across the assembled ranks, watching deadpan as the children squealed and jumped about. Vassilis had a strange expression on his face, combining mirth, shock and resignation.

'I don't believe it,' he whispered. 'Nothing has changed since I started school thirty-five years ago.'

Greek children are deeply familiar with these rituals; they were acting them out all across the country that day. The symbols are the tangible signs of being Greek, and are heavily weighted with historical significance. Not only popular with nationalists and the devout, they are widely approved of by a people who fear that their identity and character as Greeks may be washed away by the flood of globalization. For my daughters, though, this was a far more extreme rite of passage than the beginning of the school year. It looked as though they would have to go through a bewildering free-fall from the familiar, maternal nest of English language and schooling, if they were going to find their wings in their father's country. What used to look merely picturesque suddenly appeared much riskier (and suspiciously fundamentalist) now that my children were involved; I thought fondly of the bland political correctness in British schools.

The headmaster barked some instructions, and the pupils turned like an unruly battalion, to face the seaside stripes of the blue and white Greek flag. Suddenly, they were bellowing out the National Anthem – a highly charged hymn to the fierce-edged sword of Liberty, and the freedom which sprang from Greeks' sacred bones. Anna and Lara both turned around to catch my eye with looks of utter incomprehension.

'What are we doing here?'

The clear, blue skies in Athens that day looked remarkably like those above New York, which we saw later on television, as they filled with smoke, dust clouds and death. It was a glimpse of hell; a new form of terror which gave us images for nightmares, and fantasies for disasters. Aeroplanes flying over Attica became sinister machines which could slice into buildings.

It was bizarre being in Greece during the weeks after 11 September. Despite the shock and the dark atmosphere of what appeared to be a changed, fearful world, most people were not particularly worried. Newspapers claimed that significant numbers believed the Americans' behaviour had provoked the attacks on 11 September; about two thirds thought the USA 'had it coming'. I was taken aback by Greek friends who told jokes about the terrorist attacks, and by how Osama bin Laden quickly became a figure of fun – a few months later, his mask was popular at carnival time. When a couple of sadistic hoaxers sent letters containing fake anthrax, it was seen as mischief rather than terrorism. The sense that Greece existed on the periphery of the West, and was always ready to criticize the USA, may have annoyed Greek Americans, but it was now strangely reassuring. Surely we were less likely to be wiped out in Athens than in London, I thought selfishly.

On the second day at school, the children were greeted with a lecture from the headmaster. The general drift was: 'no balls, no games, no collecting of those card thingies. And there's no toilet paper in the toilets because it's dirty and attracts flies. You can ask your teacher if you need paper.' I imagined the humiliation in class. The previous day I had taken Lara to the children's lavatories where we came across half a dozen cockroaches in the final stages of life, twitching outside the cubicles. The conveniences themselves were of the old, squatting-over-a-hole variety, where you have to jump after flushing to avoid getting your feet wet. There were also plastic baskets meant for used paper; a strange, unappealing hangover from the days when drains were too narrow to handle paper.

It was surprising, though, how quickly we all got used to our new life. We became friendly with some of our neighbours, and got acquainted with the local shopkeepers. Hercules the postman nearly ran me over a couple of times (he rode his moped on the pavements to save time), but it wasn't long before we were passing the time of day. He'd regularly smoke a leisurely cigarette on Eurydice Street, waiting for me to come down all the steps to collect some parcel or registered letter. In the mornings I'd stand outside the school railings with the other mothers, watching the children line up for prayers as if it were the most natural thing.

'At ease! Attention!' the teacher on duty would shout, military style.

'Have we got a test in history tomorrow?' the mothers would

ask one another, peering across the school yard to see which child was saying the prayer that morning.

'Yes, we've got to learn all the last three chapters. I don't know how we're going to do it.' It quickly became obvious that the mothers' main preoccupation was with schoolwork, and it was a serious subject. 'Yesterday, Angelos's teacher told them to learn the names of all fifty-one prefectures by today,' bemoaned one mother. 'We had to sit up until eleven o'clock doing it.'

I'd always had the impression that Greek children led a charmed existence. You see them playing happily in playgrounds at midnight, or chasing around tavernas in the evening, before falling asleep in their parents' laps. I knew that they had three months' holidays in the summer, and I imagined that after they got out of school at one-thirty they would be free to play outside with friends, and live the sort of childhoods their contemporaries in England could only dream of. It was now dawning on me that the truth was more complicated. Part of the problem is that the schools demand an extraordinary amount of homework from the children; in Anna's class, the nine-year-olds were given at least three or four hours of 'reading' (homework) a day. The policy is that the more 'reading' you do, the better it is. But perhaps even more significant is Greek parents' overwhelming ambition for their children, and tremendous love of 'letters'. The respect for *politismos* – a word meaning both culture and civilization – is universal and unquestionable.

Vassilis's older sister Stella came to see how we were settling in. Dressed in tidy, understated clothes, with clipped, smooth hair, she has the air of a kindly but anxious school prefect, who always chews her fingernails to the quick. She occasionally smokes awkwardly, looking like the prefect trying her first cigarette. As always, she spoke about schools; she and her husband were struggling to give their two sons what they believed was the best education possible.

'You may think that life has got better in Greece,' said Stella, 'but that's because we all go mad working so we can send our children to good schools and universities, and pay for all the extra lessons. I finish work at the bank, and then I go off to my other job at the adult education centre. Then I come home and spend all evening with Petros [aged ten] doing his homework. And every day after school, he has to go and learn foreign languages at the *frontistiria* [private crammers], because they are not taught well enough in school. It's a scandal. You know that parents here spend about the same amount on *frontistiria* for secondary school students as the government does on state schools? We're propping up the inadequate schools, and the owners are making a fortune. It's a rip-off.'

We compared complaints for a while about the levels of stress on our children. I admitted I was shocked by the pressure on pupils not to go to school 'unread'. Stella needed little encouragement.

'The whole thing is barbarous,' she said dramatically, chewing on a stump of her finger. 'If there's one politician I'd like to shoot, it'd be the Minister for Education.' She had just read a survey claiming that Greek children had the lowest capacity for critical thought in Europe, and was afraid that all the parrot-fashion learning by rote at school would destroy the children's capacity for free thinking. It seemed that Greek children were not only working the hardest, they were also learning the least.

I was becoming increasingly gloomy. I knew that I still had to coax Anna through several dense pages covering 'the descent of the Dorians from the North' for her test the next day, and now, according to statistics, it was going to make her end up brain-dead. Had we really done the right thing, I wondered, bringing our children to this country, and putting them into an education system which was so flawed? As I struggled against the dread that I might become one of those horrific ex-pats, who only see problems everywhere in Greece, it did occur to me that most Greek people I know can hold their own in a debate with the vehemence and alacrity of a dueller. If there is one thing that characterizes Greek conversation, it is a lack of reticence in expressing opinions. In fact, such is the natural argumentativeness and critical nature of many Greeks that what is a perfectly normal conversation can appear on the outside like a frantic matter of life and death. When my mother first heard Vassilis and me speaking together in Greek, she often thought we were in the middle of a terrible row.

* * *

Soon after the children started school, it was Vassilis's turn to begin his new job in the Ministry of Foreign Affairs. He invited me to see his office one day, and we walked through the old, scruffy building which was just about to be renovated. Long, dusty corridors gave onto rooms where civil servants sat drinking the ubiquitous *frappé* (iced Nescafé), smoking furiously, and playing patience on their computers. They were perhaps the bureaucrats known as 'chair-centaurs,' who are supposedly so inseparable from their desks that they seem to be welded to their chairs, as the centaur's human top is joined to his horse legs. As we explored the Ministry, I had the paranoid sensation that every person we passed was a potential ally, enemy, or someone who could stab you in the back. People greeted Vassilis in the corridors, and I scrutinized them suspiciously for evidence of their intentions.

We climbed up a narrow back staircase and emerged on a huge roof terrace. The building had once belonged to a rich, nineteenth-century benefactor, and he had chosen a good position for his handsome neoclassical mansion. We could see straight past the Parliament building to a picture-postcard view of the Acropolis, glowing yet solid in the morning light. The Parthenon looked as gracious and feminine as a ship, floating above the unsettled, noisy city sea below.

We left the ministry in search of a coffee and a *tiropita*, the cheese pie which many people eat during the morning instead of breakfast. For some reason, breakfast is despised, even by children, and the *tiropita* is just the thing to take the edge off hunger before a late lunch. Bakeries and sandwich shops sell an array of pies: flaky and large, crusty and small, 'traditional' with feta, twisted with mixed cheeses, brioche style with ham, and slices cut from a giant pie. And that's before you look at the spinach pies, sausage pies and custard pies. We sat down outside a small café. The coffee was a perfect Italianate cappuccino and the cheese pie was a delicious light, crisp puff of pastry oozing with warm, creamy white feta.

The streets by the Ministry are the heartland of politicians and journalists, and Vassilis seemed to greet half the people passing by.

'It's so strange,' he said. 'I'm not always sure where I know them from. It could have been from anywhere in the last twenty years.' He looked puzzled.

'So you're back,' said a man in a suit, stopping to shake hands. He had a knowing expression, smiling sympathetically at Vassilis's well-known predicament; many Greeks have been away, and they long to return. Then they come back and it can be insufferable.

If Greeks have a passionate pride and love for their country, they also hold feelings of shame, pity and disappointment. 'Welcome back to *Psorokostaina*,' wrote a friend by text message when I arrived in Athens, using Greece's simultaneously disparaging, warm and familiar nickname, which has the tone of 'Old Blighty'. It was taken from a nineteenth-century beggar woman, and its quality of seedy poverty and misery mixed with affection has been best translated by Patrick Leigh Fermor as 'Mangy Betty'.

It might be hard settling into a new life as a foreigner in Greece, but at least you know what you are. Vassilis was now a foreigner *and* a Greek. Recently, a taxi driver had noticed Vassilis's unfamiliar intonation and asked him how he knew such good Greek.

'You must have grown up here,' said the cabbie, imagining he was complimenting a foreigner (much to Vassilis's vexation).

'It's your fault I've got an accent in Greek now,' Vassilis said, turning teasingly to me. 'It's come from ten years of talking with you.'

I felt a little bereft saying goodbye to Vassilis outside the Ministry, as if he had gone off into an unknown world, and I went over to look at a bronze bust of a jowly man on a pedestal. I read the name – George Seferis. He was the Nobel Prize-winning poet, who combined his art with diplomacy, and was ambassador in London in the 1960s. He knew about the fumbling disorientation of the returning exile, and what happens after a period of *xenitia* – time spent abroad and inevitably entailing nostalgia and longing. One of his poems applied especially to Vassilis's predicament.

> *My old friend, what are you looking for?*
> *After years abroad you've come back*
> *with images you've nourished*
> *under foreign skies*
> *far from your own country ...*

. . . My old friend, stop a moment and think:
you'll get used to it little by little.
Your nostalgia has created a non-existent country, with laws
alien to earth and man.

* * *

I'd been searching for someone to help us with the housework, and then one day the pharmacist put me in touch with a person she thought might do. Effi came on a week's trial, and entered our life like the cavalry, with noise and stampeding energy.

'Only Greek coffee for me,' she said, patting the large gold and diamond cross on her chest, as she sat sipping her coffee and smoking a 'little cigarette' before she got going. She had made the coffee with care, so that it was just right – medium sweet, heated slowly in the little copper *briki* and just lured upwards without boiling, to produce a froth on the top.

At forty-seven, Effi was a carelessly handsome, strong woman, who always wore tight jeans and unusual, high-heeled gym shoes. She saw herself as having come down in the world; her drunkard, long-gone husband had been a sea captain and she had brought up her two children alone.

'There's nothing shameful about working to keep your family going,' she asserted, adding 'but I don't tell my neighbours what I'm doing.' She liked recounting her life story from every conceivable angle. I'd try to tactfully leave the room after a while, but Effi would continue her monologue at long distance, merely raising the volume a little. Later, when there was nobody close enough to hear, she even talked to Lily, our whippet-cross.

Effi solved her problem of being thought a cleaning woman by calling herself our 'manager', or even 'sergeant', and she resolutely acted as a guide to the etiquette of Greek life. She remained mildly wary of Vassilis.

'He's like me. I understand him,' Effi said over and again, as though this implied something suspicious. She was determined that her fellow countryman would never pull the wool over her eyes. She evidently thought that I was more like the lamb destined for the slaughter, perhaps because I'd retained some of my polite, roundabout, English ways.

'Would it be possible, if you don't mind, that you could possibly ... pass the bread please,' comes out totally inappropriately in Greek. It may be a poetic language, but when it comes to practical matters it's just 'Pass the bread'. As if to remind herself, Effi kept telling me rather unconvincingly: 'You're the boss. You're the woman of the house.'

To begin with, Anna and Lara were bewildered by Effi. She was determined that they should speak to her in the proper respectful way, which meant they should add *Kyria* (Mrs) before her name, and address her in the formal second person. Naturally, she spoke to them in the friendly singular (the equivalents to the French *vous* and *tu*). The girls were reluctant, and couldn't make the adjustment. It was partly that they had only spoken Greek within the intimate environment of family and friends, but I suspected that their mother tongue was also making it harder. English is strongly egalitarian compared to Greek (and other European languages), allowing even the youngest child to address the most eminent adult simply as 'you'. I too found the strategy of ranking and formality in Greek awkward at times. Whereas Vassilis could sense when it was right to plunge straight into the friendly singular with strangers, I was diffident, not wanting to cause offence by being too forward, or fearing that I was being stand-offish. The divisions are subtle tools; I was regularly put in my place by young adults, who showed respect by refusing to speak with me as an equal.

Although Anna and Lara quickly learned to speak to their

teachers and the parents of their friends in the correct manner, to her chagrin, they never did with Effi.

'When they were young, even my own children spoke to me in the plural,' she remarked one day. I wasn't sure whether she was saying this for effect, as it was not something I had ever come across except in nineteenth-century French novels, and when I mentioned it later to Vassilis, he muttered something about how only fascists did that kind of thing. Whatever her particular brand of politics (and it's true that she did say she wouldn't say no to a little dictatorship, just for a few years, to get the country back on its feet again), Effi's language reflected the great panoply of approaches which has been the bane of Modern Greek. She proudly peppered her everyday demotic speech with quotations in Ancient Greek, and she had a penchant for the now outmoded *katharevousa*, or purist Greek. Many of the sayings and phrases she used were unintelligible to me (as they would be to many younger Greeks) but they were part of the language Effi's generation was taught at school.

Vassilis was dismissive about the *katharevousa* business too.

'We were made to learn it at school in the 1970s because of the dictatorship, but it's irrelevant now – it's not a part of our language any more.' I was indignant, having just been reading about the history of Greece's 'language question'.

'It may be finished with now,' I argued, 'but surely part of Greece's insecurity about its identity is linked with its indecision about language. You've been fighting about it ever since the 1830s – you can't just say that the problem has disappeared completely.'

The Greek language famously united the Greeks as a nation during centuries of Ottoman rule, but after independence in 1832, some believed that the living, changing, demotic Greek (*dimotiki*) had become messily debased, and 'polluted' by its contact with other languages, including Turkish. The cleaned-up, artificially constructed *katharevousa* appeared to be some kind of solution for the new state; it was closer to the ancient language, and would restore a bit of dignity.

Although the masses never spoke it, *katharevousa* became the language of literacy, and was widely used in schools, universities, newspapers and the legal system until 1976. The resulting 'language question' was powerful enough to provoke political riots and social divisions. When parts of the Bible were translated into demotic Greek in 1901, there was horror among conservative elements; Athenian university professors and their students led violent protests, resulting in eight deaths.

Everyone believed that language was the key to national identity, but whereas *katharevousa* tended to attract the political Right, supporters of demotic Greek were often associated with the Left. The Colonels' Junta (1967–74) appreciated *katharevousa*'s 'cleansed', rigid regulations, and its association with ancient glories. It was only after their fall that *katharevousa* was finally removed as the official language; anything associated with the dictatorship looked bad in the new climate of freedom. Today, most spoken and written Greek is what emerges from the demotic melting pot, with an increasing influence from English. Now, slang words such as 'cool' and 'down' (as in miserable) can be declined as Greek verbs, and making a personal 'connection' can be a *koné*. In spite of, or perhaps because of, its adaptability, Greek is still a language containing references and styles which span nearly 3,000 years.

This complicated linguistic inheritance will belong to my daughters in a different way. Every day they were getting deeper into a set of references and symbols which was not mine, however fond I had grown of it. Anna and Lara were steadily crossing from mother tongue to father tongue, as Greece also became their *patrida* or fatherland. It is said that if you learn a language before you are twelve you can become like a native speaker, and it was extraordinary to witness it taking place. I watched Lara copying out the alphabet, amazed at her six-year-old dexterity in managing the complicated curls and bends of the letter ksi (ξ), or the bold upside-down V of the lamda (Λ) that starts her name.

Both children were starting to automatically use the diminutives that add an intimacy and sweeten the most ordinary words, so that water becomes 'little water' (*nero–neraki*), bread 'little bread' (*psomi – psomaki*), or hand 'little hand' (*cheri–cheraki*). They were also learning the wishes and greetings that are used to mark almost every activity. Apart from the ordinary 'good mornings', people wish you good week, weekend, month, summer, winter, holidays, reading, work, rest, travel, return, appetite, digestion, entertainment, sleep, progress and success. When you leave, you are bade goodbye and 'to the good!' And there's even 'good freedom' for a pregnant mother awaiting the birth of her baby.

Like everyone who learns a new language in its country of origin, the territory of curses and insults was too tempting for Lara and Anna to miss. Sometimes I'd hear them discussing their least favourite schoolmates, using a bizarre mix of English and Greek.

'Oh, Katerina is *malakismeni* [literally, masturbated but implying stupid], I hate her.'

'Yes, but Artemis is *vlameni* [demented], and *ilithia* [idiotic].'

They insulted the boys by using the word for 'wanker', *malakas*, and became highly adept at using this astonishingly versatile and common epithet. It is not only a slur on somebody ignorant or incapable, but is used by friends as an affectionate equivalent to the English 'mate'. Thus, teenage boys can interject '*ela malaka*' ('Come on, you wanker') between every other word, but it is still strong enough to be used as a satisfying insult by an angry driver or an abandoned girlfriend.

Lara's favourite new acquisition was actually non-verbal: the *mountza* – a highly offensive gesture, in which the palm of the hand is stretched out, fingers splayed towards the adversary. She practised diligently, and occasionally (before I could stop her) demonstrated her new skill to horrified passing motorists.

* * *

Coming back to Greece was never going to be easy, but there were two clear points when something changed. The first came on my birthday. The children picked flowers, hung up balloons, and organized a candlelit tea table, helped by a school friend. When they ceremoniously brought in the cake, there was a pivotal moment of hesitation, before they evidently made an unspoken agreement. Rather than appear foreign and different from their friend, they launched into singing 'Happy Birthday' to me in Greek, something they had never done before. I was surprised that they already knew the words.

'May you live, little Mum, and grow old, with white hair . . .' they sang. '*Chronia Polla* – Many Years! And may you live to be a hundred!' said Vassilis, adding the traditional birthday greetings. 'Cut the cake, *Mama*,' said Lara in Greek.

It marked a change of gear. The children were sweeping me along with them as they became Greek. I realized that this would change me too, and that I wanted to mark that process by becoming a Greek citizen. Obviously, a Greek passport didn't make me a Greek; I remembered a humorous book by the Hungarian George Mikes about surviving as a foreigner in 1940s England; it could apply to the alien in Greece:

'Once a foreigner, always a foreigner. There is no way out for him. He may become British; he can never become English. So it is better to reconcile yourself to the sorrowful reality. There are some noble English people who might forgive you . . . who realise that it is not your fault, only your misfortune.' Nevertheless, just as a marriage certificate is no guarantee of love, it is an indication of intention, and I decided at that point to become a citizen of the Hellenic Republic, even if that didn't automatically make me a Greek.

The second moment of change came after the Greek dancing and guitar teacher from the children's school organized a soirée for all his pupils and their families. A tall man, with dark, bruise-like shadows around his eyes, Panayiotis Mavropoulos lived for Greek music and dance, and transmitted his passionate enthusiasm to everyone he met.

'We Greeks have had a particular relation to rhythm and language, since ancient times,' he said to me one day, when I'd gone to collect Anna and Lara from a dance class. 'I never had a classical training, but folk music runs deep inside us. In Greece we live with our emotions; we cry more easily than others . . . And we live with death, even though people are more distanced from it nowadays.'

I'd watched him during the lesson, taking the pupils through their paces in a traditional, island ring dance. Then, at the end, he switched the tape to a *zeibekiko* song – the provocation to an expressive, male, solo dance with its roots in the Orient. It is associated more often with a late-night session in a smoky taverna than with children whose only dancing space is the cramped entrance hall of a badly equipped school building. As the beautiful, sorrowful song began with its characteristically swaying 9/8 rhythm, Panayiotis and several of the more experienced pupils started dancing. With seemingly drunken, heavy steps, one arm raised to shelter the eyes, as if in defence, each of them then swooped and dived as if falling, only to twist up lightly again and continue their lonely movements. One girl was dancing expressively with her eyes shut, mouthing the words of the song, excluding everything outside her personal space at that moment.

'Did you see the girl who was dancing alone in there?' asked Panayiotis, when all the children had gone out into the school yard. 'She loves that song. Her mother died when she was born, and although she's only eleven, she can express all the song's pain through her dancing. Did you notice the words?' I admitted that I hadn't, and Panayiotis sang them softly for me:

> *It was chance that you gave birth to me,*
> *That you gave me life.*
> *Mother, where am I living?*
>
> *The little boat which carries me is going to sink,*
> *Tell me where I should hold on.*
> *Where should I stay?*
>
> *Our lost hope, our fate is written*
> *On the Devil's book*
> *And he'll make it come true.*

Panayiotis's evening out at a taverna looked unpromising initially, with dozens of families squeezed into too little space. Most of the adults were smoking and chatting, while the children rampaged between the tables. I wondered whether Panayiotis's idea of bringing the children to a real *glendi* (a festive party) wasn't perhaps a little artificial, but I was soon proved wrong. There was none of the awkwardness that I expected from a gathering of school children and their parents, but instead an ease that came from knowing the rules, and respecting the alchemy of music and wine to produce *kefi* (high spirits and *joie de vivre*).

'You can't even start to understand anything about Greece if you don't realize that everything is expressed through poetry and song,' said Vassilis, pouring some more of the sour red wine that had been brought from the barrel in metal jugs. 'It's not chance that almost every other person in Greece is a poet. It may seem as though we are all melting into a global, Americanized culture, but not in music. And because nobody outside Greece can understand the language, it remains like a secret.'

As we spoke, a group of Panayiotis's guitar pupils moved up onto a low, makeshift stage. A serious, dark-haired boy of about thirteen plucked out a melancholy tune, and sang in a clear, steady voice, a song of yearning, nostalgia and love. Even though we were all sitting in a comfortable restaurant in a modern suburb, and the boy was probably from a perfectly happy family, he seemed able (just as the motherless girl had in her dance) to carry the suffering of generations of Greeks with a knowing innocence. His singing carried hints of the *mirologia* or death laments of his forebears, and of the songs of misery, protest, departure and separation which have always blossomed in Greece's worst times of defeat and disaster. It was a demonstration of what Seferis called '*o kaimos tis Romiosynis*'; an almost untranslatable phrase meaning the suffering, pain, nostalgia and longing of Greekness. 'Wherever I travel Greece wounds me,' he wrote in one poem. The overwhelming emotion of pain in the music was all the more convincing for its understated singer. I tried not to let Vassilis see me wiping surreptitiously at my eyes; it was too much of a cliché to cry.

After we had heard some more songs and eaten dinner, Panayiotis stepped up with his oriental lute to introduce the dance band which turned out to be the illustrious Dora Stratou group, which includes some of the best performers of traditional dance and music. They sat down and, with an easy expertise, launched into a series of folk songs. As the clarinet wailed and purred, a grandmotherly blonde woman sang songs which sounded like merry tales of village wells with fresh water, of black eyes and red lips, of sheep bells in the mountains, of fishing boats in the moonlight. On closer attention, the great darkness that haunts so much of Greek popular culture was even there in the skipping dance tunes; it emerged that the black-eyed girl drowned in the well, the sheep were killed by a wolf, and the sailor was grief-stricken at leaving home. A group of young people and children got up from the tables, and hesitantly at first, but with increasing verve, danced in an uneven circle in front of the musicians. Their arms grasped one another's shoulders, and a girl with just-budding breasts showing through her T-shirt led the dance, a white handkerchief twirling in her hand.

At one a.m. we drove home from the taverna. The children sat in the back of the car looking tired, pink-cheeked and happy, after hours of dancing. I felt as though I had made contact again with the Greece that I had loved before – a glimpse of the life I'd dreamed of returning to. It made me want to explore Athens and to find out what was really going on in the lives of its contradictory people. As they drifted off to sleep, Anna opened her eyes for a moment and mumbled: 'Mum, could I start guitar lessons?' Perhaps even my dream of my daughters turning into teenagers who sang nostalgic songs wouldn't prove so wrong.

CHAPTER 3

THE THREE HILLS

The sentimental traveller must already mourn that Athens has been selected as the capital of Greece. Already have speculators and the whole tribe of 'improvers' invaded the glorious city . . .

J. L. Stephens, *Incidents of Travel in Greece, Turkey, Russia and Poland*, 1839

I'd been meaning to go in search of the place I'd first stayed on arriving in Greece as a twenty-three-year-old student. I hadn't been back there since and wanted to start again at the beginning.

I had driven out from England with my boyfriend Jeremy in a Citroën 2CV full of whatever an anthropologist was supposed to need for research in 'the field': a grammar book, a first aid kit, Marmite and a clackety old typewriter (this makes it sound like the 1930s but it was still normal in the mid-1980s). My suitcase contained what I thought were suitable clothes so I wouldn't offend the locals; pre-fieldwork seminars had included discussions about modesty, morality and appearance, and I'd packed more skirts than jeans and nothing with too many holes.

For the first few days 'the field' was the area around Omonia (Concord or Harmony) Square. Then, as now, it was the guts of the city – a bubbling, noisy belly filled with commerce, poverty, intrigue and outsiders. We were so green we didn't yet know that most visitors to Athens stayed in hotels in the tourist area of Plaka, and after searching for the cheapest thing on offer, we settled on the Hotel Mediterranean. It looked appealing, with its art deco entrance hall and cage lift, and although there was an impressive number of people coming and going, and various noisy arguments, we thought this was just local colour; it took us at least a day to realize that they were mostly prostitutes with their clients.

On a hot, humid October day, I retraced my younger self's steps around Omonia. The air smelled of sweat and the pavements were sticky after yet another autumnal rainstorm. I meandered around the side streets. Dozens of pungent-smelling garlic tresses were laid out to dry on the pavement in Epicure Street, and Euripides Street was packed with busy shopfronts displaying strings of sausages and slabs of dark red *pastourma* (air-dried beef). There were handmade aluminium pots and cans of every shape and size; a thousand different mats and brooms; ropes and nails; herbs and spices; caged songbirds and docile rabbits for the pot. Wooden buckets revealed great wedges of white feta, now officially an exclusive, patented Greek product after Danish impostors had been seen off with a court case.

Amongst the Greek shopkeepers and customers were the people who have brought some of the greatest changes to the capital in recent years. They are the groups of Albanians, Kurds and Iraqis standing on street corners, talking and waiting;

Chinese with street stalls filled with cheap acrylic clothes (collected nightly on mopeds from the ships in Piraeus); Africans selling pirate CDs and fake Louis Vuitton bags; Russians, Pontians and Poles, sitting on benches by the metro, smelling of Russian cigarettes; and Pakistanis with shops stocking unfamiliar, brightly coloured sweets. The alien Urdu script displayed on the outside reminded me of my slow deciphering of Greek shop signs when I'd first arrived in Athens. The immigrants weren't there at all then; now they are a large part of its population.

'It's like the Tower of Babel,' say the Greek Athenians about their immigrant neighbours who fill the capitals' basements and cheap, ground-floor flats. Over a million have entered Greece since the collapse of Communism, and a large proportion of them arrived illegally from Albania.

I found the old 'milk shop' where I remembered having my first Athenian breakfasts: small ceramic pots of creamy sheep's yogurt topped with a thick skin, a basket of crusty, white bread and a cup of Greek coffee. It had all seemed very unfamiliar then; almost daring. A flash forward to seeing me sixteen years later, buying similar pots from my local supermarket, accompanied by my two Greek children, would have been quite a shock. The shop window still displayed generously sized terracotta dishes of different varieties of yogurt, and little bowls of rice pudding sprinkled with cinnamon, but few of the people sitting at the tables outside were Greek.

In Omonia there is little of the modernizing and homogenizing which is taking place so rapidly in other areas of Athens, even though the City Hall and the Stock Exchange in Sophocles Street are just around the corner. You may spot the local politicians and the new breed of bankers and stockbrokers, but this is still the district of newcomers – both from the rest of Greece and from elsewhere. This is where the city looks eastward, and retains its oriental legacy; you can imagine yourself back into Ottoman times, when there were mosques as well as markets and merchants.

A visitor walking around during the eighteenth century would have seen many of the same products on sale: regional specialities were oil, honey, wax, aniseed, soap and leather. In the 1830s, a British traveller, Christopher Wordsworth, described the Athenian market as supplying: 'barrels of black caviar, small pocket-looking-glasses in red pasteboard cases, onions, tobacco piled up in brown heaps, black olives, figs strung together upon a rush, rices, pipes with amber mouth-pieces and brown clay bowls, rich stuffs, and silver-chased pistols, dirks, belts, and embroidered waistcoats. . .' He would have heard many different languages. There were Turks, Jews, Armenians and Slavs as well as Greeks, and there had been Albanians for centuries.

The Hotel Mediterranean looked exactly as I remembered it and the rooms were still impressively cheap.

'But no bathroom,' said the man at reception challengingly. 'In a few months we're going to fix up the whole place in time for the Olympic Games. We'll put in bathrooms, and the prices will go up.' I was glad to have had a last look at the dishevelled yet still appealing hotel, before it was brought into line with EU directives on hygiene and lost its old character. A sad, heavy woman with peroxide hair glanced at me with dull, suspicious eyes from her leatherette chair in the lobby. I couldn't tell whether she was Greek or not and I wondered whether the place had kept its old clientele of home-grown streetwalkers; prostitution too, has been swamped by foreign recruits.

At night, Omonia Square fills up with young, miniskirted women from the former eastern bloc and Balkan countries and heroin addicts. There is much worried talk about human trafficking, of sex slaves, of men paying prostitutes not to use condoms, of Aids – problems which barely existed when I arrived in Greece. In fact, when, a little while into my fieldwork, the female owner of a night-club-cum-brothel near Nafplio offered me a 'well-paid' post as one of her 'hostesses,' it was probably one of the earlier opportunities for foreign women to enter the profession. At the time it seemed like taking the participant-observation method one step too far.

Although Athenians are shocked by the numbers of the latest arrivals, waves of incomers are nothing new; the twentieth century supplied enough wars and disasters to make for an almost continuous state of flux. The Balkan Wars and the First World War were followed by the 1922 'Catastrophe', the national disaster brought about by the Greek army's invasion of Turkey and its devastating defeat. The Turkish army's destruction of the mainly Greek city of Smyrna eventually led to over a million Greek refugees arriving from Turkey. Metaxas's dictatorship in the 1930s was followed by the Second World War and then the Civil War. And it wasn't so long before the Colonels' dictatorship in the 1960s . . . There was little time for stability or normal life until the mid-1970s. The major difference is that in the past, the settlers tended to belong to the Orthodox Church, although even this often turned out to be an awkward classification system. The last decade or so has been the first time, however, that Greece has acted as a magnet for non-Greek speakers.

The foreign economic migrants are flooding into Athens now, rather as Greeks from the provinces did after the Second World War and the subsequent Civil War. The capital's small but powerful middle class had been all but destroyed during the 1940s, and the city was swamped with Greek provincials over the next decades. Most came because they had no choice, but the movement to the capital was known as *astyfilia* – literally 'love of the city'. Men arrived with a small suitcase and dreams of a modest job. Some of them even paid in the beginning to be given work and accommodation as caretakers in apartment buildings. Often they'd sleep ten to a room until they could get themselves sorted out, and families could follow. Now, the Albanians are doing the same thing.

After leaving my old hotel, I walked to the central fish and meat market. It is a high-ceilinged, light construction full of elegant archways and attractive wrought iron which dates from the 1880s, but your senses are left with little time for appreciation of the architecture. The pavements outside were crowded with baskets of nuts, raisins and dried figs sprinkled with oregano, buckets of squirming, snotty-looking snails, every variety of olives, piles of salt cod dripping crystals on the pavement, and vast, sticky, circular cakes of halva in every flavour. Inside, the fish men were spraying water over mounds of iridescent seafood, unravelling fish guts into buckets, and scraping glittering scales with knives.

'Fresh, local, for your babies!' they shouted coaxingly. Many stalls had a little handwritten sign with the name of the island where the fish came from: cod from Naxos, sea bream from Kalymnos, red mullet from Chios.

I passed into the meat market, which began with a horror movie scene of ripped-out hearts, lungs and livers, amputated feet, and vast, lolling tongues all dangling from hooks. A tray of diminutive, skinned lambs' heads lay staring, ready for the oven. I passed one of the working canteens which stay open all night, and serve *patsas*, the legendary soup made from offal and pig's trotters which is supposed to work wonders on threatening hangovers at the end of a night out. It has long been an institution after late-night escapades, to end up at four a.m. in Omonia, with steaming bowls of *patsas* and the first editions of the morning's papers, before going home to bed in the early dawn.

'Local, only Greek!' called a man in an apron splattered with a macabre Jackson Pollock arrangement of blood, indicating a row of lambs swaying by their hind legs. One of them had a Greek flag stuck in its anus.

Out on the pavement I took a deep breath, glad to have escaped the cloying smell of blood. Here, there were a few people who had taken the bus in from some mountain village to sell things. One woman was selling bunches of spiky, dark rocket, and an old man sat on a folding stool next to a small, open, 1960s suitcase. He was selling five thick, creamy-yellow, long-sleeved woollen vests, two pairs of long johns and some bunches of dried hillside oregano.

'All Greek,' he said, seeing me pause to admire the garments, which looked as though they hadn't been long off the sheep's back. 'Exquisite,' he murmured flirtatiously to my back as I passed on.

This preoccupation with Greekness only really began after the War of Independence, when defining what it meant to be Greek became a vital element in creating a new state. And it never ceased being a national sport. When the Greeks won their freedom from the Ottomans in 1834, their first capital was the smart little Peloponnesian port of Nafplio. It was thought to be far more suitable than the goat-infested ruins and the insignificant, predominantly Turkish-Albanian settlement which existed in nineteenth-century Athens. One hundred and fifty years later, Nafplio also charmed me enough to convince me to choose it as the location for my fieldwork after my first few weeks at language school in Athens.

My diary records that the first weeks in Nafplio were not always easy; there were already signs of strain with Jeremy. We temporarily rented some rickety rooftop rooms, which I described as being 'smaller, seedier and colder than we would have liked', albeit with a wonderful view. On our first evening, I wrote that 'this is the first time I have felt like escaping and dashing back home. Entering the field is really quite a frightening event.' A month later Jeremy was to return to England and my diary begins to show the first signs of real excitement. 'Walking home late at night through Nafplio's quiet, beautiful streets I felt really elated, and excited to be alone here in Greece.' It was the beginning of what felt like shedding my old skin as a snake does, and becoming a changed person as I fell in love with a whole country.

Greece's history might have been completely different, if the Great Powers (France, England and Russia) hadn't decided to step in and create a monarchy. They picked a youthful Bavarian prince called Otto as first King of the Hellenes. It was the new King's German entourage, fascinated by fantasies of classical Greece, who decided to change the capital to Athens. It was a move they hoped would resurrect the bonds linking modern Greeks to their glorious (ancient) past. They wanted to give some patriotism and dignity to a people who had been 'enslaved' to the Ottomans for the last four centuries, and turn them into reborn Hellenes.

Although the Greeks were certainly second-class citizens under the Ottomans (they paid taxes while Muslims didn't, and they were tried in separate courts) it is a dangerous over simplification to say that the Greeks had been merely 'slaves'. They also included rich, accomplished and politically influential figures within the Ottoman Empire. With their love of travel and adventure they were the most successful shipbuilders and merchants (the forerunners of today's shipping magnates), and in Ottoman histories it is often Greek names which crop up as bankers, physicians and advisers to sultans. These educated, cosmopolitan Greeks from Constantinople, Vienna and Alexandria did much to spread Greece's cause during the War of Independence, and they were keen to play a part in establishing Free Greece's first city. Still, not all of them left their comfortable positions amongst the Turks, and by the middle of the nineteenth century there were still far more Greeks outside Greece than inside. When Athens was still a small town with 30,000 citizens, there were 120,000 Greeks in Constantinople and 60,000 in Smyrna.

By the twentieth century, there had been such success at classifying a homogenized, faith-based version of what it meant to be Greek that a Greek Jew or a Greek Catholic (let alone a Greek Muslim) was seen as somehow 'less Greek'. Today, Greeks outstrip all Europeans in terms of national pride and patriotism; they have forgotten that they were always just one ethnic group among many, and that religion was only one criterion for belonging. When it was proposed, a few years previously, that identity cards would no longer carry the holder's religion, the Greek clergy were up in arms, and there were huge protests. Nowadays, the Muslim-Turkish minority, who come to Athens from the northern region of Thrace, may have established their own neighbourhood in the Gasworks (Gazi) district, but even in death they are not accepted. The local, public cemetery refuses their bodies, which have to be sent all the way back to Thrace to be buried in their own graveyards.

I walked down Athena Street, away from the market in the direction of the Acropolis. It was packed with pedestrians hurrying about their business, lorries manoeuvring around roadworks and angry taxi drivers swearing, their left arm raised outside the window in protest or perhaps in appeal to a higher power. The air smelled of hot metal, oily tools and exhaust fumes. Every so often, between the incoherent assortment of impersonal, modern buildings, I noticed the noble remains of a grand, neoclassical house. Some were abandoned and disintegrating and others were in a state of more genteel decay, but they hinted at the way that Athens looked after it became the new capital of Modern Greece. Architects and planners had set to, with grandiose fantasies; there was even talk of erecting King Otto's palace up on the Acropolis.

Soon, in the tiny, born-again city there were monumental public buildings, parks, a large cathedral, a university, a library, theatres, elegant boulevards, fashionable cafés, and bands that played music near the royal palace in Constitution (Syntagma) Square, as ladies with parasols strolled by. Things hadn't been this good since the second century AD when Athens experienced a last classical blossoming, instigated by the Roman Emperor Hadrian. His visionary architectural renaissance had soon been crushed by barbarian invasions in the third century, just as the mid-twentieth century hordes were to do almost 2,000 years later. Old photographs of Athens from the 1890s show Athena Street as a broad, tree-lined avenue with large, dignified homes. Omonia Square was a verdant little park, with the occasional horse-drawn carriage or tram passing by, where smart Athenian women were dressed in the latest Parisian fashions and the men adopted 'European' suits and hats. Only a sprinkling of figures in national costume indicates that this is the Balkans and not Western Europe.

People really believed for a time in the nineteenth century that Athens might become a model European city. It hadn't been a blank canvas, but there were not the complicated historical layers that are found in cities such as London either. Photographs show the important new buildings sitting alone, like plywood stage scenery. And in certain ways it was a theatrical pastiche. A small but influential group of Bavarian courtiers, politicians and architects were trying to make a complicated, Orthodox, Balkan people into good, modern Europeans, who would obediently wear their ancient ancestors' laurels with pride.

The German and Greek architects in Athens came up with a hybrid of what they saw as a mix between classical Greek buildings and European architecture – the Greek neoclassical style. This became so popular that it was adopted as part of the country's vernacular architecture; and from the nineteenth century until the middle of the twentieth, villagers mimicked the designs of grand Athenian mansions, with their relief columns and wrought-iron balconies. You can still see these beautiful houses in every shape and size all over the country, where their owners have not knocked them down to build rural imitations of the 1970s multi-storey apartment block.

The new classicism dominated architecture as a philosophy and national style. It lasted until after the Second World War, and though central Athens can give the impression of being an urban tangle of characterless concrete boxes, there are many lovely examples of neoclassical buildings. You only have to look up above the gaudy shop signs and neon lights. Then, between the dingy 1970s apartment blocks and the slick 1990s banks in aluminium and smoked glass, you start to notice the carved marble balcony supports and elegant proportions of Athens's early dream buildings. Most characteristic of all are the beautiful terracotta roof-tile decorations, which give a playful, folkloric twist to the classical formality. They often incorporate mythological motifs – Aphrodite and Dionysus face each other across the rooftops, and Hermes' winged head surveys many streets with a slight smile on his sensuous lips.

* * *

Over the next days, I paid two visits to Vouliagmeni's little town hall, to initiate what I knew would be the long procedure of applying for citizenship.

'There's a *xeni* [foreign woman] here,' shouted the woman behind the desk disdainfully to a colleague. 'She wants to be registered. Should I send her upstairs?'

I felt annoyed, sensing my cheeks flush, and noting the odd distaste that sometimes accompanies the word *xenos* – a foreigner, stranger or outsider. In the past, a *xenos* arriving in a village or an island was treated with kindness and interest. This was not only a point of honour; the stranger was also a novelty, a source of entertainment and news, interrupting the well-known, sometimes dull rhythms of a rural community. Known as *filoxenia* (literally love of the stranger or guest), hospitality is still considered a national characteristic by Greeks, but it is inevitably threatened by city ways. And xenophobia (literally fear of the stranger) is also a Greek word; racism in Greece is often dread of the unknown. The Greeks, like the Russians, can be the most hospitable and welcoming of people, but they can also be uncompromisingly suspicious and even hostile to the outsider. Some of the worst culprits of xenophobia towards both foreign and Greek strangers tend to be the employees in public offices, who put up a barrage of hostility to the interloper who dares interrupt their peace.

When there is a personal link, however slender or distant, everything changes. My second visit to the town hall was altogether different. This time, I took the precaution of going armed not only with the requisite papers (it emerged that Vassilis had to transfer all our family registration papers to Vouliagmeni), but with Vassilis for support, and, above all, an introduction from the parents of one of Anna's school friends. Now, I had become an individual; I could join the official's own network. By setting up a chain of obligations, I would become someone who might even help her one day, in a world where knowing or 'having' someone can make all the difference. 'Do you have someone in that ministry/hospital/office?' people ask, fearing to go anywhere without a recommendation.

With smiles and kindness, we were welcomed as prospective citizens (and voters) of Vouliagmeni, and given several piles of documents to fill out to get things going.

'When this goes through, we'll be able to give you your special pass to the beaches and for parking,' cooed the woman who had been so catty before.

Later that week, my brother-in-law, Christos, offered to help me continue my exploration of Athens. He'd take me to his favourite place, he said. Setting out from central Athens, we were soon driving up a steep, increasingly potholed road into what looked like a scrubby, rocky wasteland.

'These are the Tourkovounia [Turkish Mountains],' announced Christos. As he drove, he pointed out the landmarks below, smoking cigarettes with one hand, and answering his mobile phone with the other. 'You can see the whole city from here,' he said as we got higher. 'It's yours now. What do you think?' The swarming metropolis looked both intimidating and strangely enticing. Like a vast, dirty-white, geometrically patterned blanket, it was glinting under a sky which had the raw, piercing blue that follows a rainstorm.

'I can't understand what you want a Greek passport for,' Christos added, puzzled after I'd described my experiences at the town hall. 'Apart from anything else, it's unbelievably difficult to get hold of. You'll have to go and stand in line with all the Albanians and Pontians, and if you don't want it to take ten years you'll have to use some *meson* [insider influence]. And it'll cost you.'

Christos is the oldest of Vassilis's four siblings, and was the first of the family to move to Athens. Armed with a university degree from Thessaloniki, he arrived with his wife Angeliki in the mid-1970s and got a job as an engineer with Athens's Water Board. They've been here ever since. Although he has an air of gravitas, with his grey beard and sad eyes, he has a winning smile and a biting sense of humour. He has become such a streetwise Athenian that he even knows what's going on underneath the surface, in the aqueducts, pipes and drains that worm their way between ancient remains and concrete, earthquake-proof foundations.

'When I first came to Athens it crushed me,' said Christos, describing the miserable bedsit which only saw the sun for fifteen minutes a day.

'It was frightful, *a-pa pa pa*,' he said, using the useful and characteristic expression meaning something like 'God forbid'. 'We used to go along to the square just to look at the sky.' Now Christos and Angeliki live in a top-floor apartment with picture windows, and a panoramic view of Athens and its skies.

'You can see how the city spread out from the area around the Acropolis,' said Christos, taking on the role of my guide, and dividing Athens up into notional sections like a man with a plan. 'Until the [Second World] War, Athens was just a small town, but now over four million people – nearly half Greece's population – live here. They've built right down to the sea, along the coast, and the whole of the Athens basin has filled up.' From here we could see Athens's mountains, Hymettus, Pendeli and Parnis, marking the physical perimeters of the city. Their very names conjure up history: the honey, marble quarries and heroes of ancient times, as well as romantic poetry and travellers' watercolours of more recent centuries.

Christos stopped the car. We had reached the end of a rough

road on top of what used to be known as the Wolves' Mountains. They were renamed the Turkish Mountains, after the Turkish army camped there in 1456, two years before they conquered the city and stayed for nearly four centuries. Here, on this hill in the middle of the urban sprawl, we had arrived in the countryside. There were beehives, chickens, and simple, poor houses surrounded by vegetable plots, twisting vines and vividly coloured flowers. All I could hear was birdsong.

'They even grazed sheep up here until very recently,' said Christos. 'And the royals hunted foxes here in the nineteenth century.'

Most of the 'villagers' who lived up here had arrived in the 1950s and 1960s from northern Greece, and built their homes illegally.

'The owners are still afraid they'll have to pull them down,' said Christos. 'It's the same story across Athens; people just built what they wanted, and worried about the law afterwards. Here, everything is forbidden and everything is allowed. Anyway, Athens has now taken on the character of the people who moved here – most of us were born somewhere else and that's the place that stays our true home. We go back for holidays, to vote, to get married and to get buried.'

Down below, we could see the working-class area of Galatsi on one side, and on the other, the smart, leafy suburb of Psychiko.

'That's all villas, and apartments which cost a million drachmas [about £2,000] a square metre,' said Christos. When we'd first been house-hunting he'd taken us there as part of a tour of different areas. It looked like an affluent ghost town; there were no shops or cafés, and nobody on the streets apart from some Filipino domestic workers.

We looked down at the city, whose reputation can provoke

such awe, fantasy and poetry that its reality can also be a grave disappointment. Picking out the different neighbourhoods, their names sounded fanciful when put together: Dove (Peristeri), Skylark (Korydalos – home to a notorious prison), Bull (Tavros), Beehive (Kypseli), Metamorphosis, Laurel (Daphne), Vine-gardens (Ambelokipoi), Muscat Grape (Moschato), Good View (Kalithea), Byron (Vyronas), and Little Column (Kolonaki). The areas merged into one another, making up an endless cubist sea of buildings.

We drove to a large café just outside the Tourkovounia village, where a few young couples were sitting on the terrace, mesmerized by the spectacular view.

'I hate the sun,' Christos said, quickly taking the shady seat at the table, and laying down in front of him the three vital life-support systems to Athenian life – cigarettes, mobile phone, car keys.

'Look how clear the atmosphere is in Athens now,' he said, lighting up and pointing across to the glistening sea, with its stately, slow-moving ships gliding into the docks at Piraeus. The dusty, mauve outlines of far-off mountains were darkening, but the legendary Attic light imposed an extraordinary clarity. It makes distant peaks appear close, and gives a thrilling sense of eagle vision and even hyper-reality.

'Sometimes in the old days you couldn't see a hundred metres because of the pollution cloud,' said Christos. 'OK, Athens needs a bit of tidying up, but we can't be like the English. You keep everything in order, but we're less oppressed; we're healthier psychologically.'

As he spoke, Christos patted my wrist, a familiar form of physical punctuation which adds rhythmic emphasis to words, and ensures the listener's attention. I didn't argue with his theory. I always enjoy this self-promoted idea of Greeks as spontaneous, warm, Zorba-like creatures of spiritual and emotional freedom. Even the most angst-ridden, overworked city dweller with credit card debts, bank loans, and a prescription for tranquillizers in his pocket will spin it, especially to foreigners. It's still a generally accepted axiom that true men have a certain recklessness and generosity of spirit; they will suddenly decide to have a night out with friends or spend far more than they can afford on a grand gesture. It allows the individual to forget (if briefly) that life is a hard road of suffering filled with mundane, practical problems. Tellingly, one doesn't tend to hear Greek women say anything along these lines; emotional spontaneity has never been considered a desirable female characteristic.

The waiter arrived to take our order and I confirmed all of Christos's preconceptions about my foreign ways, by shamelessly ordering 'hot tea' (as opposed to canned iced tea). This is something few self-respecting Greeks will drink unless they are ill; afternoon tea has all the negative associations of prudish, formal Englishness. The waiter raised his eyebrows ironically at my request for some milk but said nothing.

Far below us, rising up out of the bristling, aerial-topped city blocks, Athens's two famous landmark hills, the Acropolis and Lycabettus, looked unfamiliarly small and insignificant. You normally see them from an entirely different perspective – looming unexpectedly at the end of narrow streets, or a raised focal point across a favourite city vista. Athens's first hill, the Acropolis, has become so much of a symbol (much more than, say, the Eiffel Tower is for Paris or the Colosseum for Rome) that it is far more than just the capital's emblem; it has become the most recognizable monument in the world – a universal icon.

In ancient Athens, the Parthenon was dedicated to the

worship of Athena, the city's dauntingly virtuous, virginal goddess of wisdom and war. Her righteous and honourable character may have been an example to the ancient Athenians, but then as now, there was an equal tendency to follow the example and the wilder excesses of the fun-loving, wine-quaffing Dionysus. He and Aphrodite, the goddess of love, were worshipped and honoured extensively at the same time. Athena underwent various metamorphoses in her long reign over Athens, the most dramatic taking place when the Greeks became Christians and she conveniently dropped her pagan cloak, reclaiming her prime position as the Virgin Mother of God. Now, the Acropolis is more like a monument to ancestor worship, authenticating the Athenians as spiritual descendants of the ancient Hellenes. Their ancestry may have become a burdensome weight, but it has also been a rock to cling to during Greece's violently turbulent history.

Just across the city centre from the Acropolis is Lycabettus. Its steep, wooded paths are popular with lovers and joggers, and it is topped by the pretty white church of St George. If the Acropolis is the sacred mountain which represents Athens's classical heritage, then Lycabettus stands as a proud symbol of the Orthodox Church and Athens's Byzantine legacy. Together they are the official twin peaks of Greek identity; the characteristics by which Athenians would like to be judged.

'Some people say that the Tourkovounia is Zeus' mountain,' said Christos, dipping easily into ancient mythology. 'But there's also a story that when Zeus' daughter Athena was carrying rocks to fortify the Acropolis, she dropped some pieces along the way, and they became Mount Lycabettus and the Tourkovounia.' As he was talking, it struck me that this often ignored, taller hill could stand as Athens's 'Third Hill' – its unofficial symbol representing the village and its ways in the city. Its name alludes to Greece's important (though less proud) Turkish legacy, and it is topped not by the formal monuments of the Church or classical Greece, but by the modest, rural houses of contemporary Athenians who work the system (even breaking the law) to make a home for their families in the city.

I put my new theory about the third hill to Christos, who wasn't entirely sure about it as an appropriate new monument for the capital.

'The Third Hill belongs to the *Romios*,' I insisted, using the alternative, untranslatable word for a Greek, which has a complex, self-denigrating, rustic character, and derives from the word for Roman (dating from the time when Constantinople was the New Rome). Pulling out all the stops, I tried to explain Patrick Leigh Fermor's wonderful description of how inside every Greek there are 'two figures dwelling in opposition': the Hellene, with his love of theory, the ideal, the ancient past and the formal *katharevousa* language; and the *Romios* with his love of practice, the real, the recent past and the demotic Greek language. Others have seen these two poles as the outsider's and the insider's point of view.

'Surely,' I argued doggedly, 'if the Hellene belongs to the Acropolis, then the Romios might visit the Orthodox Church on Lycabettus. But his home would be on the Tourkovounia.' My brother-in-law made a few diplomatic noises, and drew deep on his cigarette. You can't pin an Athenian down that easily.

CHAPTER 4

WAR WOUNDS

. . . And between his eyebrows
A small red-black bitter well
A well where memory goes cold.
Odysseus Elytis, 'The Heroic and Elegiac
Song for the Lost Second Lieutenant of the
Albanian Campaign'

I didn't know Vassilis's Uncle Yiannis and Aunt Xanthe well, though I'd met them occasionally at family gatherings, and the odd baptism and funeral. Still, I was eager to visit them, and to hear some more about Athenian life in the old days. Vassilis had told me about how he and his siblings used to come by train to visit them in Athens. As thirteen- and fourteen-year-olds, his two boy cousins would show him the city, taking him out on 'brothel crawls'. They'd dash inside, take a quick look at the prostitutes on the pretext of asking about prices, and then run off with their fantasies. On summer evenings, they'd sit on the balcony overlooking the open-air cinema next door and watch the films over and again.

'I knew *Barbarella* by heart after hearing it for three weeks in 1968,' Vassilis told me. 'We got to know the films so well that we'd shout out the actors' lines in advance, and annoy the cinema-goers below.'

Yiannis and Xanthe live in Pangrati, the district near the old Olympic Stadium, which used to be rather smart, but has become one of the most densely inhabited areas of Athens, with large numbers of foreigners and economic migrants. Despite all the changes, it still feels like a true neighbourhood – *yeitonia*, an inherently nostalgic concept, which conjures up the narrow streets of childhood memories, and the central square where children play, neighbours gather, and men drink coffee in the coffee shop. Pangrati's streets are lined with the omnipresent six-storey Athenian apartment blocks, but they are buzzing with small local shops, bakeries, boutiques and cafés.

Xanthe gives the impression of being one of those carefully stylish Athenian ladies in her seventies, with pearly fingernails and conservative, tasteful clothes. But I could see that she had the hard centre of a survivor. She had studied at the Athens Music School, brought up three children, given private piano lessons, and was now one of the great army of Greek grandmothers who play a major part in bringing up their grandchildren. Yiannis is a solid paterfamilias in his eighties, who can never resist a quick one-liner in support of the Orthodox Church, Aristotle, or his beloved village.

Their little third-floor sitting room had a balcony overlooking the street, and I watched a gypsy trio pass by, playing accordion, clarinet and tambourine. Smells of cooking wafted up from neighbouring homes, as Yiannis talked to me about 'the straight road of Christianity' and showed me his array of diplomas, degrees and awards hanging framed on the walls (interspersed with family photographs and icons). Xanthe brought in a dainty china coffee service and several plates of cakes and biscuits, and when she finally located the silver tongs for the cake and served the coffee, she started to tell her story. It emerged as a twisting Athenian epic, covering much of the twentieth century, from the angle of 'a true Athenian'.

'Actually, I'm a true *Pangratiotissa* [woman of Pangrati],' she said, and although only one of her grandparents was actually from Athens, and her father was born in Turkey, she is certainly more of an Athenian than many of the capital's inhabitants.

'I was born here,' she said, pointing implausibly at the 1960s third-floor flat where we were sitting. In those days it had been a house, when the entire street (and most of Athens) had consisted of detached houses with gardens. Pangrati was a pretty select place to live then. Her mother's parents had both worked in the Royal Palace at around the turn of the century, and the family was well placed in high society; there were servants and a villa down by the sea in Faliro.

'My grandmother was secretary to Queen Sofia, and my grandfather was an equerry to King Constantine. Grandfather was very, very handsome, with huge moustaches like the King, which were fashionable then. When the Palace made an order that only the King was allowed to keep his moustache, my grandfather refused to shave his off; he was so annoyed that he left the court.' In those days, moustaches were still a sign not merely of manliness, but even of Greekness. Until the twentieth century, every Greek man had a moustache which was an indication of his background, education, ideals and aspirations. The authentic man of the people (wearing the white *foustanella* kilt or baggy breeches) had generously proportioned whiskers, while the 'Frankish' bourgeois man (dressed in a suit) went for the clipped facial hair of the European.

The provocative contemporary writer Ilias Petropoulos published an intriguing study of the moustache in Greece and came up with some fascinating examples: the 'snot moustache' is two lines below the nostrils; the 'sauce moustache' is a very thin line of up to five millimetres in width; and '*à la Kaiser*' has a flourishing up-turn in imitation of the German ruler. In the early twentieth century, it needed unbelievable daring for the first Greeks to go out with a shaved moustache, 'like a monkey's arse'. Today, moustaches are still prevalent: you don't laugh up your sleeve but 'under your moustache', and when your 'moustaches are laughing' you're over the moon.

When Aunt Xanthe's grandfather left the Palace he opened up a café-taverna.

'It was here in this street,' said Xanthe. 'There were thirty employees and it was very popular with high society. The clientele was almost entirely courtiers and royalists, and it was more like a private club.' Xanthe pointed out a framed photograph of her mother soon after her marriage: a short, stout figure covered in jewels. 'My parents got married by arrangement. That was normal in those days,' she said. Her father moved in with his in-laws, and opened up a large and successful furniture factory and shop.

When the Second World War started everything changed. The first thing to go was the seaside villa, then the furniture factory, and by the time of the Nazi occupation (1941–4) they were down to selling their valuables.

'I remember my parents taking handfuls of jewellery and silver, just to buy enough to eat,' said Xanthe. 'Apart from a bracelet which we sold to buy me a piano, everything else went on food. People were completely ruined. My father eventually found some work in the factory of an ex-employee of his, and was paid in bread. He used to hide the loaf under his jacket so it wasn't stolen on the way home, and would often go without so that my brother and I would have something to eat the next morning. It was difficult, because we'd always been well off and had everything we wanted, and suddenly we were hungry.'

While British civilians were complaining about wartime meat rations, the Greeks were living through the devastation of Nazi oppression and real famine. The very word *katochi* (occupation) still summons up a chill atmosphere of dread. It remains a defining point in Greek consciousness, which echoes other collective memories of the worst oppressions of Ottoman rule.

'In the beginning we had the Italian occupation,' said Xanthe. 'That wasn't so bad – kids here would exchange cigarettes with the injured soldiers in the hospital for a bit of bread. But with the Germans it was different; they were very hard. The grocers' shops were shut, and you could only buy from black market dealers if you had money. We used to go searching on the hills for wild greens, but there wasn't even any oil to put with them.'

'I remember seeing children with swollen bellies coming to pick through the rubbish in the field next to our house where the cinema is now. One day there was this boy there . . .' Xanthe paused. 'He was scratching away with his fingers, when he just fell down dead in front of me. It was terrible. People used to collapse in the streets all the time from starvation and from the diseases which were spreading. I'd stand on our balcony and look down on the open lorries driving past. They were filled with corpses which they'd collected off the streets. Sometimes families just abandoned their relations' bodies in cemeteries or parks at night so they could keep the ration cards. But usually there weren't any rations. People couldn't even give a proper Christian burial for their families; they were just piled into mass graves. For us as an Orthodox people, that was very bad. It was a dark time.'

During the first, most terrible year of occupation, hundreds of children starved to death every day in Athens. In 1941, around 40,000 Greeks died of hunger alone. By the end of the war the number had risen to hundreds of thousands. Conditions were slightly better after the Allies eased their embargo, and also in the countryside; Yiannis remembered that people managed to grow their food up in the mountain village where he lived.

'We didn't have oil, but we'd get it from people down in the plain in exchange for wheat or eggs. It wasn't like in Athens where there wasn't any food. The Nazis took it all.' When the Germans left in 1944, Yiannis went to Athens.

'I had a small suitcase with a blanket and some food in it,' he said. 'And I hitched lifts all the way with a fellow villager. We managed to survive by selling onions on the street.'

The desperate situation encouraged many people to become more radical. There were rumours that the Germans were starving the Greeks to death on purpose, and the resistance movement (EAM – the initials of the National Liberation Front) developed into a strong Communist organization, backed up by its own army and various mountain-based guerrilla groups. Many of them worked in collaboration with the British Allies. Nazi reprisals to the resistance were viciously savage: resistance fighters were summarily executed and villages were burned. Civilians were indiscriminately murdered in revenge attacks, and the death of one German soldier could lead to the slaughter of hundreds of innocent Greeks of all ages. Alongside this carnage, most of Greece's Jews were rounded up and sent to their deaths. Almost all 50,000 members of Thessaloniki's thriving and historic Sephardic Jewish community were killed in Nazi concentration camps.

When Xanthe's family ran out of jewellery they were forced to sell their house.

'A black-market man paid us the price of five containers of oil for it,' she said, smiling wryly. 'But by the time he gave us the money, inflation had made it into worthless paper, and we just put it in the attic. Later, we couldn't even pay the rent to stay in the house and the owner tried to evict us. My mother was going crazy – we'd lost everything. Then, when the Germans left, a law came through announcing that anyone who had sold their house during the Occupation could buy it back at whatever price they'd paid. We couldn't even afford that, but we managed to pay half and divided it with the black-marketeer. At least we stayed in our home.'

'We lived through the worst periods in Greek history,' said Yiannis, dipping a biscuit in his cold coffee. 'Just when most European countries were starting to rebuild their cities and their lives after the war, Greece started another cycle of death that was even worse. It was brother killing brother during the Civil War.' Yiannis had begun to study law at Athens University, but that was interrupted by the upheavals, and he became a non-commissioned officer with the government forces.

The Civil War was a time of unspeakable horror and crimes on both sides: families were broken apart and villagers were massacred by their neighbours. Hatred was reinforced by relentless poverty, and the bitter enmity polarized the Left and Right for at least another generation. The situation was so complicated and painful that it's almost impossible, even now, to describe the facts without appearing to take sides. What is clear is that once the common (German) enemy had gone, the old battles between the Right and the Left re-emerged with a vengeance. In their carving up of the map into communist and capitalist, Stalin, Roosevelt and Churchill agreed at Yalta that Greece would go with the West; as in other times of crisis, its fate had yet again been determined by the Great Powers.

Needless to say, reality was more complicated than the theory. The Communist resistance fighters were still supported by the Soviet Union, while the British backed the right-wing and monarchists, and were soon fighting their erstwhile comrades of the anti-German resistance. During the infamous *Dekemvriana* of December 1944, dreadful fighting took place across Athens, between the Communist-controlled resistance army and British troops. The polarization only got worse. The Communists abstained from the country's first elections in 1946, and the reactionary forces acquired increasing levels of power.

I'd met a taxi driver who described how his family (like many others) had sheltered an English soldier during the Occupation.

'He was with us for six months,' he said. 'I was just a boy, but I helped feed him and care for him. It was a big risk; the Germans hanged people for less. It was a crime just to listen to the BBC. And do you know what? Five years ago he returned to our village with his wife and we had him to stay for a month. We couldn't believe it after all that time.' He looked thoughtful, then continued. 'But after the war the English didn't treat us well – they came like conquerors. It didn't give us a good picture of the English.'

While Yiannis was fighting his fellow countrymen up in the Grammos Mountains on the Albanian border, he was wounded and brought to Athens. It was a time when the islands, mountains and countryside were emptying; life there had become too brutalized and poor to bear. During the 1940s about 1,000 villages were destroyed, agricultural production fell by over seventy per cent, and about eight per cent of the entire population died. The proportion of people living in rural areas fell from about two thirds in 1940, to less than one third in the 1990s. Greece became an urban country in less than half a century.

'I went to visit Yiannis in the Military Hospital,' recalled Xanthe. 'We'd never met, but we'd started writing to one another a year or so previously, after he placed an advertisement in a paper for a correspondent. Lots of soldiers did that then. I was wearing a tight dress,' she added, stroking her bosom tenderly. Despite all the suffering, it was still these details which counted for a pretty young woman. 'Close-fitting and décolleté, with organza over the arms and a skirt cut on the bias. Later, when I saw him in his uniform and his hat he looked very handsome; we got engaged, and were married the next year.'

As I was leaving, Yiannis dug out some religious tracts he thought I'd enjoy. Since his retirement from the Ministry for Public Works, he'd had more time for a little writing himself, and he threw in various pages of his thoughts on the meaning of life and death. Xanthe put some pomegranates and sweets for the children in a little bag. She also showed me a black and white photograph of them as newly weds. They were a handsome couple; Xanthe with the sculpted hair and dark lips of 1940s Hollywood divas, and Yiannis with his stiffly upright, military bearing. The country might have been going to hell around them, but together, they had the indomitable air of youth.

* * *

Stepping out into the characteristic Athenian street of anonymous apartment blocks, it was odd to think that, like so much of the city, until the 1960s it had been an open road lined with spacious houses and tree-filled gardens. Like the vast majority of Athenians, Uncle Yiannis and Aunt Xanthe had given up their house (with their co-owner) in the late 1960s, taking advantage of the newly popular part-exchange system. This process lay at the root of Athens's dramatic architectural transformation – a response to the dire post-war need for housing, and a way for ordinary people to make money. The system was simple: an owner gave his house and land to a builder or developer, who built a block of flats. When it was finished the original owner received a flat to live in, plus one or two more to rent out or put his children in when they grew up.

Thousands of Athens's detached family homes and beautiful, neoclassical buildings were destroyed within a decade or two. The dramatic expansion of the capital solved unemployment and housing problems – some building firms even worked in exchange for apartments during the 1950s. But the weak, over-manned and bribe-taking bureaucracy allowed the new buildings to shoot up with minimal interference from government or planners. In the horrendous aftermath of war, hunger, poverty and emigration, few thought about green areas or public spaces, let alone style or quality; it was enough just to have a home. The sad results remain only too visible; shoddily built constructions using cheap materials, which in turn created dark, narrow, congested streets.

As I walked down into the centre of town, I marvelled at how Athens has managed to keep so much charm in spite of the abuse it has suffered. Even in the most modernized districts there is often a sense of neighbourhood. You still have the same neighbours, even if you now see them across fourth-floor balconies instead of on the front door steps, and the local kiosk, grocery, coffee shop and church still hold central positions in daily life. Among the more positive side effects of the post-war concrete jungle in central Athens, my favourite is the arcade or *stoa*. These walkways and tunnels thread their way like rat-runs beneath many of the larger office blocks and public buildings. Between Constitution Square and Omonia they are everywhere.

The Athenian *stoa* ranges from the chic and stylish (with dauntingly grand jewellery stores and purveyors of smart fountain pens and leather cases) to the dusty, forgotten remnants of the 1960s (with tiny outlets for out-of-date electrical appliances and places selling flesh-coloured bloomers and old women's cotton print dresses). In between you find the practical and charming arcades (with brass-plate engravers, hat sellers and tobacconists), and those that have become like modern shopping malls (with jeans, bikinis and record shops). There are also the specialist ones: the *Stoa* of Books (which organizes exhibitions and poetry readings), and the unforgettable *Stoa* of the Immortals, with its rembetika nightclub and tiny ouzo café leading off the meat market.

Whether it is a gloomy, neon underworld, whose shopkeepers look as though they've rarely seen a customer, or a glamorous arcade with glass and wrought-iron ceilings, these enclosed galleries usually have a café, even if it's only a window one and a half metres across, serving coffee and cheese pies. They provide shelter from the cold and wet in the winter, from the burning sun in the summer, and a moment of respite from the noise and bustle of the street. And where else would you find peach-coloured, cone-shaped satin bras that date back to a time before anyone had heard of Madonna?

Walking to the metro station in Constitution Square, I paused to look at the Evzones outside the Parliament building. They were putting on a fascinating, choreographed performance for the changing of the guard. Two lanky youths dressed in soft, white leggings and stiffly skirted *foustanella*, moved with exaggerated slowness, ponderously raising each stretched leg to a horizontal position. Just as a little flash of blue underpants showed, they gave a flick of their red wooden clogs, like marionettes. At times, the two men even touched toes in midair, the woolly pompons quivering, and their glazed eyes focused in the distance.

On the other side of the road, the celebrated Hotel Grande Bretagne was wrapped in scaffolding and plastic sheeting. All its innards had been scooped out to turn it into something super-luxurious for the 2004 Olympics, and it was now a hollow, vulnerable-looking shell. Guidebooks claim that 'almost everyone of fame or importance who has visited Athens' has stayed there. When it opened in the 1870s it was the city's first really smart hotel. The *Wehrmacht* requisitioned it during their occupation (they were said to have contemplated changing its inappropriate name), and in 1944, after they'd left, Winston Churchill (*Tsortsil* as he's known in Greek) narrowly escaped being blown up by a bomb planted in the sewers underneath it. The old GB Corner bar was always a favourite place for a cocktail amongst smarter ex-pats, and its interesting ambience married the unlikely combination of Greek and colonial. I felt a little sad to see all that gone; the new, slicker version would never recapture that old-fashioned gentility.

Syntagma still has the old men who tout lottery tickets and sell sesame-covered *koulouria* (bread rings) from large baskets, but it has changed since I first knew it. Constitution Square has been tidied up. The giant, gaudy billboards advertising Bodyline diet centres and cigarettes, which adorned the rooftops, have disappeared. Malodorous fast food outlets have replaced the old pavement cafés. And their most obvious customers have gone too. Back in the 1980s, the cafés in Syntagma were filled with male 'harpoons' or *kamakia*, hoping to 'catch' female tourists. You couldn't miss them. Wearing tight white trousers (or ironed jeans with creases), black slip-on shoes, open shirts and gold chains, they had ravenous eyes and dreadful pick-up lines. Anywhere a female tourist went, the *kamakia* went too.

When I'd arrived in Nafplio, I'd been intrigued (and occasionally appalled) by the Athenian *kamakia*'s provincial cousins. I'd just missed the infamously competitive 'Octopus Club', whose members counted up how many female 'victims' they'd seduced by the end of the season. But there were still plenty of freelancers. Dressed in vintage frocks picked up at

Oxfam and plimsolls (my idea of respectability at the time), and riding an aged, man's bicycle around town, I must have seemed pretty strange to them. I was blonde, evidently foreign, and during my first winter in town (before I became a familiar fixture), I was like a game bird out of season; it was the harpooners' instinct to move in closer.

My fieldwork diaries reveal my diffidence; I wasn't used to being stared at so obviously, and I didn't know how to react as an anthropologist. A haughty turn of the head would do in Athens, but I had all my research ahead of me in Nafplio. Initially, I had a not dissimilar problem during my numerous house visits to the people of the town. I was unfailingly pressed to sample traditional 'spoon sweets' (fruit preserves) and cakes, and in the early months it seemed rude to refuse the hospitality. I found my weight ballooning. For a time I was a plump game bird.

I eventually learned to politely refuse the sweets, and my solution to the approaching *kamakia* was to bring out a notebook and pencil and ask for information. I intended it as a damp blanket for romantic prospects (which it undoubtedly was), but as I got to know some of the characters (with marvellous nicknames like Prince, Butterfly or Hawk), their 'sport' became increasingly interesting. The more I learned, the more I became convinced that it wasn't 'just for sex', as most people said.

'Harpoons' thought that the unsuspecting visitor was tricked by their cunning advance and suave deceit. Claiming to be architects and doctors, they ignored the idea that the visitor might actually prefer a fisherman or a waiter on her holidays abroad. Different nationalities were graded according to a scale of perceived difficulty (Italians almost impossible, Germans, Americans and Britons easy), but a Greek woman was never tackled. 'She smells of sheep,' they'd say disparagingly of their own kind, knowing they had no hope. Their success in 'spearing' the 'whores' or 'chickens' was described as 'slaughter', 'roasting', 'beating' or 'throwing down', and their failures or a brush-off as 'eating dog poison'.

The description of *kamakia* in my thesis was formalized to fit the requirements of academe, though the mix of slang, sexual innuendo and anthropological theory hovered on the brink of comedy. My theory was that *kamaki* was a 'system of male competition, whereby men without material and social status established other grounds for prestige'. Instead of money, education or respectability, the harpoon won success by 'scoring' women.

The 'hunters' both desired and despised the foreign women, something which encapsulated to me the complicated sense of antagonism that Greeks often had towards 'Europe' and America. On the one hand, tourists represented the affluence and attraction of countries perceived as more advanced than Greece. On the other, tourists were 'immoral' hedonists who used Greece as their sunny playground, so that lying to them and sexually conquering them provided the perfect combination of pleasure and revenge. Student protesters might march on the US Embassy; *kamakia* could just screw an American tourist for a similar sense of satisfaction.

Given the hostility of the 'harpoons' to foreign women, it was surprising that a fair number ended up marrying their Shirley Valentine 'victims'. Whereas Greek wives were seen as snaring husbands, the foreign ones were viewed as dupes. 'Take shoes from your own place, even if they're patched,' was a popular proverb in those days. The idea was that it's better to marry an old boot who is local than a more seductive proposition from elsewhere. That way you know what you're getting. I became acquainted with many of the outsider wives, who were pitied by most locals and often ended up keeping house while their husbands went back on the prowl. Now, I remembered these marginalised women with their bilingual, bi-cultural children in a different, more sympathetic light. It had been easy to feel a little superior then, almost 'one of the boys'. God only knows what 'the boys' thought about me with my little notebook and my endless questions.

I may have fought off the *kamakia*, but I ended up breaking the basic anthropological rule of non-committal, morally impeccable behaviour, by acquiring a local boyfriend. With hindsight, my attempts to keep the relationship secret were hilariously inadequate; I erroneously imagined that if I was tactful in the town and home before breakfast, all would remain undisclosed. I quickly learned a great deal about the dreadful pressures of small-town gossip; how to deflect questions and how to deceive convincingly. 'Why tell the truth when you can lie?' was the principle. In those days, a 'nice girl' in the provinces had to watch out for her reputation, or she could be labelled a slut; something which could also have an unpredictable, probably detrimental effect on fieldwork. In the end, nothing dramatic occurred, perhaps because I didn't have parents or relations to put pressure on me. And by the time I left Nafplio in the late 1980s, the 'harpoons' were already starting to die out, Greek women were becoming much freer and Aids had put a damper on so-called 'holiday romances'.

Now, over a decade after I'd finished my thesis, the 'harpoons' kept popping up in my life, despite their demise.

'This is Sofka. She wrote her thesis about the *kamakia*,' friends would say on introducing me to someone. Everybody would laugh at the incongruity of a foreign woman pinning the 'harpoons' to a page of analysis. I hadn't discovered a good response: it was pathetic when I laughed coyly, lame when I replied: 'Actually, it was only a chapter,' and too earnest if I started banging on about the theory.

'It was just about sex; simple as that,' people still tended to say.

'I'll tell you about *kamakia*,' retorted some of the older, more flirtatious men, 'but only in practice; not the theory.' Their eyes would light up at the memory of their lecherous youth, when they were 'always hungry'. Greece had somehow seemed more remote and innocent in the days of the harpoon hunters.

* * *

Not long after I visited Uncle Yiannis and Aunt Xanthe, Anna and Lara's school organized its regular annual parade to commemorate one of the few clearly victorious, heroic moments of Greece's Second World War. *Ochi* Day, on 28 October, is a major national holiday, celebrating the resounding 'No' (*Ochi*) that Greece said in 1940 to the invading Italians, and the subsequent military victory over the fascist 'macaroni-eaters' in the freezing Albanian mountains. For a while, until the Nazis arrived six months later, the Greeks were united in victorious patriotism, having succeeded in rejecting an occupying force. It was one of the few times in modern Greek history when the Greeks said 'No!' and weren't trampled over by invaders. So it is hardly surprising that there should be such a popular celebration of this symbol of resistance, even if it was said by one unpalatable dictator (Ioannis Metaxas) to another (Benito Mussolini).

During the week before the holiday, Anna and Lara joined their schoolmates to practise marching, military style, around the local streets of Vouliagmeni in preparation for the annual parade. Throughout Athens, roads were hung with Greek flags, and special shops and stalls sprang up, selling nothing but stripy blue and white flags of every size and quality imaginable, and quaint posters of old-fashioned, bayonet-bearing Greek soldiers in clogs, charging into the snow and surrounded by olive branches and patriotic slogans.

Newspapers were filled with articles about the current significance of 'No Day', television and radio shows remembered the war, and political parties shamelessly declared their own versions of 'No': the Government favoured 'no to terrorism', and the left-wing alliance, Sinaspismos, supported 'no to globalization'. A few dissenting voices said no to parades and celebrations. Greece was behind the times, they said, in persevering, almost uniquely in Europe, with such outmoded practices.

Most off-putting was the now annual scandal of people debating whether it was appropriate for Albanian schoolchildren to walk at the head of the parade, holding the Greek flag – a privilege accorded to the best students. A few unpleasantly nationalistic, usually rural officials regularly emerged to make a fuss if the top student happened to be Albanian. The media were only too happy to exacerbate the fray.

'What next?' people ranted. 'Soon we'll have Turkish children carrying the flag for our Independence Day parade.'

No Day turned out blazingly hot; the beaches were full of people taking their last bathe of the season. We had left early from a weekend expedition to an island with some friends, who were incredulous that we should be returning for the parade. I had felt slightly ridiculous as a foreigner, trying to explain to a group of Athenian parents (whose children all attended private schools, which don't organize these patriotic events) why we thought we should go back to Athens for the Monday bank holiday.

'The children have been practising all week,' I said defensively, 'and the headmaster was so severe to the pupils about people who don't turn up for the marching.' We were apparently living in another Greece from our liberal-minded friends.

In Vouliagmeni, nobody needed convincing about the importance of the day. The streets were crowded with proud parents and interested locals admiring the neighbourhood's youth as they gathered to march. Even Effi had come along to cheer on Anna and Lara, and was striding around jauntily, greeting friends and acquaintances.

'It's not like it used to be,' she sighed. 'We used to feel really proud. We walked upright,' she said, stiffening her back militarily. 'They don't feel the same now.'

Teachers tried in vain to put some order into the rows of children, who were all dressed in neatly pressed blue clothes or national costume.

'I need black shoes,' Lara had announced hopelessly that morning, as we dug out the least dirty pair of trainers, which she told me were banned.

'Oh, I'm so embarrassed in this,' said Anna (who would never willingly wear a skirt), looking unfamiliarly feminine and lovely in her *Amalia* – the national costume of long, blue skirt and heavily brocaded, red velvet jacket and cap, which is named after Greece's first queen. She quickly joined her friend Aphrodite in a gaggle of other *Amalias*, and they whispered and laughed at the sweaty-looking boys in white leggings and *foustanella (*pleated, white kilt).

As I listened to the teacher calling out the pupils' names, some of the ancient ones still gave me a jolt with their incongruity and romantic allure. It must be hard, I reflected, to live up to the implications of dazzling beauty and eroticism of Aphrodite and the purity and wisdom of Athena. And how do the raucous schoolboys feel about being called Socrates and Plato? Of course in Greece these names are taken for granted. Nobody finds it amusing to tickle babies called Themistocles or Clytemnestra, and it seems natural to deal with officials called Pericles or Solon, waitresses called Electra or Hera, and shopkeepers named Homer or Xenophon. And if girl babies are more often called after goddesses, nymphs and mythological heroines it is only for a lack of famous female protagonists in ancient history.

These forenames only became popular among modern Greeks in the nineteenth century after the formation of the Greek state, when taking ancient names was an efficient method of emphasizing the desired link between the ancient and contemporary Hellenes. Most Greeks are still called after saints, and the Greek Orthodox Church was, to say the least, ambivalent about the idea of baptizing the increasing numbers of babies with pagan names. Eventually, however, there was an effort to incorporate them into the Christian realm; a number of saints were established with ancient names, and even people without a specific saint can celebrate their name day along with the other lost boys and girls of the festive calendar on All Saints' Day in June.

The parents were dressed, like the teachers, in a version of Sunday best. Fashionable mothers wore elaborate high heels and tight jeans covered in lashings of sequins, embroidery and snakeskin patches, while the less style-conscious came in shiny jackets with outdated shoulder pads and awkward, squeezing shoes. The fathers carried cameras and patted each other on the back.

'*Chronia Polla!* Many Happy Returns!' we all said to each other in recognition of the celebration.

The traffic was diverted as the procession proceeded through the main seafront road to the war memorial, and martial music blared out from loudspeakers. The first time I'd been to this kind of parade had been in my days as an anthropologist, a few days after I arrived in Nafplio. I understood then about the theoretical power of ritual in a parade, but I hadn't realized how different it is when you see your own children participating, and how your emotions are manipulated by the event. I felt strangely touched. The best pupils carried the largest flags, and the youngest ones clutched little plastic ones, as they marched past the enthusiastic crowds of relations and onlookers, who waved and clapped, straining for a better view of their children.

On the surface, the whole thing looked a bit like the sort of event you'd find in a Fascist or Communist state, but the children's chaotic marching, the genuine enthusiasm and jollity of the onlookers, and a characteristically nonchalant disrespect for authority gave the whole occasion an air of fun and pantomime rather than pomposity. The parents chatted happily as the priest got on with his business of chanting the prayers, and onlookers made cynical little comments as they clapped the Mayor, the local politicians and military men, the local choir, the athletics clubs and even Vouliagmeni's animal lovers' society, who all laid their wreaths by the war memorial.

Afterwards, I asked Lara if she had understood what it had all been about. What did all this flag waving and marching in memory of something so long ago mean to her?

'Well,' she said, pausing to think, 'I'm not sure, but I know it was good that we said no.'

CHAPTER 5

A DREAM CITY

Here the sky is everywhere,
On all sides shines the sun,
And something like the honey of Hymettus is all around
Kostis Palamas, 'Athens'

By November we had started to feel at home in Vouliagmeni. The autumn days were warm and we were settling into our new routines. Bitter oranges were ripening on the trees near Eurydice Street, and sometimes small boys would pick them, rolling them into the road as cars went by. As the fruits were squashed into the tarmac, the boys laughed and jumped with pleasure, and a sharp, citrus tang filled the air. The hills by our house were covered in delicate mauve and white anemones, and we planted a couple of olive trees, some climbing jasmine and a few rosemary bushes in our small, rocky garden. One day, I came across some old people near the dry-cleaners, whacking the branches of an old olive tree with long sticks. Hard, shiny olives were tumbling down into the fine, black nets laid out across the pavement. It could have been a scene from any time in the last few thousand years, if you ignored the tarmac and the large jeeps speeding by every so often. If this was living in the suburbs, then that was fine.

There were times, though, when it was hard being a *xeni* – a foreign woman. The more I saw Vassilis rediscovering his own roots, the more I realized that I didn't have any. Vassilis found himself hearing songs he hadn't listened to for over twenty years and knowing all the words. I saw him looking surprised at himself, singing along on auto-pilot, and being transported back to his teens.

I began introducing myself with the Greek version of my name – Sophia. People found it much easier than the foreign-sounding Sofka. At the children's school I was *Kyria* (Mrs) Papadimitriou, a surname which in England had provoked as much bewilderment as my own. In Greece, however, it was refreshingly ordinary. In fact, it was the first time in my life that I'd been able to use a name that was generally recognizable and pronounceable, and could book appointments without giving explanations and spellings. Sophia Papadimitriou. A new me.

Sometimes, though, my attempts to become Greek only emphasized how little I belonged. The hours I spent waiting in the local Aliens' Office and municipal buildings trying to get my papers in order were a kind of purgatory; Eurydice waiting to cross the river Styx on her way to the underworld. I sat there, pondering on the implications of committing myself to being a foreigner for the rest of my life, hoping the experience of my mythological namesake wouldn't turn out to be too appropriate.

The Aliens' Office was an unapologetically horrible department in the police station, filled with hopefuls like me. We were all trying to get to grips with the appalling amount of paperwork required to gain legal status. It is notoriously difficult, and time-consuming. And if it was hard and sometimes humiliating for me, what was it like for the less educated Albanians, Romanians, Ukrainians and Poles without money, contacts and above all confidence? I imagined the problems of those who didn't speak Greek, when almost all signs and forms are in Greek and few civil servants speak another language. People hung around smoking by the 'no smoking' signs, and a radio was tuned to a station playing irritating popular songs. There were icons everywhere of Saint Artemios, the patron saint of Greece's police force. Over the fuse-box was a cardboard cut-out of the handsome, fourth-century military man, armed with an elegant spear, plus bow and arrow.

'E-oo-ri-dees . . .,' said the woman who was filling out a form for me in triplicate by hand. She was tall and curvaceous, with raven-coloured, waist-length hair and high heels, and didn't know what to make of my middle name.

'Eurydice – it's the English version of Evridiki,' I said helpfully, seeing that my Greek middle name (which means wide or universal justice) was being turned into a travesty of itself. I was ignored.

'Marital status? Height? Colour of eyes?' I realized I didn't know how to say hazel in Greek.

'Greenish?' I replied hesitantly. 'Hmmm, strange . . .,' said my interrogator critically, examining my eyes. 'We'll say green,' she resolved. 'Religion?'

I was pathetically pleased to answer 'Orthodox', which was technically true, though I'd rarely been to the Russian Orthodox Church in London after my baptism. I imagined the policewoman was expecting another answer, and that my reply somehow made me less of an alien.

As we were dealing with the paperwork I asked how long she thought it would take for my application to go through.

'Don't expect anything for two years, and it could be longer,' she answered, combining the smugness of the public employee with a small glimmer of cunning and challenge in her eyes. 'That is unless you've got some "inside influence." Then you might be able to push things along . . .'

There was carbon paper all over the place, and no computers. The policewoman told me to remove my rings and roll up my sleeves, and proceeded to squeeze some tar-like black paste from a tube, spreading it onto a metal-topped block of wood with a roller. It looked as antiquated as something Sherlock Holmes might have used. Taking my fingers one by one, she rolled them in the black goo, and pressed an imprint onto the appropriate place on all the three forms. She kept going until she'd done whole thumbprints and then palm prints and I was covered in the sticky substance. I asked her if she did the serious criminals too.

'Oh yes, we get them all coming through here,' she replied proudly.

Afterwards I couldn't get rid of all the black; it was as though I'd been marked by some strange rite. I tried to keep my hands hidden when I collected the children from school. Who'd want a criminal or an alien for a mother?

* * *

I was becoming increasingly enthusiastic about my exploration of Athens, but there were times when it seemed as though the crazy race to prepare for the Olympic Games was getting out of hand. The year 2004 had been a mythological date – a dream time for a new dream city of the third millennium – but now it was suddenly looming. Every day there were more cranes along the skyline, and it was hard to avoid getting snarled up in traffic jams caused by convoys of JCBs and cement mixers. The roads were lined with gangs of Albanians digging pipelines and erecting scaffolding, tunnels were being gouged out of the earth all around town, and the juddering of pneumatic drills resounded from street to street.

Many projects now had to be completed in double and triple time; building sites were often busy and floodlit at two a.m. Billions were going into all the Olympic paraphernalia: stadiums, marinas, rowing lakes, press centres, the Olympic Village. New stations and train routes were being constructed, pedestrian precincts were being laid by the kilometre, and most of the smartest hotels and many museums had closed for a couple of years of renovation. They were even putting back the tram line which Aunt Xanthe remembered from the golden days of her pre-war youth, linking the centre of town with Athens's long seafront promenade.

'Well, it can't get any worse, can it?' said Vassilis's sister Stella, evidently taking some pleasure in her gloomy optimism. She'd taken to ringing me up from work, during quiet moments, and we'd have long discussions about the difficulties of living in Greece, and plot the reformation of the entire education system. The latest bugbear was the state of the roads, and in particular the proliferating potholes, which were never fixed. There was now a pothole helpline, and people were counting them ('40,000 in Piraeus alone,' announced one journalist).

'Did you hear about the man who was driving along, when the road opened up beneath him?' asked Stella. I'd seen the pictures in the paper, of a huge, hellish crater, fifteen metres deep, where the main road had suddenly given way. The geologists who had made the survey for the new metro tunnel underneath were now in serious trouble too, but miraculously, the driver had escaped with minor injuries.

'They say that he was arguing with his wife as they drove

home at four a.m.,' said Stella laughing. 'And he said, "if I'm being unfaithful, let the earth swallow me up."'

The surprising thing was that almost every Athenian seemed positive about the Games. There was a determined belief that this would be the birth of something glorious for Athens, and few people were complaining about the problems in the pregnancy. In many ways, this constructive chaos suits the Athenians; the noise and tension is part of what gives their city life. An Athenian friend who spent much of her childhood away from Greece remembered how she loved coming back to Athens so much that she enjoyed inhaling the thick fumes of exhaust and pollution in the city centre.

After the chaotic suffering and tragic mistakes of the last century, there were clear signs of a renaissance of urban culture in the twenty-first. Some optimists even suggested that Athens's characteristic post-war concrete blocks would not last more than another few decades; their poor quality meant they will have to be pulled down, they said, and the whole architecture of the city will alter yet again.

Dramatic changes were already happening in some areas. When I visited a friend in Maroussi, I was bewildered by the transformation. I'd previously known it as a quiet, northern suburb, not so unlike the leafy outpost described in Henry Miller's *The Colossus of Maroussi* – a paean to the massive-framed literary figure, George Katsimbalis, whose huge appetites and talent for storytelling so impressed the American on his pre-war travels in Greece. Now, however, parts of the district had exploded into an incongruous forest of towering glass edifices housing multinational companies, looking as though they were accidentally dropped on Athens while on their way to Dallas. Maroussi was also where they were preparing the centre of action for the Olympics; a futuristic stadium had been designed by the illustrious Spanish architect, Santiago Calatrava.

I took 'the electric' (train) from Maroussi back into town. Built for a steam engine in 1869, this line was until recently the only way of beating the traffic, and traversing the city, albeit only along one axis. Running all the way from the smart, northern suburb of Kifissia down to the port at Piraeus, it links two points which have long been opposite extremes of the social spectrum as well as the train line. Now, 'the electric' looks like 'old Athens'; 'new Athens', on the other hand, is clearly to be found on the metro.

Changing lines that day, from 'the electric' to the two-year-old metro, was like changing countries. Even the people looked different, as they walked down the immaculate escalators into a Hellenic Switzerland; a fantasy underworld, where everything was squeaky clean marble, and large, open spaces decorated with a tasteful mix of modern art and ancient artefacts. There were carefully presented museum exhibits of archaeological finds unearthed while digging the tunnels, playful murals by contemporary artists, and even piped music.

I walked from the metro station to a café where I'd arranged to meet Vassilis, and turned off the thundering main road into a square. It was an unexpected oasis of calm and shade. A few men lay asleep on benches under the trees, and a little group were playing backgammon on a rickety table by a flower stall. Some handsome young sailors walked past in baggy white trousers and clumpy black boots. Opposite the square was a squat, Byzantine church, overshadowed on all sides by tall office buildings. This is a common sight in Athens; there's even one minuscule chapel which has been left *in situ*, despite a whole modern block (housing the Ministry of Education) having been built over and around it. Now, painted a playful mauve, it sits pluckily in the gloom under the cantilevered first floor, between the concrete columns.

I sat down to wait for Vassilis at the café, and watched people drinking coffee. The rituals were the opposite of the Italian, who quickly downs his espresso at the bar for an injection of caffeine. In Greece it not only takes time, but is a weighty business.

'It's our form of psychoanalysis,' says Kostas, my brother-in-law. He loves the coffee shop so much that he has his 'first coffee' there at seven a.m. before work, in addition to his serious, early evening session with all the regulars.

Vassilis was late, something which sometimes made me feel all English and finicky; Greeks actually say: 'We're English,' when they do arrive on time. Recently, we'd invited some friends to Sunday lunch at two p.m. The first guests arrived at three-thirty, the next at four-fifteen, and the last lot (who admittedly did ring before four) showed up after five. One explanation is that it's normal to set out at the time of the appointment, so the further you travel, the later you'll be. But it's also linked to an acceptance of one's human weaknesses and of refusing to be tied down and obey the rules. Of course, most Greeks know how to work the system, and set the invitation time for an hour or so before they actually want their guests. So there is some kind of coordination to it, as I'd discovered when finding myself as that awkward social pariah, the first guest at a party.

I ordered a coffee and gazed at the people sitting around me. They were talking animatedly, waving their arms, flicking keys and worry beads, and tapping their hands on the tables or their companions' arms. Everything about their conversation was more than what northern Europeans are accustomed to. Greeks speak louder, interrupt more often, and if they can't use their bodies as well they feel drastically handicapped (you can always tell a Greek driver when you're in the car behind by the flailing arms). One man was slicing the air with his free arm as he spoke on his mobile phone, a device which was surely invented for Greeks. Mobiles not only enable you to keep talking when alone, but allow for last-minute plan changes, and a speeding-up of pace when things get dull. People like them so much that they are rarely switched off (few situations are considered worthy of that honour), and there are currently enough phones in circulation for every man, woman and child in the country.

In the distance, Vassilis was walking towards me with our old friend, Stelios Kouloglou. They were guffawing with laughter. Seeing them together took me straight back to memories of 1990, when I'd been rash and in love enough with Vassilis to uproot myself again and move from London to Moscow. Stelios had been one of his two flatmates, both foreign correspondents reporting on the collapse of the Soviet Union. Paolo Valentino, the other, was a debonair Sicilian, who cooked exquisite Italian food every evening, and whose favourite word was 'decadence' (applied to shavings of parmesan dipped in honey; best quality Uzbek marijuana; and parties he organized with Russian models and poets, Italian actors and rock singers, Greek students and diplomats and a sprinkling of every kind of journalist). They'd been a trio of tall, handsome, dark-haired bachelors and there were times when I felt as out of place as a hen at a stag night. Nevertheless, I adored Stelios and Paolo, and was cherished as the token female member of the gang. Together, we had witnessed the crumbling of Communism, consuming outsize jars of black-market caviar and quantities of viscous frozen vodka.

Shortly after Vassilis and I left Russia, Anna was born in England. We brought her to Greece as a young baby for our wedding – a quiet affair in late November on the rocky island of Hydra. I invited Stella, an old friend from my Nafplio days, as a witness and we asked Stelios as the other. Civil marriage had only been made legal a few years earlier, and the approach was appealingly amateurish. On finding out that we didn't have a yacht for the purpose (Hydra has long attracted the smart set as well as writers, painters and weekending cognoscenti from Athens), the female official at the town hall asked us where we would like the ceremony.

'Over there by the sea,' I said, pointing vaguely, and we trooped along the coast path to a convenient spot under a pine tree. Vassilis clutched the new baby, Stelios carried a bottle of champagne and some glasses, and I had a small bunch of flowers I'd managed to pick – sprigs of perfumed jasmine, and some shamelessly bright pink bougainvillaea. In acting as our marriage sponsor, albeit outside the proper, religious service, Stelios had become our *koumbaros*, bound to us for life.

Vassilis and Stelios sat down with me at the café. Stelios's wild-eyed, naughty-boy look was not compromised in the least by a few grey strands showing through his dark, cropped hair, and he was in an extremely good mood. His investigative documentary series on TV had been awarded a prestigious prize, and it looked as though he was winning a ferocious battle with one of the rabid, 'tabloid'-style television channels which he had accused of lying and misleading the viewers on its news programmes. Even better, the bookshops were full of his new novel *Never Go to the Post Office Alone*, based on a romance he had in Moscow with a beautiful and mysterious Bulgarian. Stelios was now a father of three with a family apartment in the exclusive, northern suburb of Kifissia, but he retained his pied-à-terre in town, and still seemed like a free spirit.

We talked about the frenzied atmosphere in Athens.

'They're hoping that it will be like the success story of Barcelona, where industrial zones were developed for the

Olympics,' said Stelios. 'And you can see that the city is really changing. It's just we're doing it '*à la grecque*' – all over the place and without knowing which direction we're going in.'

Foreign newspapers were already bringing out articles suggesting that Athens would never be ready in time, and that Greeks were not up to the job.

'Everyone gets so upset here about the criticism,' said Vassilis. 'But it's ridiculous, this inferiority complex we have towards Europe. Greeks all think that "Europe" is the centre of Paris or London. They forget that Europe is also council estates with drugs and crime and mafia villages in Sicily. We may be a small country, and we don't have industry, but at least we don't have working-class ghettos.'

'That's true,' added Stelios. 'Athens may be an ugly city, but there's a high quality of life and it's very lively.'

It was funny how often conversations started out with the premise that Athens is an unbearable, inadequate 'cement city', and ended up eulogizing its advantages. Stelios was getting into his stride now, counting up the blessings:

'The warm climate allows us to live outside for half the year, and it's also extremely safe – there's very little violence and crime . . . In fact, if Athens was beautiful too, it'd be the perfect city.'

* * *

I said goodbye to Stelios and Vassilis and decided to get a taxi home, standing at what looked a likely spot by the edge of the road. There's a definite knack to obtaining a taxi in Athens, which is something between catching a fish and public speaking to a restive crowd. You wave at any taxi, whether it has other passengers in it or not, and as it swerves over towards you, slowing down slightly, you shout out your destination. The taxi may be empty and ignore you, or it may be almost full and stop.

So you keep shouting until one pulls over. Sometimes the driver graces you with an unequivocal refusal, but more often he gives a little roll backwards of the head and eyes, accompanied by a *tsssst* sound – the expression for no. At other times, you are just left to wonder whether he didn't feel like it, or didn't fancy going in your direction.

I kept on shouting 'Vouliagmeni,' which is asking for trouble, as it is off the main routes, but eventually a taxi with a female passenger stopped. As the woman didn't show any sign of moving up, I got into the front seat next to the young driver. I felt as pleased as though I'd just hooked a trout, and generally full of positive thoughts about how democratic and ecologically sound the shared taxi system is.

It was a little less pleasing when we had to go off my route in order to take the other passenger to her destination (everybody pays their full fare regardless of other occupants and diversions), and surprising when the youthful driver stopped at a garage and announced: 'I have to do something.' To my puzzled expression, he replied: 'or I'll burst.' He returned a few minutes later, looking relieved. Taking a swig from a glass of cold, watery-looking Nescafé, which was stuck into its special holder on the dashboard, he took out a packet of cigarettes. I decided to try my luck. Following a recent campaign and change in law, smoking in public offices and taxis was forbidden, and there was even an order (to general shock and disbelief) that restaurants should offer non-smoking sections.

'Please could you open your window if you're going to smoke, as it bothers me in cars,' I said politely. The youth flicked his lighter, lit the cigarette, opened a slit in the window and turned to me.

'Where are you from?' he asked, turning to look at me with genuine curiosity, and blowing a stream of smoke into my face.

The organizers of the Olympics were becoming worried about Athens's ill-assorted, often untrained collection of cabbies, and about how visitors to the capital would react to their mysterious ways, not to mention lack of foreign language skills. It had recently been announced (and met with rather the same disbelief as the anti-smoking regulations) that they had decided to prepare a fleet of elite taxi drivers. They would not only be given lessons in the appropriate manners for foreign visitors, but taught a few basic sentences like 'Good morning' and 'Where are you going?' in English. But as another cabbie had recently remarked to me, 'you can never put a Greek in a cage'; it was hard to imagine a courteous new breed of Athenian super-cabbies.

Back at Eurydice Street, Lara was helping Effi make *koulourakia*, little round biscuits flavoured with orange zest, and the house was filled with homely baking smells. The afternoon was still warm, and Effi was sitting on a rock in the garden having a cigarette break.

'What can I do, Sophia?' she said to me, inhaling with evident pleasure. 'I don't have a man, so smoking is my only pleasure.' Women often said something like that. 'It's my only vice,' they claim. Smoking embodies countless Greek ideals about spontaneity, living in the moment, conspiratorial pleasures and rebellion. It also forms such a perfect accompaniment to lengthy cups of coffee and wine-filled evenings that it sometimes seems surprising that there is anyone in Greece who doesn't smoke. Newspapers report that one in four ten-year-olds smoke, and that most children are unaware of the health risks. Anna and Lara claimed to detest cigarettes, but their favourite popular song was as much a romantic hymn to smoking as to love. They sang it over and again:

> *To the cigarette which I'm holding, to my only God*
> *Let the dawn never come.*

To this angelic body, to this mouth I'm kissing
Like this I'll love you for a lifetime.

'Cigarettes and sweet things,' continued Effi. 'Sometimes I go out at midnight in search of chocolate profiteroles. I get desperate. Can you explain that? Anyway, when are you going to find a husband for me? You said you'd help. You must have a nice friend, but he's got to be someone special . . .' She was off on one of her monologues, which could last for twenty minutes if uninterrupted. They usually centred on food, Greekness and men, but it was mostly rhetoric; she'd already heard my cod-Freudian theory that her longings for sugary pleasures were a substitute for other physical satisfactions.

I suggested a swim to the children, but they weren't interested, so I packed a basket with a towel and a book, and set off alone.

'Have a swim for me!' called Effi. I walked down the lethally steep descent of Orpheus Street to my favourite place for a quick bathe – the little municipal jetty. In the summer, the small strip of sandy beach and the quayside itself were packed with sunbathers, but by this time of year there were only a few dedicated winter swimmers and the odd fisherman.

'What do you catch with that?' I said amicably to a shaggy-haired old man, who was cleaning a fishing net.

'Fish,' he answered tersely.

'Where do you go to set the nets?' I asked, hoping he'd turn out friendlier.

'To sea,' he replied, and I moved on.

I dived off the rusting, metal ladder into the cool water. It tasted saltier than usual. A smell of fried calamari was wafting over from the nearby ouzo bar, and I looked across to where a young couple were eating a lazy, late lunch, with tall glasses of cloudy, white ouzo. I swam quickly, parallel to the rocky coast, passing two elderly ladies floating companionably in flowery bathing caps.

'Isn't it lovely?' one of them called to me. 'Good swimming!' shouted the other. I reached a small bay, with a flimsy wooden diving tower built on the rocks. In the summer, it often had a line of skinny boys flipping and tumbling into the deep water below, but now it was deserted. I lay spread-eagled in the water for a moment, looking up at a seagull wheeling overhead. High above, a tiny aeroplane heading south towards Africa was making a vapour trail in the blue-violet sky. These were the best moments of the day, when everything made sense and I knew exactly why I had moved to Greece. As I walked home up Orpheus Street, it was as though Eurydice had not stayed underground after all, but had made it back to the land of the living.

* * *

That weekend we went down the coast a little way to Varkiza. There was a long, sandy beach there, and on it, our favourite taverna serving the best fish soup. On Sundays, it was always filled with families and groups of couples out for leisurely lunches, sitting outside if the weather permitted; Greeks always prefer eating alfresco, even if it means wearing a coat. I enjoyed looking at the grandmothers in their Sunday best after church, the perfectly lipsticked wives in high heels, the children running down to the sea and being scolded for not eating enough, and the husbands with fat bellies ordering generous quantities of seafood.

After we had eaten, Vassilis and I sat drinking cups of grainy Greek coffee and watching Anna and Lara playing on the beach with a puppy. There were dozens of abandoned dogs at Varkiza, but this one was evidently too young to keep up with the others.

'It must have been left here a week or so ago, the poor thing,' said Panos, the taverna owner, bringing us a plate with slices of home-made halva. 'We've given it something to eat, but there are so many dogs here now, it's become quite a problem.'

I'd always liked Athens's street dogs. You see them on every street, sauntering along, meeting up with friends outside some café, and often crossing at traffic lights with pedestrians. They lounge about in shop doorways, lying lazily on their backs with their legs in the air, or flopped despondently, as though they are sleeping off a hangover. In some parks there are packs, which frolic and chase cats, and as few of them are sterilized, litters of puppies are born and become increasingly feral. These independent, urban animals are said to travel vast distances in their wanderings, perhaps with some atavistic memories of life as wolves.

But I had stopped seeing the street dogs as a merry band of outlaws after the day when I went to our local post office – an old metal trailer with a window flap, sitting on the pavement. I had to step around a large, handsome, yellow dog which was lying in front of the postbox. As I leaned over to post my letter, I noticed a fly crawling around its eye. It was dead.

'They've been putting down poison,' said a man outside the shop over the road. 'Several dogs have been killed recently, and they're not sure who's doing it. Usually it's older people. Either they're disturbed by barking, or they just don't like dogs.'

When we got ready to leave Varkiza, the children arrived at the car clutching a small, hairy, black and white bundle.

'No,' said Vassilis firmly.

'Absolutely impossible,' I confirmed. 'Anyway, we've already got Lily.'

'We're not going without her!' shrieked the girls, as the skinny puppy wagged its little tail and stared up at us with liquid brown eyes. Panos looked out from the taverna, smiling sympathetically at the family crisis. After about ten minutes of arguing I showed the first fatal sign of weakness: 'Maybe we could take it as an outdoor dog?' I said.

We named her Bella. She ate voraciously, quickly putting on flesh, and growing larger, hairier and more boisterous by the day. From time to time we tried the idea of outdoor dog, but she was aggrieved by Lily's indoor status. She destroyed the plants, smashed the flower pots, and gathered up collections of our neighbours' slippers, toys, tools and rubbish, depositing them on our doorstep.

'She belongs on the street; she doesn't know how to behave,' said Effi, seeing me trying to train Bella. 'She's not suited to life in a house.'

In the past, dogs belonged only outside in the street; they went with dirt, chaos and even immorality. They were the *koproskyla* or 'shit-heap dogs', an insult which is still hurled at strays. There were so many dead dogs on Greek roads in the 1980s that I used to have nightmares about them; I was sickened by their stiff, stinking corpses, which were left to rot where they fell. But Greek dogs weren't always outcasts; archaeologists have even discovered tombs of some privileged ancient dogs which included ornamental collars and perfume bottles alongside the skeleton.

Things have changed now from the older, more brutally practical, rural ways which dominated human–animal relationships in Greece. Families keep dogs and cats as pets in Athens, and even if a proportion of them are later abandoned (keeping a boisterous husky or Alsatian in a small flat isn't easy), a new generation of mostly urban Greeks has become more sensitive to and romantic about domestic animals. There's an animal sanctuary named after Argus, Odysseus' faithful old dog, who breathed his last when he finally saw his master return home after his long travels. And the smarter districts, such as Kolonaki, have fixed stands with water and feeding bowls for strays. Outside Athens there is even a pets' cemetery, filled with small tombstones, wreaths of plastic flowers and ceramic statuettes of dogs.

With the Olympics coming up, there were new problems for homeless animals. The authorities were rumoured to be so keen to tidy up the city for the foreign visitors who were coming for the Games that they would be taking extreme measures. I'd heard that the capital's ownerless animals, the 70,000-odd dogs and cats who live rough in Athens and its outskirts, were going to be rounded up and sent to camps, where sooner or later, many would probably be killed. It might have been an efficient and hygienic solution, but the increasing number of the capital's animal associations were in uproar.

'We need compulsory registration of all pets, sterilization of strays, and then they should be released back on the streets. That's what we want,' said the representatives. The protesting was a sign of how things were changing, and it looked as though they were having some success.

In the past, people who cared about animals' well-being in Greece tended to be slightly dotty foreign women, and although Greeks now play a larger part in animal welfare, many of the eighty or so animals' associations and charities were set up by outsiders. Some of these charitable souls lived in Greece, and dedicated their lives to alleviating the plight of Greek animals on the islands and around the country. Others were simply tourists, who were shocked by large numbers of skinny cats clawing at their table in a fish taverna, or by old donkeys which looked maltreated, and went back to Britain or Germany determined to do something.

Meanwhile, I was beginning to understand better the predicament of the irresponsible people who dumped their pets. Our house had turned into a wild, noisy, hairy place, dominated by dogs and children chasing and barking. Vassilis discovered he had high blood pressure; Bella was the final straw. One day, he finally snapped and announced that there was not room for him and Bella in the same home. It seemed like time to act.

For a while things looked dicey. Eleni at the local greengrocers (who is active in animal welfare, and keeps a pack of strays in cardboard boxes outside the shop) told me that I wouldn't find anybody to take on a stray. 'They only want Dobermanns and Rottweilers these days, and they have to be pedigree puppies,' she said. 'We couldn't even find a home for an abandoned, blue-eyed husky, and the shelter is refusing to take on any more animals. The only solution is to send her to Germany. We sent one last week.' The dogs were apparently adopted and taken to a good home.

In the end, Bella went to live with a Vouliagmeni family who still run an old-fashioned smallholding with olive trees, goats and chickens. As I arrived with Bella, the owner drew up in his car too. He opened the rear passenger door and a large nanny goat stumbled out from the back seat, bleating with pleasure to be free in the air again. After a trial period the smallholders declared they were impressed by Bella's barking skills ('She barks if a fly goes past,' they said delightedly) and let her have the run of the place with their other six dogs. I felt guilty and the children were furious, but I realized that we'd been lucky. Vassilis's blood pressure went back to normal, and at least Bella didn't have to go to Germany.

CHAPTER 6

FREEDOM OR DEATH

And on the banner the undying mothers, bowed over it for years, had embroidered with their black and grey and snow-white hair the three undying words:
FREEDOM OR DEATH.

Nikos Kazantzakis, *Freedom or Death*

Almost every week I would get stuck in traffic or stranded without a taxi because of protests and marches in Athens. The centre of town becomes paralysed: the arterial roads around Constitution Square are blocked off; appalling road diversions are put into effect; and extra police forces are drafted in. To add to the impact, thousands of furious drivers sound their horns in frustration. Frequently, I'd discover that the pandemonium was being caused by a small group of individuals: angry pensioners from airline companies, 250 school caretakers, or a band of disgruntled market stall holders or public employees with a few megaphones, whistles and banners. The havoc they provoke presumably gives them a marvellous sense of power, if nothing else.

Everyone in the capital is familiar with strikes, stoppages, marches and demonstrations. Athenians may be put out by them, but many people enjoy attending events where a love of freedom can be combined with gregarious inclinations and a mistrust of authority with a pleasurable degree of noise and commotion. The dustmen's walk-outs leave the streets with mountains of festering rubbish for days on end, airline employees leave travellers stranded in the airport, and taxi drivers strike so regularly that it is almost routine.

'At least the traffic flows more easily,' people say phlegmatically, as they cope with the public transport system. Medics, civil servants and teachers are not averse to abandoning their posts either, and when children count up their school holidays, they make sure to calculate several days off each year for their teachers' protests. As teachers belong to a variety of unions, pupils never know in advance what will happen. Sometimes, I noticed Lara and Anna repeatedly making the sign of the cross before we arrived at the school gate.

'We're praying our teachers will be on strike,' they explained.

University lecturers were striking so much that many students were unable to take their exams; students and secondary school pupils stage their own sit-ins, and even consumers like to rebel. I'd already joined (admittedly somewhat passively) a boycott of all shops for one day because of price rises, and it was a pleasure to support a television boycott from seven to nine p.m. in objection to the dreadful quality of news coverage.

Some protest marches have become institutions, and one of the most significant takes place every year on 17 November. This is the date associated with the toppling of the Colonels' dictatorship in 1974. On 17 November 1973, the army sent in tanks to repress students who were holding a sit-in at the Athens Polytechnic, the most prestigious centre of higher learning in Greece. It was never established exactly how many casualties resulted (relatives were fearful of reporting them to the authorities), but recent studies claim that around thirty-four students were killed and many hundreds wounded. This massacre of the country's youth was pivotal in turning the public mood against the Junta, and it remains one of the major emotional and political points of reference of twentieth-century Greek history. The annual march attracts a wide range of supporters, from grieving relatives to angry vandals, and from Communist Party members to student anarchists.

Our first Athenian 17 November fell on a Saturday. The children had a celebration at school on Friday morning and were given the rest of the day off. Anna had been sick with nerves before reciting a poem in front of the whole school and the parents. It was about an idealistic girl who committed suicide after the Polytechnic slaughter. The school was filled with posters, period photos, and a collage containing hundreds of student faces peering out from behind railings. We heard the historical, crackly tape recordings of the students' radio station:

'This is the Polytechnic . . . This is the Polytechnic . . . People of Greece, you're hearing the truth now. We are unarmed . . . Our only weapon is our faith in freedom . . .'

A young teacher gave a talk on the 'kids who gave their lives for freedom', the importance of questioning authority, and how you shouldn't believe everything you are told. There was an implicit parallel with the fighters of 1821, who took the revolutionary oath 'Freedom or Death'. What sometimes appears like a natural tendency towards anarchic disobedience (parking illegally, smoking where it's forbidden, or ignoring rules wherever possible) has been carried to its logical conclusions when necessary. This can mean death. Every Greek knows the story of the nineteenth-century women of Souli in northern Greece; rather than be captured and enslaved by the Turkish soldiers, the village women took their children and danced their way off the edge of a cliff.

On the anniversary itself we were invited to a wedding by some distant cousins of Vassilis; their grandfathers had come from the same village. We sat in the large church in the suburb of Neo Psychiko, watching the young couple go through the timeless rituals: the delicate, white crowns crossed over their heads by their wedding sponsor, and the pelting of the bride and groom with rice – a symbol of fertility and plenty – as the priest leads them three times around the altar in the 'Dance of Isaiah'. Vassilis's sister Stella whispered rumours in my ear. During the Civil War, the cousins' branch of the family had been hounded out of the village for their Communist beliefs. They had suffered humiliations and beatings; a young woman was dragged into the village square to have her hair shaved off.

'The family all have typical left-wing names,' Stella continued. 'Eleftheria [Freedom], Irini [Peace], Sophia [Wisdom] and Sotiria [Salvation]. They were all used by people on the Left.' Names of hope for a Communist Greece which never happened.

Later, there was a sumptuous lunch at Athens's smart Jockey Club, an unexpected haven of parkland and racing tracks just off the polluted thoroughfare of Mesogeion Avenue. Stella pointed out another cousin, a well-groomed woman of a certain age.

'Her sister left Greece for the Soviet Union like thousands of Greeks during the Civil War,' she murmured. 'And she disappeared. They never heard of her again.' These were shocking details; who'd have guessed that in this exclusive club, amongst a sea of smart, chiffon-clad matrons and respectable, be-suited men, there lurked a history of persecution?

'Uncle Yiannis never told me any of that,' I said, feeling vaguely let down. 'He said the village had been neutral in the Civil War.' Stella shrugged.

'What do you expect?' Given the scale of the horrors taking place, these were the small, often forgotten details of history.

Only a few touches hinted at the political sensitivities of the groom's family, though I later speculated that the date set for the wedding had not been a coincidence. When the newlyweds arrived at the Jockey Club, they played a song by the popular left-wing composer Theodorakis: a rousing march, synonymous with protest, which gives the sense that people can do anything, even topple dictators, if they come together.

> We're two,
> We're three,
> We're a thousand and three

In the car on the way home, the radio reporter was describing the 17 November march; tens of thousands of protesters had already gathered. I'd always been curious about the event and I persuaded Vassilis to take the children home, and drop me at a metro station. The demonstration was to start at the Polytechnic, which has become a place of myth, martyrdom, pilgrimage and protest. It is an inspiration to both creators (poets, writers, composers) and destroyers (terrorists, hooligans). Although the building is frequently vandalized and even set on fire, no police have been allowed in since the fall of the Colonels.

Surrounded by some of the ugliest, greyest, tallest blocks of flats in the city, the Polytechnic is a beautiful sanctuary, with tall palm trees and elegant if decrepit colonnades. Its tired pastel-

and ochre-coloured walls are covered with a solid border of sprayed graffiti to the height where an arm can reach. Despite the building's grandeur, it is crumbling so badly that it sometimes gives the impression of an ancient classical edifice rather than a neoclassical imitation.

I arrived at Omonia station and emerged into an eerie hush. There were no cars and scarcely any people. Only a few Eastern European and Filipino immigrants were lingering in the square. Something very strange had happened. I began walking towards the Polytechnic, but long lines of policemen were blocking all access. They'd put down their riot gear and were chatting and smoking. Athens had been transformed into its own antithesis – a peaceful, car-free, empty metropolis.

'I'm trying to get through to the Polytechnic,' I said to a policeman.

'It's all blocked off until midnight now,' he said categorically. 'Anyway, the march left two hours ago. They'll be approaching the American Embassy by now.'

I'd got the timing wrong. Feeling slightly foolish for missing a crowd of 40,000, I went back to the metro and crossed the centre of town to the Athens Concert Hall stop. This time I walked up the steps into chaos. The air was acrid with wafting tear gas and my eyes started to water. In one direction I spotted a group of thugs in balaclavas smashing marble paving slabs, and in the other, someone had thrown a Molotov cocktail at a bus ticket booth. Flames were leaping up several metres, licking around the branches of a nearby tree, and producing a large plume of noxious black smoke. In the centre of the broad avenue were the marchers. They were passing by in orderly groups: students who resembled their parents in the late 1960s, with long hair, patched jeans and afghan coats; respectable old Communists (the men in tweed jackets and fisherman's hats, the women in sensible skirts and lace-up shoes); young Communists, hoisting white sheets painted in blood red with the familiar KKE (Communist Party of Greece); trade unionists with their rabid cheerleaders; and shaven-headed youths wearing Doc Martens, who clutched the thick wooden poles for their flags and banners like threatening weapons. There was even a group of Pakistani migrants who had joined in and were flourishing placards in Urdu.

I followed them for a while, until we reached the American Embassy. Dusk was falling, and the Embassy was completely shut up; not a light showed anywhere. The message seemed to be: 'Shout as loud as you like; we're not listening.' A row of blue police buses was parked nose-to-tail before the railings, with a phalanx of riot police in front. Vassilis rang me on my mobile. He was back at Eurydice Street watching everything on television.

'I think you should leave,' he said, sounding worried. 'I can see anarchists throwing petrol bombs. It could get nasty.' I told him that things seemed to have calmed down where I was, and there was no sign any more of the violent hooded youths. Nevertheless, people were shouting with genuine anger in their faces; it was the first time I had seen anti-Americanism in action, rather than discussed over dinner.

'*Greece, Cyprus, Palestine,*
No American will remain!' they chanted over and over.
'*The people demand:*
Out with the Americans!'

There are over a million Greek-Americans. Many of them manage to combine a cultural conservatism and loyalty to the old country with an intense reverence for the American Dream. After 11 September, the old-world Greeks and those of the new often found themselves in confrontation. Although every Greek village has its returned migrants (with their baseball caps, incongruous ranch-style houses, and their awkward hybrid 'Gringlish'), emigration and the relentless 'Coca-Cola-ization' of Greece have not fostered brotherly love. When President Clinton had visited Greece a couple of years earlier, he made an emotional apology. It might have been the sentimental theatre he was so good at, but his admission that the United States had failed in its 'obligation to support democracy' was the first time any formal acknowledgement had been made of America's secret dealings with the dictators. It was balm to old wounds.

I was relieved that I wasn't American, although I realized that being British was only a little better. I had also begun to feel somewhat ridiculous, dressed in my party clothes from the wedding. The black trouser suit and new, pointy boots were inappropriate enough, but the frivolously colourful, beaded bag was bordering on provocative.

'Please pass, Madam,' said a photographer, with an ironic smile, bowing to let me by.

Each group of marchers paused for a few minutes in front of the dark, silent Embassy to shout its slogans. People yelled with fury and passion, and the emotional intensity of the march was immense; it was easy to envisage the mood tipping over into violence. The Greek thirst for freedom (which has often been a fragile prize) is matched only by their hatred of tyrants (who have so often triumphed). It might once have been the Turks who threatened these values, but it was now the Americans. The lingering reek of smoke only added to the atmosphere of battle.

In the end though, everything finished peacefully enough. The protesters passed on up the road, efficiently rolled up their banners, loaded them onto trucks, and dispersed. The trucks were parked near to one of Athens's few skyscrapers, topped with a huge neon sign advertising Interamerican (actually a

Greek insurance company, but one which regularly pays the price for its name at demonstrations).

I was tired and desperate for a cup of tea, but I couldn't find anything except a traditional coffee shop. I was reluctant to enter, as I knew I would be an uncomfortably ill-fitting customer. The *kafeneio* is still a place for men. They not only drink coffee (made to each individual's taste) and sip ouzo (with a small plate of snacks), but play backgammon, read the papers and discuss politics without women, at any time of day or night. In the end, my desire for tea won over my scruples, and I entered a glass-fronted *kafeneio*. A noisy group of men with country accents were seated at a green baize table. They all stopped talking and shamelessly eavesdropped, as I walked over to the bar and asked the young man with a ponytail whether they had tea.

'Yes,' he said, coping bravely with the difficult moment when I asked if I could have a little cold milk in it. I sat down, listening to the promising sounds of a camper gas being lit and a *briki* being stirred.

After about ten minutes, I was brought a large, mug of pale, greenish tea. I took a sip. It turned out to be a herby, mint-flavoured mountain tea, kept for people with colds. The sense of disappointment was crushing; it bore no relation to my dreams of a nice cuppa. What with all the added tension, I just hadn't thought to say 'European tea'. Admitting defeat, I left as soon as I judged was polite, walking back down the avenue in front of the US Embassy. The traffic had been let through again, and it was almost as though the scene of half an hour before had not taken place. Street cleaners were out, sweeping up the debris; a few television reporters were filing their stories for the evening news, and the policemen had piled into their buses.

* * *

In Greece, 17 November is not only associated with martyred students and left-wing marches, but with more recent bloodshed. When a group of Greek terrorists began a long campaign of shootings, bombing and robbery in 1975, they chose carefully when they named themselves 17 November, or more precisely, the 'Greek Revolutionary Organization 17 November'. It was an attempt to automatically legitimize their actions by association. None of their members had ever been arrested, although they had murdered twenty-three people in over twenty-six years, including officials from the Junta, US, British and Turkish diplomats, and Greek politicians and businessmen. The shadowy members had taken on mythological status; even those who detested every element of the terrorists' extreme-Left ideology sometimes grudgingly admired their audacity.

By the time we arrived in Athens, attitudes were changing. Security surrounding the forthcoming Olympic Games had become a serious issue and after 11 September, the pressure was on to find the killers. In fact, the transformation had already begun just over a year before we moved to Athens, with the murder of Brigadier Stephen Saunders, the Military Attaché at the British Embassy.

Saunders had been driving to work one June morning, and was stuck in the usual rush-hour traffic on the broad, busy Kifissias Avenue which links Athens to the northern suburbs. In a characteristically well-planned attack, two men on a moped drew alongside, and the pillion passenger pulled out a rifle and shot the fifty-three-year-old Saunders several times through the car window. Fatally wounded, the Englishman pulled himself out of the car and collapsed on the road, at almost exactly the spot where two other 17 November murders had taken place.

Later, the terrorists' communiqué would accuse Saunders of having been involved 'in the planning of the barbaric air strikes against Serbia', in a war which most Greeks had strongly opposed. But by then it was too late for the Brigadier to plead innocence. The apparently invincible killers had struck again. There were no leads, only a general atmosphere of hopelessness. Over and over again, Greek television showed clips of the bloodstained car seats, the fragments of glass on the road, and policemen milling around looking inadequate.

It was not so much Saunders's horrible death as his widow, Heather, who provided the catalyst for the national change of heart. When she appeared on television the same day, bewildered and weeping, it was the first time that Greeks had seen something like this. Victims' relations had rarely been given or sought a voice in the media, and the public response was overwhelming. It's hard to admit it now, but when I saw Heather Saunders crying on television, it was the first time that I truly felt sorrow about 17 November's terrible crimes. Like many Greeks, I too had been partly seduced by 17 November's despicable logic that they could decide whether individuals were wrongdoers, and whether they deserved to die. When I lived in Nafplio in the late 1980s, it was easy to believe in the idea of social crusaders cutting through the sordid reality of shady dealings and corruption, and that their 'executions' had some justification. Nobody I knew then spoke of the victims or the suffering; the killers were like modern Robin Hoods; they were cleansing Greek society of its rotten elements.

The terrorists took the Greeks' greatest fears and obsessions, and twisted them into their favourite kind of adventure story, where the small guys manage to outwit and defeat the lumbering authorities. The killings fitted straight into a natural set of reference points, which drew on the wellspring of anti-Americanism and suspicion of authority. It was like a small, Greek Odysseus taking on the huge, foreign Cyclops. From the Byzantine

Emperors and Ottoman Sultans, to the Bavarian and Danish royal families of the nineteenth century, and the dictatorships and occupations of the twentieth century, Greece rarely lacked for high-handed or cruel rulers. When tax revenue offices and large international banks were bombed, many ordinary Athenians couldn't fail to feel at least a glimmer of satisfaction.

Most of our friends had become much angrier about the terrorists too. One of them was Stelios, who was disowned and disinherited by his father in his youth when his Maoist beliefs made him refuse to take over the family pharmacy business. Like most of his comrades, he gradually settled down, becoming a more comfortable, liberal left-winger. But not until after his father's premature death; he paid a bitter price for his principles. Those of his contemporaries who remained faithful to the ideal of armed struggle were thought to be among the founders of 17 November.

Stelios agreed to meet me one day to talk about all of this, and we fixed a rendezvous in the central square of Exarcheia, a district near the Polytechnic, which has long been associated with radicals, anarchists, students and drug-users. I had been in nearby Kolonaki, and walked the fifteen minutes or so, along the lower slopes of Lycabettus. It is a progression from one world to another. Leaving behind the expensive boutiques, fancy cafés and stylish women, you arrive in an area with run-down buildings, bookshops and cheap cafeterias, where most people are under twenty-five. In between is the middle ground of Skoufa Street, where the perfectly placed café Filion has been the haunt of the politico-arty-intellectual set for decades. Still better known by its previous name, Dolce, it is near enough to the action in Kolonaki, but close enough to Exarcheia to lend some street cred.

Exarcheia is one of the few places in Athens where a pink,

Mohican haircut won't raise many eyebrows, and where grunge is de rigueur. There is graffiti everywhere:

'KILL THE COP THAT'S HIDING INSIDE YOU'

'SINCE WE CAN'T CHANGE THE LAWS OF NATURE LET'S CHANGE THE NATURE OF LAWS'

'LICK ICE CREAM NOT THE BOSS'

'ONE SOLUTION – REVOLUTION' [in English]

'TERRORISTS ARE THE BOSSES'

In the old days, you expected anarchists with home-made petrol bombs to be lurking behind every lamp post in this refuge for the Left. The familiar, husky voice of one of the most popular, politicized troubadours, Dionysis Savopoulos, wafted from apartment windows. His defiant, often surreal ballads are Greece's equivalent to Bob Dylan, though he cleverly combines rock with rembetika and popular Greek music. Now he looks like a twinkling, tubby grandpa, but he remains very popular, especially with the generation of people he won over in the 1970s and 1980s. Today's students are more likely to be listening to foreign rap, heavy metal or popular home-grown rock bands, and while the odd Molotov cocktail still gets thrown at the local police station, the youth of today don't have the same cause to be angry.

It was warm enough to sit outside, and I placed myself at the centre of a sea of pale, denim-clad students drinking the ubiquitous frothy, iced Nescafé *frappé* at a café in the square. Stelios arrived looking tired. His elderly mother wasn't well, he explained. He had spent much of the previous night in the hospital. We ordered coffee, and then for the first time since I'd met him, he told me about his awful experiences during the Junta.

'I was often beaten up,' he said almost casually; a personal nightmare had turned into a story; into history. 'They arrested us all the time, and locked us up. We students used to gather to talk about politics, and about how to establish free elections in the university. But the law forbade meetings with over five people, and it was illegal to discuss politics.' Stelios and a group of Left-wing students were eventually removed from university by the Junta, and were sent instead to the army.

'We stayed there for six months and I was made to dig all day, or clean toilets. My hands still have calluses from the digging. We were treated very badly.

'But what was really terrible about the Junta was the lasting damage it did,' continued Stelios, turning away from his personal story. 'It destroyed the cultural spring that was flowering during the 1960s. Greece had been opening up and becoming more cosmopolitan; it was the time of glamorous holidays on Mykonos, painters and writers gathering on Hydra, films like *Zorba the Greek* ... And we had great musicians like Hadzidakis and Theodorakis. Then the military stepped in with their slogans like "Greece of the Christian Greeks" and their obsession with ancient Hellenism and the Orthodox Church. They even banned certain songs; it became an act of bravery to sit in a taverna and sing a song by Theodorakis. You have to remember that the authorities had spent much of the previous fifty years chasing Communists. With the Junta, a Greek version of McCarthyism began all over again, supported by the Americans and especially the CIA.'

If you hated the dictators, you hated the Americans. But it wasn't until after the collapse of the Junta, when democracy was restored, that 17 November carried out their first murders. They were offered freedom but they chose death; this time, though, it was other people's deaths. Stelios admitted that he didn't mourn the early victims. When three men walked up to Richard Welch, an official at the US Embassy, and shot him in front of his wife and driver just before Christmas in 1975, it was hard for Greeks to mind. When it transpired that he was also the CIA Station Chief in Greece, it looked like revenge for seven years of a barbaric regime.

'People said he deserved it,' said Stelios simply.

A drug addict was doing the rounds of the café asking for money, and Stelios lit a small cigar and paused. There was a pleasant clack-clack sound of some speedy backgammon players at a nearby table. I remembered Edward Lear's wonderful description of the numerous nesting storks he came across in a Greek village on his travels:

'The clatter they make with their bills is most curious, and makes you fancy all the town are playing at backgammon.'

'Eventually, 17 November lost sight of what they believed in,' Stelios continued. 'They started robbing banks, and their communiqués became increasingly nationalistic and rabid. They were really harming the country. But I think that even then, public opinion didn't really turn against them until Saunders was killed in 2000. Now they say that the net is tightening on them.'

Stelios had to leave to tend to his mother, and we parted in the busy square. I decided to ring up some new friends who lived nearby. I'd met them as I'd encountered most people in Athens – as part of a *parea* or company of friends. You only need a few links in the city to quickly become part of a wider network. Old friends of mine turned out to know Vassilis's friends, and new connections were always being made. Athenians often say: 'Athens is just one big *parea*,' but it appeared to me to be one small *parea*; everyone seemed to know everyone else.

'Come over now,' said Margarita on the phone.

Margarita Anagnostopoulou is a striking Australian Greek with flowing tawny hair and a penchant for military boots. Her parents fled Greece after the Civil War and she had come to her unknown 'homeland' to research for a doctoral thesis on women partisans in the Civil War. I walked around the park on Strefi Hill – a welcome green prominence in the middle of Exarcheia's otherwise unrelenting low-lying basin of urban sprawl. The houses there have become some of the centre's most desirable addresses, and the previously dilapidated neoclassical buildings in the area are being rapidly renovated.

Margarita's husband let me into their airy, 1950s apartment, dressed only in a pair of Lycra cycling trousers, and laden with an impressive number of mops and brooms. Yanis Varoufakis may be a university lecturer in economics, but he evidently takes the cleaning seriously; he'd been carrying out a vigorous housework session to the Eurythmics, and he looked as though he enjoyed it. But, I reflected, only in Exarcheia would you find a Greek man in flagrante delicto with the mops.

'He's not my slave – it might look like that, but it's not,' said Margarita, laughing, as we went into the kitchen to get a drink. Although she was now settled and married to a Greek, Margarita often felt uncomfortable. She was connected yet disconnected, she was Australian yet Greek, she loved Greece yet it drove her crazy.

On the fridge was a snap of Margarita's family on a sunny, Australian veranda. Her father was due to return to Greece after fifty years the next summer and everyone was nervous. When he last saw his country it was in ruins; the Marshall Plan was being put into effect, and American aid was just beginning to alleviate the widespread hunger, while propping up the Right-wing regime. He had fought with the Government Army, whereas Margarita's maternal grandfather fought with the partisans.

'We have a running joke in our family, though it's a bitter one,' said Margarita, recounting the sort of Oedipal tragedy that was all too common during those years. 'It's possible that it was my father's bullet that killed my mother's father; his regiment was fighting in the same place at the time of my grandfather's death.'

Yanis put on a shirt and joined us. We talked about mutual friends and upcoming concerts, but the conversation kept turning back to politics, as it does so often in Greece. Yanis's father had paid a high price for his Communism. During the Civil War, he had been exiled for two years on the notoriously horrific prison camp island Makronisos, now a memorial to the atrocities.

'They tortured him terribly,' said Yanis. 'He still has the scars. Have you heard how they used to tie people up in sacks with several cats and throw them into the sea? They'd pull them out just before they drowned, but after they'd been scratched to pieces. All that was to persuade people to sign the "declaration of repentance." But my father said that denying your belief in Communism and abandoning your comrades was the greatest humiliation of all.' These macabre stories reminded me of Christian martyrs, who clung to their faith when faced with the choice of death or denial.

The poet Yiannis Ritsos shared a tent on Makronisos with Yanis's father in the late 1940s, and then ended up imprisoned on Agios Efstratios ('Ai Stratis'). He put his poems in a bottle and buried them. Poems like this had the same resonance in the late 1960s:

Dear Joliot, I am writing you from Ai Stratis.
About three thousand of us are here,
simple folk, hard workers, men of letters,
with a ragged blanket across our backs,
an onion, five olives and a dry crust of light in our sacks,

folk as simple as trees in sunlight,
with only one crime to our accounts:
only this – that we, like you, love
peace and freedom.

On the night of the Colonels' coup in 1967, Yanis was six years old.

'The soldiers arrived at five a.m. and broke down the door,' he remembered. 'They were very organized; anyone who had a "file" from the Civil War was arrested. I remember all the shouting, my mother screaming, and then they took my father. It all finished very quickly. The terrible part came afterwards, when we had to wait for weeks to learn whether he was dead or alive.' It is still impossible in Greece for politics to be merely abstract ideals, coffee shop gossip or party members sparring. Anti-Americanism is not merely a philosophical position; it is still inspired by personal memories of oppression and even torture and dawn raids, and heightened by powerful family loyalties.

I'd been so absorbed in the stories that I'd forgotten the time, and suddenly found I was running late. Yanis offered to take me back to the centre on his motorbike. We sped around the base of Lycabettus back to the chic side in a few minutes, with Yanis giving a running commentary.

'I love this trail bike,' he shouted over his shoulder. 'It's perfect for the potholes, and it's high enough to go over car mirrors. You avoid all the problems; you don't get stuck in traffic and it's much better than walking. It transforms Athens into a beautiful city.' It was true; Athens looked magnificent whizzing past from this angle. It was as good as flying.

CHAPTER 7

CREATURES OF THE NIGHT

Because the fun never stops before daylight.
Greek National Tourist Office
brochure on Athens

'Have you been to "the *bouzoukia*" before?' Christos shouted in my ear, trying to communicate above the metallic twanging of half a dozen bouzoukis.

'Only to the "dog-places,"' I replied. 'In my student days in Nafplio.' Christos laughed. It was amusingly incongruous that his well-brought-up, foreign sister-in-law should have frequented these dodgy dives. But I'd enjoyed myself. I was intrigued by the intrinsic excesses of the 'dog-places' and the 'dog-women' who sang there; they combined a sweaty, seedy eroticism with the pathos of Greek popular music, which was unlike anything I'd seen before.

These days in Athens you can take your choice in terms of

'going to the *bouzoukia*', from the small bars with long-haired troubadours to the vast, glittering, laser-lit, pop-bouzouki shows where the major stars perform. These places have international names like Privilege, Venue, Mercedes and Fever, and you need to book weeks ahead or have some serious political or social clout to get a good table. If you want the rougher end of the market, with the big-haired, heavily made-up singers who often double up as hostesses, then there are still 'dog-places' to be found among the rubbish and dogs' corpses at the edges of the National Highway.

Vassilis and I had chosen Harama (Dawn), a historic bouzouki club, and we'd arrived there, as instructed, by eleven-thirty, with Christos and his wife Angeliki. Things were still so quiet that Thursday evening, that the *Maître* (as he's known) gave us a table right next to the slightly elevated stage – the highly sought-after position known as 'first table by the dance floor'. Our sense of triumph only increased when a group of ageing, former divas of the *bouzoukia* were shown to the table next to us. They looked glossy and knowing; the aristocracy of the night.

We were waiting for Glikeria, the star attraction, who had long been seducing audiences with her performances of popular songs, but by twelve-thirty the place was only just starting to fill up. We were onto our second bottle of red wine, we'd finished the platter of sliced fruit sprinkled with cinnamon, and we were still watching the warm-up singers. Vassilis had taken against a short, Balkan version of Gerard Depardieu, who was singing his heart out a mere two metres from our table. A line of darkly handsome, if expressionless musicians sat behind him in a row, plucking nimbly at their bouzoukis and the instrument's tiny brother, the baglama.

Harama was made famous from the 1940s onwards by the celebrated bouzouki player and singer Vassilis Tsitsanis, and the place still has a theatrical if seedy, post-war atmosphere: worn, velvet curtains, rough walls covered with posters for old brands of cigarettes, and slightly absurd-looking uniformed waiters. Tsitsanis used to thrill Athenians with his virtuoso playing and soulful, rough-edged singing of rembetika songs. Originally these emerged as the music of the *rembetes* – prisoners, drug addicts and illiterate immigrants, who sang in jails, hashish dens, port-side dives and brothels. Some say the word comes from the old Turkish *rembet*, meaning 'of the gutter', but there are many alternative etymologies. The songs tell stories of doomed love affairs and prostitutes, of heroin and TB, and of prison life and love for a mother.

Known by some as 'the Greek blues', rembetika were also associated with the *mangas*, the macho spiv or wide boy, whose strange mix of provocative nonchalance and lethal egotism established one of Greece's old archetypes which still has currency. The *mangas* had his own slang containing Turkish and even Venetian words, whose origins went back to the eighteenth century when the Ottoman overlords were briefly substituted in parts of Greece by the Venetians. A *mangas* played his music on instruments which were easily made and transported; it was something spontaneous. Both the bouzouki and the baglama could be constructed from pieces of firewood, dried gourds or tortoise shells, and the diminutive baglama was convenient for hiding in prison. There were times during the twentieth century when a man would come under suspicion from the police merely for possession of one of these instruments, such was their association with the disreputable, underworld life of the poor, the excluded and the dispossessed.

Rembetika started out as a dangerously dissolute, male music, and its performers were uninterested in (and rejected by) both the Left and the Right in politics. However, with the influence of European dance music and the impact of the radio, rembetika gradually became a cherished element of a mainstream repertoire dominated by the bouzouki.

Soon, popular bouzouki songs and rembetika were sung by women as well as men, and by the middle of the last century, 'going to the bouzoukis' was something enjoyed by both the bourgeoisie and the masses. When Tsitsanis sang these songs in the 1940s, they implied a particularly Greek defiance to the foreign occupiers; they were songs of rebellion, even if they spoke of love or drugs.

> *I came into the teké* [café and drug den]
> *To smoke a narghile*
> *To smoke and blow my mind*
> *And forget the bitterness.*
> *In all this darkness*
> *I feel fine when I'm stoned.*

It was no coincidence that composers such as Mikis Theodorakis and Manos Hadzidakis used the oriental, modal tunes of the rembetika as an inspiration and form for their work. Theodorakis often described his experiences during the Civil War in the late 1940s on Makronisos, the prison island. He learned to dance the zeibekiko and sing rembetika with the other Left-wing prisoners, and his first symphony had its debut there, with an orchestra of violins and mandolins in a tent. Music was a way of surviving in a country which was almost destroyed.

Things were warming up in Harama and Glikeria finally emerged. A girlish fifty-year-old, with a deceptively youthful, round face and compact figure, she looked familiar from television appearances. Like many of the most successful singers in Greece, she is not too aloof to do a winter's season of almost daily live shows at a music club where her admirers can drink, eat and dance up close to their favourite musicians. Glikeria was wearing a tight, black, lacy skirt to her ankles and high heels – a strangely old-fashioned look compared to the overtly sexy, showy clothes of her younger colleagues in the Greek pop-*bouzoukia* world, although perfect for the *Smyrnaika*, the songs from Smyrna, which she began to sing.

> *I swear, upon your two sweet eyes,*
> *If I don't make you my partner,*
> *My Smyrna girl, I shall die.*

The songs take you back to the atmosphere in a city which was not only famous for its music (travellers told of dances occurring at any place and time, even on the decks of boats), but also for its tragic end, when the Turkish army burned it to the ground in 1922. Its predominantly Greek population was killed or fled, and large numbers of them ended up in Kaisariani, Harama's neighbourhood. At certain points, between verses, Glikeria launched into her famously passionate, drawn-out calls of *'Aman aman'* – a Turkish word, roughly meaning 'Mercy, mercy'. Closing her eyes, she let rip with a haunting, guttural, eastern sound that is guaranteed to give goose bumps.

As Glikeria sang, the levels of *kefi* rose tangibly. Christos and Angeliki were singing along, leaning back in their seats and letting their cigarettes burn to sticks of ash. Their faces, which had looked so tired, with smudges of purple-grey around their eyes, were now animated and bright. Angeliki is a Cretan, but with her hennaed, curly hair cut in a 1930s-style bob, her delicate frame and her elegant, city clothes, she could have passed as a lady from Smyrna. Vassilis looked interested in the performance; enjoying himself, but at a distance. I wondered whether we both looked like foreigners.

There are some singers who believe that they haven't done their job if they don't have the women dancing on the tables, but the customers at Harama looked happy enough, singing, swaying and clapping along to the songs, and toasting each other with fat, clinking glasses of whisky with ice – '*Yeia mas!*' – Our health. Waiters transported innumerable bottles of *ouiski* – the preferred drink for a night out at the *bouzoukia*, although mysteriously, no one was getting drunk. Greeks have become the greatest consumers of whisky in Europe, and it is popular amongst young as well as older drinkers (adverts for it tend to be fun, sexy and youth-oriented). But they evidently know how to handle their drink better than northern Europeans.

The cost of an expedition to a music club is gauged by the advertised price of a carafe of whisky, which is presumed to be shared between four people. You normally pay about the equivalent of two labourers' daily wages, making it an expensive business. However, this is all part of the atmosphere of overindulgence and recklessness, and of living for the moment. You are meant to throw money around as though it doesn't matter (even if it does), and it is not unheard of for men to spend a month's wage, paying for their friends at the *bouzoukia*.

The plate smashing I remembered from the old 'dog-places' is now banned. It had always looked ridiculous to me in any case. Customers paid large sums for a waiter to go and drop great piles of specially produced plaster plates on the stage, and then a minion with a broom arrived to sweep up the debris. 'Break them all, and I'll pay,' goes the cheerful old song. But there was none of the exuberance and devil-may-care thrill you'd expect from somebody breaking real china for himself. Some people break a plate or a jug at funerals or after a death; it supposedly gives Charos (the Greek equivalent of the Grim Reaper) a fright, and I imagine it feels appropriate too. The bouzouki version, on the other hand, was not only ersatz, but by proxy; it seemed like an unsatisfactory way to express one's appreciation.

There are still other ways of getting rid of your money besides the overpriced food and drink, and tipping and bribing the waiters; sometimes people even throw money at the singers, or tuck it into their clothes as a sign of appreciation. A pretty but unsmiling young woman was wandering about selling small baskets of flowers, and I thoughtlessly asked Christos how much he thought they were going for. Soon there was a large pile of carnation heads on the table in front of us, and we joined in the general assault, pelting Glikeria as she sang, until the stage was ankle deep in bright red and white pompoms. I later found out that each basket cost the equivalent of ten packets of cigarettes, and you need several to make any impact.

Every so often, the dour flower-seller was commissioned by someone in the audience to walk onto the stage with several flower baskets, and pour the contents onto the floor, something she carried out with the casual manner of someone emptying the rubbish. On finishing, she thrust a handful of the carnations into the singer's hand and indicated the patron. Even in the middle of a huge, moaning, shuddering *'Amaaaaaaaaaaaaaaan!'* Glikeria still managed to make a gesture of recognition to her admirer, and threw a few bruised flowers back at the appropriate table.

A man in his sixties got up from a nearby table, and walked onto the stage in front of Glikeria. Dressed in an outdated, caramel-coloured suit, he danced with jaunty, jerky little steps, kicking his feet up and slapping their soles. Although he looked comical, and was far from impressive in his technique, his right to express himself in front of everyone was respected. It is an almost sacred moment when an individual (traditionally a man) lives out his own ecstasy or despair on the dance floor. However, what can look like an emotional free-fall has specific rules and a certain method to it. The dancer is not part of the audience in the traditional or passive sense of the word, and although he is moving right next to the singer, he is certainly not a performer. Friends of the dancer may crouch at the edge of the dance floor, clapping in rhythmic support of this highest point in the expression of *kefi*, but nobody else should dance. There have even been knifings in the past over this point of honour.

I asked Vassilis whether he'd ever consider dancing like that.

'Never,' he answered categorically. 'For a start, I never learned how. When we were growing up it wasn't popular like now. We listened to rock music then. Traditional Greek dances became associated with the Junta and nationalism. But the zeibekiko has come back into fashion. It's a showy, solo dance. Like the tsifteteli [a Balkan take on the belly-dance], which those young women are dancing now. When I was young it was only gypsy girls who danced it; you'd never see anyone respectable dancing so provocatively. Now it's danced by the same people who go to the disco.'

As we got ready to leave, we discovered that Christos had already surreptitiously settled the bill and would not hear of sharing. A telltale smile of victory played on his lips as Vassilis and I protested. It was a familiar and delicate predicament, where old rules of *filotimo* (one's sense of honour and pride) and manliness are at stake; there is a certain humiliation in being paid for, just as there is triumph in paying. Subterfuge is normal in paying bills, and those who have been paid for sometimes appear angry, and certainly show no gratitude. The only retort is: 'Well, it'll be my turn next time.'

'Why are you leaving so early?' asked the doorman, part

plaintive, part challenging, as we left the club at about two-thirty. He waved off our excuses of work the next morning as if they were an insult. If you have truly entered into the spirit of the bouzoukis, you shouldn't be thinking of such things; time should be suspended. Even mid-week, the shows continue until about four a.m. It is a matter of honour to cope with this painful regime; the spirit must triumph over the body.

Even I (who have always needed my sleep) was becoming accustomed to going out to dinner at ten or eleven p.m., and staying up until three a.m. or later. I remembered, somewhat ashamedly, how I had once requested to meet some friends for dinner at eight-thirty. I had been howled down:

'What do you take us for, Germans?' one of them had said. In Greek there is a verb for staying up late or all night – to 'un-night' or 'de-night'. You can't live life to its full without some 'un-nighting'. It is also an explanation for silence and bad moods; when you see someone nursing their coffee and cigarette with exhausted tenderness, he or she need say no more than: 'I un-nighted,' for all to be understood and forgiven.

Staying out late seemed to be something like learning to ski (though I never truly mastered that either), and required both a change in attitude and certain precautions; pacing the evening, drinking the right amount and choosing good companions were obvious elements, and sleeping afterwards in the legendarily refreshing, dry Attica air was essential (I couldn't do the same in England). I realized that I could never become one of Athens's creatures of the night who regularly 'go to burn it' until dawn, but I had come a little closer to understanding why they do.

Angeliki, who is a lawyer, trumped everyone by announcing that rather than go to bed, she was going straight to her office. She had a court case to prepare for the next morning, and had intended to start earlier than usual anyway.

'It's OK, I'm used to it,' she said, pulling her coat around her against the cold. The night air smelled of damp earth. Angeliki coughed a nagging, raw, smoker's cough, and her eyes took on their purplish tinge again.

* * *

During our first winter in Athens, Vassilis and I often found ourselves in Psirri. In just a few years it had become one of the city's most lively areas for nightlife. Neither of us knew the quarter before, but friends kept inviting us there to try out the latest restaurants, and to attend parties and gallery openings. During the day, Psirri is an artisans' district; its narrow roads are filled with small ateliers with leather and metal workers, mechanic's shops and storehouses. At night however, it undergoes a metamorphosis into the only area where you can choose between visiting a chic Indian restaurant, a designer-kitsch gay bar with fusion cuisine, or a converted warehouse specializing in mussels. It is also gaining in popularity as a venue for the more offbeat, experimental theatre companies which are constantly springing up in the city. Athenian audiences are keen enough to provide work for 120 active theatre troupes. While the summer sees an annual blossoming of ancient Greek drama, the winter is the time for the increasing numbers of modern Greek plays, in addition to translations of Ibsen, Chekhov, Brecht, Shakespeare and contemporary European playwrights.

One December evening, we went to Psirri to see a new play. We arrived early and went for a walk, peering into the restaurants and bars, and inspecting the new crop of restored buildings. Between freshly painted places dressed up as traditional tavernas and island ouzo cafés, were fancy wine bars and cutting edge dance clubs preparing for their late-night visitors. It all looked slightly artificial, with the fresh, self-conscious feel of a film set. Crowds of people were walking along the main pedestrianized street with us: young men in tight jeans with nervous eyes, flicking bunches of keys; groups of girls with over-lacquered hairdos; and couples being pestered by gypsy children to buy single soft, wilted gardenias.

'It's a "brides" bazaar,' said Vassilis, referring to the traditional stroll where young, single men and women walk up and down the main street, eyeing up their prospects.

Athens often appears to be changing so much as a city that it's easy to assume that social and family customs are changing too. But according to sociologists, that is not the case. Marriage remains overwhelmingly the preferred state, and while it's true that the older generation does pressurize the young to conform, there is little determined effort to sidestep customs. It is still considered normal for young adults to live with their parents until they marry, and although dowry was abolished in the 1980s, parents usually try to provide a home or financial assistance to a daughter when she gets married. It's just called 'help' now instead.

Unlike northern Europe, where single-parent families and unmarried mothers are increasing each year, in Greece the conventional family, with marriage at its core (and grandmothers as back-up) is almost as strong as ever. Whereas about a third of babies in Britain are born out of wedlock, in Greece they only account for about three per cent. It is true that this remarkable traditionalism goes hand in hand with the highest rate of abortion in Europe, something which often stands in for contraception. However, it is arguable that the more cavalier approach to pregnancy, and the fair number of shotgun weddings, are in some ways further indications of the strength of marriage as an institution.

The ideal of the household based around the married couple is so powerful that calling a person a 'householder' (*noikokyris*) is one of the highest compliments, implying stability, trustworthiness and honour. 'Household-like' signifies order, cleanliness and even godliness; Anna's school Religion book states that Christians keep their churches beautiful and 'household-like'.

Continuing our stroll, we arrived in a small square known as Heroes' Square after the tough old veterans of the 1821 revolution, who favoured the area. Then, as now, it was filled with drinking holes, and even King Otto used to visit them incognito for a taste of Athenian low life. A great admirer of the former warriors' costume (*foustanella* with red velvet jacket and a cap intricately embroidered in gold thread), he insisted on being buried in these clothes. Right up to the end, Otto still showed some affection for his adopted kingdom, even though his subjects had deposed him.

Some of these heroes of the Revolution became part of the new political regime. Their names are known by every Greek school child: Makriyiannis, Mavrokordatos, Botsaris, Kolokotronis, Miaoulis. And of course, Bouboulina, the daring female admiral who defies all Greek stereotypes in having combined being a mother, a brave fighter, a strong drinker, and a leader of men. Their portraits and weapons now sit quietly in the National History Museum. The place bristles with impressive moustaches and long, slim rifles and swords, inlaid with sparkling jewels, mother-of-pearl, silver and gold.

The less principled of the fighters ended up as Psirri gangsters. They were still armed after the Revolution, and established a menacing home-grown mafia. Something like their contemporaries in the 'Gangs of New York' (as depicted in Scorsese's film), they often aligned themselves with politicians, who used them to intimidate their opponents or voters. Some of the Psirri gangs had their own slang and bizarre dress codes; the snappily dressed

Koutsavakidhes, with their twisted moustaches, were the antecedents of the *mangas*. They donned strangely elongated, pointed, high-heeled boots, black hats tipped far back over greased-back hair, stripy trousers, yellow shirts and black jackets which were worn only on one arm, the other being left dangling.

Along with the numerous bandits outside the capital, the Koutsavakidhes and other mobsters turned the newly Free Greece into a perilous, violent country for its first fifty years. This was the darker side to the classy, neoclassical city, which was blossoming so promisingly. One police chief who wanted to humiliate the Psirri ruffians devised the perfect punishment. Gathering them together in the central Klafthmonos Square, he took some large scissors, and ceremoniously snipped off their fancy moustaches, the ridiculous tips of their pointy boots and their pretentious dangling sleeves, and left them to shuffle, shamed though free, to their homes.

Just before the era of the Athens gangs, Psirri had also been home to Lord Byron, when he came to Greece as an ardent supporter of the War of Independence. I had long wanted to see where his lodgings had been, and after asking for directions, we eventually arrived at number 11 Thekla Street. We found ourselves outside an unremarkable, grimy warehouse. Standing there for a while, we tried to imagine how it might have been in the days when Byron flirted outrageously with his landlady's three teenage daughters. He immortalized the youngest daughter (Theresa, then aged twelve) in a poem which allowed her to spend the rest of her life living off her reputation as Byron's romantic love.

> *Maid of Athens, ere I part*
> *Give o give me back my heart.*

It turns out, though, that although Byron serenaded the pretty young girl, he was in fact enjoying a dalliance with a handsome Greek youth. The Maid of Athens story was, in the end, no more than a fiction, blown up by Theresa's mother, a public hungry for romance, and a philhellene who knew how to sidestep the rules. Such was the aristocratic poet's popularity in Greece that portraits, statues and streets bearing his name are to be seen all over the country. The Athenians even named a whole district after the Greek version of Byron – Vyronas.

Leaving Byron's old haunt, we arrived at the small theatre, which was showing a play called *National Anthem*. It had evidently been some kind of warehouse or workshop until recently, and the auditorium was a large, undecorated room, filled only with a U-shaped banquet table, laid for a feast. Along with the limited number of spectators, we sat at the white-clothed table and waited. During the play, the actors poured us red wine and served a steaming chickpea broth – a reference to Greece's simple, peasant foods, and symbolic of a whole (disappearing) way of life. The performers jumped on the table and chairs, sang traditional love songs, danced to waltzes and disco music and said prayers. Most striking of all, they shouted down the National Anthem.

'You'd never have found something with such self-irony in Athens even a few years ago,' said Vassilis in the interval. The fragility of the Greek nation state had always been confronted with unquestioning devotion to its symbols, especially the flag and the National Anthem. In this theatre, however, Greece's almost sacred tenets of patriotism, religious identity and food were mocked subversively in front of the bemused yet appreciative audience.

Afterwards, in spite of the chickpea soup, we were still hungry. On the off-chance, we entered a small, Greek-Argentine restaurant-bar next to the theatre. Lit with hundreds of candles,

El Peccado (Sin) was almost as theatrical as the show we'd just seen. Groups of handsome, quick-eyed people stood at gilt ecclesiastical tables drinking cocktails, or sprawled on sofas beside erotic murals and religious paraphernalia. A DJ played tangos, Greek songs and sambas.

Near us, a bald man smoked a large cigar while playing with a string of worry beads. He flicked them to and fro across the back of his hand, making an elegant little twist at the end of the small routine, so the dark oval-shaped beads clicked round to begin again under his hand. I noticed Vassilis watching him admiringly. I'd imagined that worry beads would have died out with the true *mangas*, and other picturesque, masculine traditions in Greece, but it seems that if anything, there's been a comeback. They are the perfect antidote to smoking, they provide activity for any situation which involves waiting, sitting, talking, or strolling, and they channel fidgeting or nerves into a positive, even creative pastime. I'd heard an expert on the radio explaining how they should be made from a living material – amber is first choice, but also bone, ivory, wood or coral.

'I can't have a companion,' he'd said, 'which I'll keep with me, and which I'll stroke, if it's made from dead material like metal or stone.'

After we had eaten, we drank sweet, ruby-coloured Vin Santo from Santorini, which slipped down like liquid silk. We lay back on our red velvet sofa, and watched a couple tango their way between some dripping candelabras. Yet again, Athens was changing. Psirri had been attracting alternative elements since the outrageously dressed Koutsavakidhes swaggered about in the new capital. But it was a sign of another transformation that Athenians could now mock their old ideals, and merge Latin American nightlife with their own as though it were the most natural thing in the world.

As we left, Psirri's twisting streets were fuller than ever with people leaving restaurants and bars, meeting friends and arriving at clubs. Athens was waking up and coming into its own in the small hours, as the night creatures emerged to make the city theirs. We found ourselves stuck in a tailback worthy of the rush hour – the less welcome side of the Dionysian impulse in the modern age. Instead of ending the revelry by falling asleep under an olive tree with a faun or a nymph, you sit in your car under sodium street-lights waiting for the gridlock to ease . . .

* * *

Sometimes in our wanderings at night, we'd come across windows glowing with red lights. I'd always been intrigued by stories about prostitutes in Greece. I'd often been told about them by men whose early erotic pleasures had been in their arms; in the past, many young teenagers were taken along by uncles, older brothers or even fathers. Like the *mangas*, the *poutana* is another archetype; another outsider and a creature of the night, who avoids the sacred vows of marriage and their hallowed place in the household.

The local *poutana* is an institution, but one which is changing. I'd heard that her position is now threatened by bureaucratic impediments and by the increasing numbers of illegal 'foreign imports' mostly from the Balkans and the former Eastern Bloc countries. These approximately 20,000 women are said to be spoiling the market, and such were the worries of lawful Greek prostitutes that they had even organized marches in Athens to protest for their rights. I'd recently met someone who worked with minorities in Greece, and was a great champion of civil liberties. He let drop that he was friends with the leader of the prostitutes' union.

'You could go and see her,' he suggested.

I wasn't sure what to expect when I turned up one afternoon

at Dimitra Kanelopoulou's place in the working-class district of Patissia. Perhaps she had a daytime office to deal with the paperwork, I'd thought. Stepping off the busy street I entered a 1930s hallway that was painted a vivid scarlet and had a fancy chandelier hanging by the door. I went up the stairs and rang the bell and a homely, grandmotherly figure with a grey bun and inelegant glasses opened the door.

'I've come to see *Kyria* Kanelopoulou,' I said, adjusting my eyes to the crimson-hued darkness. I'd arrived in a place that looked like a cross between a Turkish harem and a nineteenth-century Parisian bordello. A high-ceilinged salon with velvet curtains, a chaise longue, a sculpture of Aphrodite and sweeties in cut-glass bowls lay ahead. Through some open doors I spotted several red bedrooms with large four-posters draped in burgundy hangings.

A gigantic blonde of about forty came towards me down the short corridor and I shook her hand and introduced myself.

'What sign of the zodiac are you?' she asked in a friendly manner, leading me into a cosy, lilac-coloured kitchen.

'Are you hungry? Would you like coffee? Or maybe tea?'

An overweight spaniel, a foundling called Lady, sat on a window seat by a poster of Marilyn Monroe, and a pretty dresser was laden with crockery and a large medical-looking box of condoms. In the corner a dozen small icons were lit by a small, hanging oil lamp. The granny turned out to be the housekeeper, *Kyria* Zoë, who made me a cup of tea, and was then sent out to buy some food and cakes.

As we spoke, Dimitra started to undress. I asked her why the house had the name Ellie outside the front door.

'That's my artist's name,' she said, pulling off her clothes until she stood before me completely naked. She looked like a mythological creature – the offspring of an Amazon and the

Minotaur, but she spoke with a warm, low voice which inspired confidence. She told me about her happy childhood in Athens, her private school, and her entry into 'the world of the night'. It was an unlikely career for a bright, middle-class girl. I sipped my tea, unable to prevent myself looking at her pendulous, veined breasts and enormous pale buttocks as she walked around in the kitchen. The unashamed, close-up flesh reminded me of a Lucian Freud painting.

'If I lived my life over again I'd do the same thing,' she said, spraying herself with an orange bottle of scent, and rubbing it over her breasts, belly and pubic hair. She offered me some politely.

'I really like it; I like men. But it's a profession which should be chosen not forced. These foreigners who've been in illegal prostitution since 1990 are like slaves.' Dimitra sat down heavily in an old armchair, and slowly pulled on some black stockings and high-heeled shoes. As we spoke, she began to put on her make-up, her long, yellow hair falling around her face. Even her lips were enormous. I wondered whether she was giving something of a performance for me, but her intelligent gaze, articulate speech, and the impressive ease with her body were all genuine.

Kyria Zoë arrived back with some pastries and takeaway food, and then went to answer the doorbell. She let in a slim, young man in a leather jacket and showed him through to a bedroom. After a few minutes, Dimitra stood up, well over six foot in her heels. Pulling a long, black satin robe around her, she left the kitchen without a word. Wondering whether the man would survive her embrace, I settled down to talk with *Kyria* Zoë, who, it turned out, had been a seamstress sewing uniforms for Olympic Airways. After she lost her job and got divorced, she found this work the best way of supporting herself and her two children.

'I've educated my children, and now both of them are

professionals. They've given me grandchildren,' she said. 'I told them what I do – that's how I helped them get on. Glory to God, they've done well. And they adore Dimitra.'

After a short time (the going rate was thirty euros for ten minutes), Dimitra reappeared, and sat back on her armchair again. I asked her what she thought about the foreign prostitutes.

'That's something else,' she answered. 'They're new blood, but they're illegal, and we don't have anything to do with them.' I'd heard that these foreigners were seen as taking away customers, and that there was no love lost between the two groups of prostitutes.

'There are about 5,000 women in our union,' said Dimitra, 'and about 500 are foreigners. We have to register with the authorities; we must be single or widowed women over eighteen, and we're checked over by doctors once a month. We're interested in health; we know how to recognize illnesses. We're a different thing altogether from the black-market prostitutes.'

I wondered why they'd been protesting recently.

'We were marching because we have problems with the law, love,' she replied, lounging back in her chair and filing her nails carelessly. 'We're here to service the psychological and physical needs of men; they need us. And most of them are married. But the laws are all there to limit prostitution. You can't have a "house" less than 200 metres from a school, a square, a church, a *frontistirio* [crammer] or a playground. That makes it impossible for us. It should be fifty metres, and even then, what happens if someone opens a crammer in the same street? The other problem is you're not allowed to have more than two women working together. I'd like to buy up a big hotel and fill it with women; we'd have saunas and massage for the men, and I'd live on the top floor . . . but it's not allowed. All the colour has gone from prostitution now.'

After another short break, when Dimitra went to see a client, she announced that she was hungry, and *Kyria* Zoë put a foil takeaway dish on a tray and placed it on her lap.

'Naturally, I like men extra large,' Dimitra said naughtily. 'Strong *palikaria!* [brave young men]! But if they have a small one,' she said, holding up her little finger and laughing, 'I don't say anything.' I wasn't sure whether she was teasing me, but her housekeeper evidently didn't think so.

'That's right,' nodded *Kyria* Zoë sagely, as though we were talking about dinner party etiquette. 'You'd never say that to a man, just as you never tell a woman that she's ugly or sterile.'

'Mmmmmmmm, spaghetti with *putanesca* sauce,' said Dimitra, forking the food into her mouth. I laughed with disbelief at the theatricality of a *poutana* eating the Italian 'whore's sauce' (so named for its quick preparation, allowing a working woman time for her profession), but Dimitra had a straight face. She explained about capers, olives and tomatoes, and how she doesn't eat meat on Wednesdays and Fridays.

'I believe in these things,' she said, neglecting to pull up the slippery robe which had fallen open over her belly. 'I light the lamp by the icons and the incense every day, I pray, and I go to church. Yesterday I went to visit a monastery – of course I didn't tell them what I do. And last year I made a pledge to give a diamond ring to the *Panayia* at Tinos; it was for gynaecological problems. We all get them – your fallopian tubes get wrecked, and there's nothing you can do. I had a year off work, and several operations. We've even got a patron saint for our union – Saint Pelagia,' she continued, letting out little burps of satisfaction every so often. 'She's the protector for all our members.'

St Pelagia was a classic case of the beautiful, high-born femme fatale. A fifth-century Syrian, who abandoned her debauched ways, she became a devoted Christian for the rest of her long life.

'I could never have a stable relationship with a man,' confessed Dimitra without much sadness, as I got ready to leave. 'You can't mix this job with a serious attachment; it'd get too complicated. Anyway, I haven't met the perfect man so far.'

As I put my coat on, Dimitra invited me to visit her again. I could go to her real home down by the sea at Faliro one day when she wasn't working. Perhaps we could even make an expedition to a holy place. I left her warm, dark, almost womb-like brothel, thinking how the leap made by Pelagia from sinner to saint was not necessarily such a large one; it is in fact a cliché. Women in the world's oldest profession are still known by the ancient Greek term meaning 'sacred slaves' (*ierodouloi*), and they have always had Aphrodite as their 'patron goddess'. In Greece there still aren't many ways a woman can evade the embrace and restraint of conventional family life; the nun and the prostitute are two established alternatives. Walking down the road towards the electric train station, I thought how it wouldn't surprise me if, some years later, I came across Dimitra (renamed as Sister Pelagia) in some island convent, her blonde tresses snipped short behind a veil, and her long, black robe buttoned up to her neck.

CHAPTER 8

FEAST AND FASTS

Athenians have the sense to eat at home except when they want to make a noise.

Kevin Andrews, *Athens: Cities of the World*

One of the things I'd fantasized about before moving to Athens was being scooped up into the bosom of a large, nurturing family. On our visits to Greece, Vassilis's four brothers and sisters and their families had looked the epitome of a chaotic, loving extended family. They reminded me of romantic Italian films, with their noise, bustle and copious meals. They sat around laden tables together, looked after each other's children, and phoned one another several times a day for advice and gossip. This was something I had never been a part of, coming from a background where divorce had sliced its way through generations, creating other, more complicated configurations. I loved the idea of joining this environment, and imagined Anna and Lara developing close friendships and alliances with their cousins, while we adults sat around on the terrace, drinking wine and shouting our opinions into the city night.

During our first months in Athens, however, we rarely saw my in-laws. When we did, it was usually for a quick coffee, and there were none of the jamborees I'd been so impressed by when we'd been passing through. 'Real life' was evidently somewhat different from the easygoing, indulgent summer holiday version I'd witnessed. It was partly that there wasn't time. Contrary to what I'd thought, Greeks work more hours than any other Europeans; it's often hard for the average wage-earner to survive on one regular salary, and it has become normal for people to have two jobs. The days when ordinary Athenians left work at two p.m., went home for a big lunch and slept for a couple of hours before drifting off to the coffee shop, had clearly gone. Almost all of Vassilis's siblings and their spouses have jobs in the public sector (a couple of architects, an engineer and some civil servants) and several work into the evenings. Most of them were too exhausted or busy to socialize during the week, and weekends were often taken up with errands, shopping and ferrying their children to extra lessons.

Worse than this, we'd been hearing rumours of cracks in the glossy picture of a loving, united family that I had always admired on brief visits. I learned that there had seen several serious rows over the last years, which had produced factions and split loyalties. It was like going back-stage on a cheerful musical and discovering that the actors were depressed.

During the lead-up to Christmas we weren't sure whether there was going to be a big get-together or not, and as nobody had said anything, we planned a quiet celebration at home. Christmas in Greece has never been a major event – its significance doesn't run as deep as Easter or New Year. Greeks have adapted their own few indigenous customs, and jumbled them up with foreign imports, to produce a curious hybrid. What I imagined would be Lara's nativity play, at school, turned out to be about a family plagued by a long-tailed, black *kalikanzaros* – a small, hairy imp who steals or spoils food, pees in the fireplace, and runs amok on Christmas Eve. There were no angels, shepherds or wise men, although Saint Vassilis (Basil) – one of the four great fathers of the Greek Orthodox Church – got a small part. Saint Vassilis may have come from Cappadocia, but he has been gradually blended with the northern Father Christmas. Both kindly old men are not only lovable and generous, but are depicted with a brace of reindeer and red, fur-lined robes. Like Santa Claus, Saint Vassilis climbs down the chimney, although he is nowhere to be seen at Christmas. Instead, he brings children presents on New Year's Eve, in time for his feast day on 1 January.

Opinion was divided on the appropriate seasonal food. The local butcher derided turkey as a recent fad, and recommended pork or suckling pig instead, but I was happy when I located a small shop supplying organic, free-range turkeys; a privileged and scarce minority in Greece. The birds had an authentically scraggy appearance, and were completely different from the swollen, pale turkeys I'd eaten in England; their scarily strong, dark legs were decorated with little tufts of black feather and looked as though they had done a lot of running.

Organic food is just catching on, but health food shops are still rare and outrageously expensive. They have the cultish obscurity of the places where my mother used to buy wheatgerm and intriguing food supplements when I was a child in 1970s London. We were doing what we could to support Greece's infant organic movement, but it wasn't easy to obtain provisions that way. Going 'biological' (as it's known) involved buying milk from Germany, rock-hard bread, maggot-filled rice and fruit which looks as though it fell off the back of the lorry. When I asked some local shopkeepers if they could find organic produce they were dubious about its quality and authenticity.

'It's all "monkey" [fake],' said the greengrocer, as he fished about for the best of the mandarins, a bag of pomegranates, and prepared me a pungent little bouquet of flat-leafed parsley, mint and feathery dill. 'Nobody checks up on these producers and they can say whatever they like.'

The weeks before Christmas were pleasantly low-key. There isn't the commercial over-kill and sense of dread that arrives in Britain after too many weeks of tinsel and mince pies. Nobody tells you how many shopping days you've got left, and you can happily buy your presents on Christmas Eve without panic or queues. I'd been getting quite enthusiastic at the idea of having a real, transplanted English Christmas, with stockings for the children and chestnut stuffing. My image of an idealized, childhood Christmas was propped up by the lack of a convincing Greek alternative.

'No Christmas pudding though,' said the children, and Vassilis agreed that it was too disgusting even to be considered.

Sometimes I worried about becoming an embarrassment to my daughters with my foreign ways. And I realized that it was only going to get worse as they became more Greek. One morning, as I walked the children to school, we came across the dustmen collecting the rubbish on Eurydice Street. I got out some money for a Christmas tip, and passed it to the driver, wishing him the customary 'Chronia Polla! [many years]' and 'Merry Christmas!' Anna looked uncomfortable.

'Mum, they don't *do* that in Greece,' she said, taking hold of my arm.

'Yes they do,' I assured her. 'I've talked with our neighbours

about it, and they said that they're going to give something too.'
I saw a look of relief sweep over her face.

It was when she asked me: 'Do they do it in England too?'
that I realized how hard it can be as a bi-cultural, bilingual child.
Not only do you have an outsider parent who is always at risk
of mortifying you, but you don't belong fully in either culture
yourself. I knew only too well the sense of humiliation which can
come with seemingly insignificant mistakes; it's often the tiny
details which mark you out as foreign.

On the morning of 24 December, small groups of children
rang our door bell from first thing in the morning.

'Can we say them?' they shouted into the intercom, before
climbing the long flight of steps up the hill to sing a Christmas
carol. Among the earliest arrivals was a young, pale girl who
desolately struck a triangle, and two grumpy boys, who sang the
little song dutifully, if somewhat tunelessly, looking down at the
ground. Anna and Lara stood grinning shyly behind the door,
spying on their contemporaries' performance.

> *Good day masters*
> *And if it's your wish*
> *I'll tell to your good house*
> *Of Christ's holy birth*

Only two native carols (known as *Ta Kalanda* – 'the carols') are
actually sung these days, and you tend to hear more American
seasonal songs. Nevertheless, the Greek ones (which are
something like the English wassailing songs) are sung enough in
the couple of days leading up to Christmas and New Year to
make up for it.

'Happy Christmas!' the children said cheerlessly on finishing,
and then spent a long time by the gate counting the small change

I'd handed out, while Lara filled me in on playground gossip about them.

* * *

Just before Christmas, we decided to feign ignorance of the family tensions, and organize a big gathering at our house on Christmas Eve. We hadn't had a proper house-warming party, and it was after all, the season for reconciliation. The turkey would be far too scrawny for eighteen people, and Effi unhesitatingly recommended suckling pig. It might not be organic, but her daughter's boyfriend had a smart butcher's shop, and could get us a nice one.

On the morning of Christmas Eve, Effi turned up with a piglet that bore a disconcerting resemblance to the body of a hefty, naked toddler. The children were part amused, part appalled, and shrieked and giggled at its sad, hairy face and its soft little trotters. We tried to curl it up as though it were going to sleep in the baking tray, but it wouldn't even fit halfway into our oven. I'd already gone right off the whole idea, but Effi suggested going the old-fashioned route – taking it to be cooked at one of the bakeries which still accept other people's food and cook it in their ovens after the bread has been baked. After lunch, she set off with the pig in search of an oven, and I started fretting about whether I'd prepared enough food for a proper Greek celebration. There were little, puffy cheese pies, bright-red pointed peppers stuffed with feta and mint, roast potatoes and several different salads, but I remembered how Vassilis's sister admitted that she had been up all night cooking the last time we'd eaten at her house. There can never be too much. I also recalled the advice of a Greek school friend of mine who warned of the pitfalls of cooking easy, quick meals, known dismissively as 'whore's food'.

My in-laws turned up looking rather stiff, and smarter than usual. They squeezed themselves into our cramped sitting room, hugging and teasing the children, and pinching their cheeks in delight. Our fire was lit against the uncharacteristic cold outside; soon Vouliagmeni's beaches would be covered with snow for the first time in nearly three decades. We'd bought the regulation mix of split pine logs (for fast burning) and bony offcuts of olive (for slow), and a fug of wood smoke and Marlborough Lights soon filled the room.

My mother-in-law had brought along a bulging bag of food: piles of the seasonal, spicy honey cakes (*melomakarona*); crumbly shortbread-like *kourambiedes* covered in powdery icing sugar; platefuls of pies – crispy 'leaves' of pastry stuffed with feta, and yellow cornmeal crust with wild greens; and jars of her sweet preserves – red quince shreds, and green walnuts (now sinister black balls) in syrup. She also evidently scattered a few religious pamphlets, children's prayer books, small wooden crucifixes and the odd miniature icon around the house while nobody was looking, as I came across them sporadically over the next few days.

Vassilis looked vaguely annoyed about the food (he hadn't yet noticed the pamphlets), but didn't say anything. I suspected that he was feeling the stifling sensation that many Greek mothers induce in their offspring by pressing food on them, even after they are grown up. Mothers use the wiles of a seductress and the threats of a harridan to encourage their children to eat. Their success is evident in the size of the Greek young, who are among the plumpest in Europe. It is commonly believed that this approach to food is one of the lasting legacies of the appalling food shortages and starvation during the Nazi occupation. After the war, when mothers were finally able to provide nourishing food for their children, they wanted to make sure that no one ever went hungry again. It is now the grandmothers who carry these memories and fears, but the syndrome continues.

At about ten o'clock, just when we were abandoning all hope of seeing Effi or the meat, she turned up with the pig. It was now looking tired and leathery, slumped on a baking tray the size of a child's coffin which she had somehow acquired. She placed it ceremoniously in the kitchen, wished us 'Happy Christmas!' and set off for her own feasting. Christos hacked it up into chunks, and although I couldn't face it, most people ate some.

'It's nice, but it smells a bit of pig,' was the entirely true but depressing verdict. More important though, all my in-laws now seemed jubilant and full of seasonal merriment. I waited for some sign of the dark currents or jagged silences that I'd expected, but nothing happened. Far from it. We seemed to be at the heart of a united family, who had either forgotten about their grievances or were doing a good job of pretending they'd forgiven all.

Everyone shouted their opinions enthusiastically, ate vast quantities, and clinked glasses of the heady, slightly fizzy, red wine from Zitsa, the northern home of one of Vassilis's brothers-in-law. In the end, it was I, the foreign 'bride' (*nyfi* – as a daughter- and sister-in-law is known) who felt out of sync with the proceedings. It was partly the panic of pretending to be in control of so much food, but it was also my gaffe with the presents. I knew in theory that Greeks exchange gifts at New Year and not Christmas, but somehow (maybe in my triumph at having managed to buy things for all of Vassilis's four siblings, their mother, their spouses and their five children), I forgot. We ended up handing out fourteen presents to people who hadn't brought any for us (and politely didn't say anything about it being the wrong day). Vassilis hadn't mentioned that we should keep them for New Year. Either he didn't know or didn't care. He shrugged when I asked him later: 'I forgot.' After so many years of living in different countries, he was no longer sure what was customary or where was home. He was hovering between cultures which he had adopted and others which he had forgotten.

'Is that why you call him "the European"?' I asked Christos 'Is it because he's been abroad so long?'

'Not at all,' he answered, explaining that Vassilis had been given the nickname when he was a child. 'He used to drive our father mad, sitting up on the roof terrace, gazing at the trains on the distant hill. He had wanted to get away from the age of about eight. Anyway, lots of Greeks have this desire to travel, to leave their home – like Odysseus. It was always obvious that he'd leave.'

In the late 1950s, Vassilis's father had been posted as a schoolteacher to a village with no proper road, where everyone was illiterate. Greece was still desperately poor and was suffering from the after-effects of the Civil War.

'My father was even instructed to *build* the school,' said Vassilis. 'So he gathered the forty village men together, and using horses to carry whatever materials they could find, they made a small schoolroom. He ended up teaching the children in the mornings and their parents in the afternoons. Later, a road was built to the village, but nobody lives there any more.' Even though Vassilis is only four years older than me, it sometimes seems as though his childhood took place in an entirely different epoch from mine. It is strange to think that my parents were dabbling with flower power, and delving into electronic music and psychoanalysis in the London of the Swinging Sixties.

'I've heard that when these Odysseus characters come back home, they sometimes revert to being "more Greek than the Greeks,"' I said. I'd been told of a syndrome whereby cosmopolitan, liberal Greek men who live abroad with foreign wives, suddenly turn conservative and patriarchal on their return to the homeland. 'Ever since we arrived, I've been waiting for Vassilis to take up smoking, grow a moustache, and start playing backgammon in the local *kafeneio*,' I half-joked.

'And what would be wrong with that?' asked one of Vassilis's brothers-in-law (a keen *kafeneio* visitor), blowing a plume of smoke out from under his walrus whiskers.

'Nothing,' I replied, 'but I thought I'd married a "real" Greek, and it turns out he's a European.' Christos laughed.

'Exactly. And he thought he'd married a real Englishwoman, but you're more Greek than he is.'

* * *

Athens had a feverish feeling on the last day of the year. It was a piercingly sunny day, and the city was full of last-minute shoppers, clutching prettily wrapped presents and bags. Gypsy women sat on the pavements selling large, wild bulbs (known as 'wild onions'), their broad, green leaves already sprouting, and tied with a red ribbon. I'd seen them growing on the hills near our house, but hadn't realized that they were supposed to bring good luck if you hang them over the front door. Greek folklorists (who always love a good continuity theory) link the custom to an old Byzantine tradition where olive and laurel branches were hung over the door all year and replaced with new ones on 1 January.

Vassilis and I had been invited by our friends Thalia and Alexis Papahelas for a *mezes* at a trendy new restaurant-bar in the smart, central neighbourhood of Kolonaki. We walked slowly past the famous cafés in its main square. Older Athenian friends say that a generation ago, you only had to walk from Constitution Square to Kolonaki in order to learn everything worth knowing about what was going on in Athens. This may no longer be the case; the city has expanded, and true Kolonaki aficionados claim that their district is now filled with wannabes and impostors.

According to one elegant Kolonaki friend, you can spot the fakes: the women from the nouveaux riches southern suburbs, in elaborate designer jeans, glittering tops, full make-up and high heels at ten a.m. Those from the more traditionally wealthy northern suburbs go for the expensive, athletic-chic look ('it's all Prada trainers and spotless tracksuits, but you can tell they don't go near the gym,' she said pointedly). Nevertheless, Kolonaki still attracts enough politicians, media stars, journalists and glamour pusses to make it lively.

'It's where "the shiny people" are,' said a friend from scruffier Exarcheia. Certainly on New Year's Eve they were looking positively gleaming.

The newer cafés with Italian names (Da Capo, Ciao), supply fancy sandwiches with real *prosciuto*, and pricey, perfectly made espressos. They are the favourites of Athenian *lifestyle* gurus, and may have the best coffee, but I prefer the atmosphere of the older establishments; places like Kolonaki Tops, with leatherette armchairs and dated Formica and blond-wood decor. There, you get a whiff of Athens's own 1960s *dolce vita*, when one side of the modestly sized square was known as the Athenian Saint-Germain-des-Prés. Sedate ladies with helmet hairdos and ornate, gilt sunglasses slowly light up their cigarettes with expensive lighters, and pass the time of day with toady old men with sunspots and blazers. I imagine they've been coming since they were the bright young things and their dapper beaux of long ago. As I passed, I eavesdropped:

'I'm exhausted, *chrysi mou* [darling, but literally 'My gold'],' said one younger woman. 'I've been to the gym, the hairdresser, the psychotherapist and the beautician, and I've still got some presents to buy for tonight . . .'

All the coffee drinkers in Kolonaki have one thing in common; they inspect the passers-by as though their life depended on it. If you don't want to feel like a rabbit passing by a confederation of hawks, it is inadvisable to walk by on a day when your hair looks a mess or if your clothes are crumpled. Even on a good day, it can be necessary to take a deep breath and look straight ahead, before striding confidently along what feels like an alfresco cat-walk parade.

The fashionable Caprice was bursting with 'shiny people'. Even those I didn't recognize from television or politics had the air of being VIPs. Everyone was taking a good look at everyone else, and walking between tables greeting friends and acquaintances. It was about four p.m. before the dozen or so people at our table had gathered for lunch. Thalia and Alexis were both hungover from a late party the night before, and when our friends Marianthi and Andreas arrived wearing dark glasses and looking pale, it was clear that they were too.

'We were dancing until three-thirty,' explained Andreas, begging a cigarette from someone, and putting one long arm around me and another around Vassilis. 'Mayhem!'

Far from dampening spirits, however, the occasion turned into a mix of hair-of-the-dog and gearing up for the celebrations that evening. It was like watching athletes warming up for a marathon of feasting. Nearly all of us were due to see in the New Year with family and relatives, before heading off for at least one party. We would cut the *Vassilopita* (the special cake containing a lucky coin, known literally as 'Vassilis's pie'), and many would also play cards – the traditional activity for New Year's Eve, when large amounts of money are won and lost through the night.

Wine was poured, food brought, and a long-haired DJ turned the music up to rock concert levels, until I began to feel my solar plexus thudding. It was impossible to talk, so everyone sang along instead.

'Happy New Year!' we shouted over the music, toasting one

another across the table. Alexis (a tall, well-built, authoritative figure, known for his serious political writing and television appearances) started banging his fork against his plate like a rhythmically talented toddler, merely to add to the noise.

The music veered giddily from old rembetika favourites to the latest glitzy Greek pop hits, and our companions belted them out too, word perfect. Hangovers banished, they sang with gusto, reaching out to slap each other's hands, or clutch a neighbour's arm, giving themselves up completely to the moment. The table consisted overwhelmingly of cosmopolitan, highly educated Greeks who had spent many years abroad. Last time we'd seen them, they'd been debating the virtues of the *New York Review of Books* and the *Times Literary Supplement*. Today, though, they were singing the same songs that other Greeks in completely different circumstances, all over the country, were singing too.

Afterwards, outside the restaurant, we talked with Andreas and Marianthi in the dimming, rosy dusk. I realized that however much I had admired and enjoyed the party, I was still aware of being an outsider. It was partly that I didn't know all the words to the songs, but also that I am more bashful than most Greeks about just letting go. I admitted that I was amazed by the inexhaustible appetite for celebrations:

'You can all just summon up the enthusiasm out of nowhere. And in the middle of the afternoon with a hangover and parties to go to that evening . . . You'd never find that in England.'

'It's like what Plato said about the Athenians,' replied Andreas without hesitation. 'They were the best out of all the ancient Greeks at feasting, banquets and music. It's in our ancestry, in our blood. We're just still doing what comes naturally.'

* * *

The final seasonal family feast turned out to be a fast. Vassilis's older sister, Stella, invited us over to celebrate her mother Fotini's name-day, on the last big holiday of the season, the Epiphany, on 6 January. You can't ignore a name-day, and though these celebrations are inevitably shared with everyone else bearing that name, they are treated with greater regard than a birthday. Many people hold open house on their name-days, and even if they don't, they may find that visitors arrive anyway, bearing a gift or sweets and expecting some kind of party, or at least cakes and a liqueur. You are expected to phone your friends, relations and even work colleagues on their special day; there's no excuse for not knowing someone's name (as there is for a birthday), and even people you barely know will wish you many happy returns. On the saint's day of a common name such as Dimitris, Yiorgos or Eleni, it can become quite a time-consuming affair.

Stella decided to hold the get-together on the day before, a Sunday, but she had forgotten that it was one of the main fasting days. She had prepared huge quantities of lamb the evening before, only to be reminded by her mother that morning that this was the sacred day of the Holy Cross. Meat was out of the question, dairy products were inappropriate and it was unthinkable that a meal in her honour should contain them.

'I just didn't think,' said Stella, looking stressed and exhausted, as we all piled into her flat. She'd hidden the roast lamb in the oven, and prepared another more suitable meal, according to the rules her mother kept.

Vassilis's mother had always been devout. Indeed she tried to persuade her husband to leave his vocation as a teacher and become a priest. One of his forebears had evidently been a cleric, as the family surname, Papadimitriou, begins with the telltale Papa- (Priest), which is part of so many Greek family names. Papadimitriou becomes the name of Father Dimitris's offspring, just as a Papantoniou is a descendant of Father Antonis and a Papayiorgiou of Father Yiorgos.

'In fact we shouldn't really have used oil either, but that's impossible,' said Stella, bringing out dishes of stuffed tomatoes, puréed split peas, roast octopus, and numerous salads. The Greek way of fasting had always seemed to me a good excuse for a meatless feast, but it was clear that the rules and boundaries were becoming less clear, especially to the younger generation. There is no longer the way of life which allows the dramatic contrast between periods of deprivation and discipline, countered by meat-eating and satiation.

'The children don't really know about fasting any more,' said Christos. 'And anyway, if you followed them all strictly, it'd be 150 days of the year: forty days before Christmas, forty before Easter, fifteen before the Virgin's feast in August, various other holy days, and every Wednesday and Friday. Only devout old women keep to all of those, but we all avoid meat on the important days like Good Friday. That's how we were brought up.'

I sat next to my mother-in-law at lunch. Fotini's pale, kind face has the sad, slightly hooded eyes which Vassilis inherited, and is framed by gentle grey curls. Her daughters persuaded Fotini to cut her hair short and practical, replacing an outdated bun, but they couldn't make her abandon the widow's clothes. Since Vassilis's father was killed in a car crash four years before, she had worn only black.

For half a life time, Fotini was dominated by her own mother-in-law. Until the old matriarch's long-anticipated death at over 100, Vassilis's grandmother was always referred to by her first name – Styliani – and never by the more usual and affectionate *yiayia* (granny). Styliani would sit in a corner, swathed from head to foot in black, ruling domestic life by banging her heavy stick on the floor. Her husband died young, leaving her alone with four children, and she had become a hard, uncompromising survivor. Once, as a young widow, she visited a grocer who owed her months of the rental money on which she survived. Carrying a very large stone into the shop, she handed it to the shopkeeper, saying: 'May you have as heavy a weight as this on your heart.' Vassilis described how Styliani had cured his childhood lisp by taking a razor blade and cutting the small flap of skin under his tongue. Soon everyone at the table joined in with their stories about the family tyrant.

'From tomorrow we're starting a diet in our house,' announced Vassilis's sister Kouli, looking pointedly across the room. Her husband, who is on the large side, was ferreting around in the oven, piling his plate with the forbidden, hidden lamb. 'We've all put on weight, and the whole family is going to lose a few kilos,' Kouli continued severely, preoccupied more with her husband's increasing girth than his breaking of religious rules. There's probably a statistic about more people visiting diet centres in Athens these days than attending a church service. Certainly, the widely positive attitude to fasting is based on combining some light dieting and detoxification rather than with upholding religious tradition.

As Kouli's husband returned to the table, he passed close by his mother-in-law. Smiling naughtily, he murmured theatrically: 'Mmmmmmm, nice fish I'm eating here,' before returning to his seat and polishing off the meat. Nobody said anything. It's not that anyone minded his regular declarations of atheism, but in a society where agnostics usually hedge their bets or keep quiet, his behaviour was still unusual enough to be notable.

Out of the window, the disappearing sun was turning the smudged, grey city pink. The meal drifted into long-drawn-out cups of coffee and cigarettes, and the conversation turned to inheritance. Since Vassilis's father died, the matter had never been taken in hand; he had left no will. But it appeared that everyone was now calm enough to carry out this most delicate of family discussions. I knew that most family feuds (not to mention much of a solicitor's work) in Greece were over inheritance. Matters are frequently complicated, as all children must inherit equally, although dowry can count as an early legacy. It is often difficult for the numerous heirs to agree; family jealousy is prevalent in this perilous area.

Everyone was shouting, but that was normal, and it sounded good-natured. Apparently Vassilis owned what is known as 'the air' (in this case, meaning the potential to construct) above his sisters' building in the village. Consequently, he should help pay for the steps. One person promised to deal with the inevitable red tape, and another had to make sure that their father's fruit trees were being taken care of so they wouldn't go to ruin.

I wandered over to where my mother-in-law was pottering about in the kitchen. I had a cold, and she boiled me a cup of herby mountain tea.

'It's fresh, picked up in the mountains,' she said, stirring in a large spoonful of honey. She still had her mind on the past; old Styliani's tyranny had been nowhere more evident than in the painful, half-hidden struggles with her gentle daughter-in-law, played out as often as not in the kitchen. Vassilis's mother laughed ruefully as she told me of Styliani's orders to ration the oil in her cooking.

'She lived through hard times and hunger – she brought up four children on her own,' she said in her tormentor's defence. 'That's why she was always careful, even when it wasn't really necessary. She'd remark how the dishes tasted much better prepared her way, but I would secretly add another cupful of oil to the food when she wasn't looking. That's why it was so tasty.' They were small, secret triumphs.

It was appropriate that the women should have been

undermining each other with olive oil, something which (even more than bread) is associated with life of the soul as well as the body. Greeks use more olive oil than any other country (each person consumes about twenty litres a year), and over three quarters of all trees growing in Greece are olives. Not only was olive oil the traditional basis of Greek food, but it was used for soap, lamp oil and medicinal purposes. Even in the cities, the olive harvest is still a part of life; many Athenians return to their village in November or December, to gather the olives for that year's pressing. Olive oil has been a part of Greek culture since ancient times. When a baby is smeared with sacred, scented olive oil in the Orthodox baptism rites, there are echoes of ancient heroes; Odysseus became golden-skinned like a god when he anointed himself with olive oil after bathing. If someone has really annoyed you or worn you out, you can say: 'He squeezed the oil out of me.' On the other hand, to 'oil someone' is to bribe them, and if you don't feel well or have a headache, a friend may naturally suggest 'doing the oil', reciting some charms while dropping oil onto water to remove the Evil Eye.

As we got ready to go, Vassilis looked happy. The discussion had gone smoothly, and a dozen young olive trees on a small strip near the road had been designated 'Anna and Lara's olives'.

'We should be getting a container of oil from our daughters' olives this year,' he announced, a grin spreading across his face.

CHAPTER 9

GODFATHERS AND FAVOURS

Who wouldn't lick his fingers if he got honey on them?
Greek proverb

After we moved to Greece, our friends Andreas and Marianthi brought us into their circle of friends, consistently introduced us to people as their *koumbaroi*, and greeted us or left us friendly, slightly tongue-in-cheek phone messages saying: 'Hello, *koumbarakia*! [little *koumbaroi*]!' The link had been made after they became godparents to Lara, when we were all living in London some years previously. Half their friends seemed to be *koumbaroi* to one another too; it was like one big, happy family; 'a *koumbaro*-company,' they called it.

'It's just an indication of affection and friendship and has nothing to do with religion or practical reasons any more,' said Andreas, after I quizzed him about the significance. But I disagreed with his purely secular interpretation. It might be true,

I argued, that like many contemporary Athenians, we'd chosen our wedding sponsors and children's godparents from among our friends, but the title stands for much more than that. In the past, the bond with your *koumbaroi* was as important as that with your family. Priests describe the relationship as sacred and existing at the undying level of the soul, and anthropologists have long been fascinated by 'spiritual kinship' in Greece. Andreas looked puzzled, but gave me a *koumbaro*-hug anyway.

The godparent is a highly revered figure, who is also bound with obligations. When someone 'baptizes the child', he or she gives the customary gold cross which should last for life, and even has the right to name the child. Infants commonly remain nameless for up to a year, or until the baptism; 'Baby' or nonsense names fill in until then. There are stories of controversial, last-minute changes where the parents were left speechless at the godparent's choice. It is assumed that the godparent will not only provide the special decorated candle at Easter time and presents on name-days, but will be a constant support throughout life.

Such is the pre-eminence of the godparent in Orthodox tradition that the mother is practically excluded from much of her offspring's baptism service. When Vassilis and I went back to Hydra (where we'd got married) to have Anna baptized, I'd mistakenly imagined some picturesque customs forming the backdrop to a party for our new baby. Unbeknownst to us, however, the priest was a hardliner who stuck adamantly to traditional practices. First, he smothered the wriggling, naked infant with oil brought by the godparents, and then anointed various significant points (ears, breast, forehead, hands and feet) with a particularly holy, consecrated oil. Next, he snipped off some of her hair, which is said to be the child's offering or gift, much as it is when a monk or nun takes vows.

The priest was wearing an apron over his robes, and his large hands gripped the slippery, protesting baby tightly around her plump, glistening torso. To Anna's disgust, the priest dipped her up to her neck in the big, cauldron-sized font. Then, all of a sudden, without warning, he tipped her upside down and plunged her head-first into the oily water. Nothing less than total submersion was correct, and this was his method. I ran towards the man I thought might be my daughter's murderer shouting: 'No!' only to reach his side as the howling, drenched creature was already being bundled into a lacy towel. By then I was crying almost as much as Anna, but I still wasn't allowed to take her in my arms; that was the right and duty of the godmother.

Afterwards, Anna was dressed up in the required finery: fancy white bootees and cap, the laciest possible dress and her new gold cross. Someone attached a little blue glass eye on a safety pin to the back of her dress; she was bound to be admired, which brings the danger of the admirer giving her 'the eye'.

I was undeniably shocked by Anna's christening. It had some of the physical intensity and even violence associated with childbirth, and in some ways, the ritual is like a second, spiritual and social birth. Anthropologists describe the Orthodox baptism as being a rite of separation from natural birth, and acting as a 'rite of incorporation into society'. Acquiring a name is highly significant; it is no chance that name-days are celebrated more than birthdays. I was not the only one who was shaken; I saw Vassilis's father, who was a real old-timer, wiping away a tear. Several of us dreamed of drowned babies that night. Nevertheless, it was not enough to put me off having Lara christened three years later, by which time we had found a kinder, more gentle priest to perform the ceremony.

Launching upended, screaming infants into the font is no longer so common, but the mother is still expected to give way to the spiritual parents during a christening. I witnessed this again when Marianthi and Andreas became godparents to the first child of our mutual friends, Thalia and Alexis. After the godparents had finished the interesting rigmarole of rejecting Satan near the church's door – as with avoiding the evil eye, they spit symbolically in his eye – the priest asked Thalia to bow down before Marianthi and kiss her hand. Thalia blushed furiously. As a worldly, well-travelled journalist, she was thrown into bewilderment by her own country's customs, and at the prospect of honouring someone who had merely been a friend until now.

'Don't be shy now, it's a tradition,' said the priest kindly. The earthly mother bent over quickly, performing a ritual that indicated only too clearly the subservience of flesh to spirit.

* * *

When we'd met Andreas and Marianthi Papandreou in England, I'd known perfectly well that Andreas's father and grandfather had both been Prime Ministers. More recently, his brother George was tipped to follow in their footsteps and was now the Foreign Minister. However, it was only on moving to Athens that it became evident to me what it really meant to go out with a Papandreou. Even half a decade after their father's death, the family were still big fish in a little pond. Wherever they went they were fêted and made much of. Andreas lectures in economics at Athens University and has little to do with politics, but he is still treated like a prince. In terms of cachet and political clout, the Papandreou family is the nearest thing Greece has to the Kennedys.

One evening, we went out to dinner in Plaka with a group of friends, which included Marianthi and Andreas. Marianthi is pretty enough to turn heads and Andreas is tall enough to draw attention even without his surname, but as we entered the warm taverna, which smelled of roasting meats and woody, resinated barrel wine, I noticed a little frisson ripple through the other diners. In contrast to the slow, easygoing approach I'd seen there before, the owner and the waiters grinned and scurried around us.

Platanos was the sort of unpretentious place which could have been swamped and ruined by the hordes of indiscriminate tourists which snake their way through Plaka's narrow streets around the base of the Acropolis. In fact though, it has retained a relaxed, family atmosphere, and the tiny square outside still has the shade-giving plane tree after which the taverna is named. Its walls are covered with mementoes and souvenirs declaring its pedigree: pictures of the Acropolis and ancient pots compete for space with paintings of fierce nineteenth-century *klephtes* (freedom-fighting outlaws), comical Karaghiozis shadow puppets and photographs of famous poets. Platanos takes you back to an Athens which even a decade ago was not a city of two-car families, mobile phones, multiplex cinemas, credit cards and consumer loans. Not that things were necessarily better then. Foreigners have frequently appreciated the more picturesque aspects of what can be merely poverty (a man on a donkey looks so much nicer than one in a car). Greeks, though, have been only too ready to embrace a higher standard of living.

The stout, dimple-cheeked proprietor ran about, pulling out extra tables and making sure we were all seated comfortably.

'You're Andreas, aren't you?' he said. 'I'm from a village in the Peloponnese just next to where your father was from. Don't you worry, you don't need to order; I'll just bring you the best of what we've got.' It was the nearest I'd ever seen a Greek get to bowing and scraping. Gradually, various plates appeared on the table: plump, stuffed vine leaf parcels with *avgolemono* (egg and lemon) sauce; fried segments of spicy, country sausage; salt cod in batter with pungent garlic sauce; *stifado*, the rich, slowly stewed dish of beef with baby onions; and slabs of salty feta from the barrel.

I was still bothering Andreas about the *koumbaroi* business, and he told me about how his father would often send one of his four children off in his place to act as godparent at provincial baptisms. Until recently, whole networks of votes could be ensured if a minister (let alone a Prime Minister) 'baptized' a baby. Andreas described how people would frequently request the honour through local party officials, and were proud to have a Papandreou as 'family'. Leading politicians sometimes have hundreds of godchildren, many of whom they'll never see again. Over the years, Andreas regularly found affectionate strangers approaching him and claiming to be the uncle or the sister 'of your godchild in Patras'.

Every so often, as we were brought a plate of some tasty *mezes* or another jug of yellow retsina from the home-made stock, the owner would come and pat Andreas on the back.

'Strength!' or 'We're here!' he'd say conspiratorially, clenching his fist, as though the late Andreas Papandreou was still the dynamic, provocative Prime Minister of the 1980s, standing on the podium, exhorting the people to create a new socialist Greece. Andreas, his namesake son, did a good impression of him holding out his arms and shouting: 'People!' in a rich, bass voice. In Greek, *laos* is a powerful word, which means populace or the entire population, and has none of the ambiguity of 'people'. The crowds would roar back: 'Andreas! Andreas!'

When I first arrived in Greece in the mid-1980s, it was just at the end of the first flush of optimism following the 1981 election of Andreas Papandreou's Pan-Hellenic Socialist Party PASOK. He had come to power with radical, populist slogans and a reputation as a rebellious 'bad boy' of the Left. All across the country you saw walls covered in green graffiti: an emerging green sun – the movement's symbol – and its slogans 'Change' and 'Greece belongs to the Greeks'. Papandreou's maverick personality and his wariness of America, the European Union and NATO, were all to strike just the right chord. His demands for an end to America's undermining and destructive domination in Greece was matched by Greeks' anger over how their small country had been treated by the USA over the previous decades.

In the early years, there was a strong sense that real changes might actually happen. A serious attempt was made to get rid of Greece's old power structures: for the first time, the poor, the disadvantaged and, above all, the left-wing were given public sector jobs; the institution of the gendarme, the notorious *chorofylakas*, who tyrannized so many villages, was done away with; women's rights were vastly improved by a radical overhaul; and people who had been underdogs for generations were given the opportunity to rise up.

'When it was our father's name-day, there'd be a huge line of well-wishers bringing endless gifts to the house,' said Andreas, reminiscing. 'Of course, it was my name-day too. When I was young, I used to stand by the door, watching the gigantic pile of my father's presents growing. I'd tell the strangers: "You know, it's my name-day too."'

Eventually, financial and personal scandals lost Papandreou the elections. Notoriously, he abandoned Margaret, his American wife of almost forty years, and married Mimi, a busty, blonde Olympic Airways air hostess half his age. Nonetheless, PASOK managed to return to power, and had clung on to it for the best part of two decades. Now, things were different; Greece had changed, as poverty and the influence of dictatorship and disasters receded. It had opened up as a modern, European country. People no longer talk of 'going to Europe' as though it were a far-off place, and confidently remark: 'We're part of the European family.'

PASOK has changed too. While the Papandreou family is part of a political aristocracy, the characteristic PASOK supporter and even the typical MP tended to come from the social (and often geographical) margins.

'You can tell how things have changed,' said Vassilis, 'by looking at the sort of cars that show up at party rallies. Everyone used to arrive in beaten-up old bangers and pick-up trucks, but nowadays it's all Mercedes. PASOK became the establishment – the party of the privileged. Ironically, it's New Democracy [the conservatives] which now appeals to the poor and the unemployed. Now, you see the old wrecks and the farmers' trucks at their gatherings. They've become the party of protest.'

While we were talking, a middle-aged man walked up to Andreas and clasped his hand.

'Lots of love,' he said quietly, looking intently into Andreas's face. 'And respect, for what your father did.' It was poignant to see this shy man honouring his political hero. Whatever the scandals and tawdry intrigues, Andreas's father was still a legend.

As a final tribute, the taverna owner offered us his last remaining deep-crimson wedges of quince baked in wine. On leaving, we were ushered out into the quiet, chilled streets, our hands shaken like old friends. Above us, the Acropolis loomed benevolently, lit up and glowing as though bathed in moonlight.

* * *

Vassilis had offered to take me to meet his friend Yerasimos, a colleague from another ministry, who spoke openly about political favours, and was happy to discuss how he doled them out.

'He believes that if a favour is done in the right way, it's an act of philanthropy and not a matter of corruption at all,' said Vassilis, as we rode in the lift up to the top floor of a modern but slightly seedy ministry building, where Yerasimos worked as the right-hand man to the Minister. Vassilis had the ease of an insider, as he whisked me past two beady-eyed men who sat jangling keys and worry beads at desks in the smoky corridor outside the Minister's rooms. These bureaucrat's equivalent of bouncers, who block public access, are a vital measure in a country whose citizens still believe that the answer to most questions can be found in some minister's office. There are always members of the public loitering outside, waiting for a chance to get a foot inside the door.

As a Greek archetype, the ministry is like the palace in a fairy tale; it is the seat of power, whether the ruler is good or bad. The minister becomes its feudal prince, surrounded by a court of advisers, minions, jesters and sycophants. There is a sense that his power is absolute and anyone who is close to him is also in great demand. Power is like honey; everyone wants a taste. Many of the country's ills are also laid at the minister's door. When there was no gym teacher at the children's school for two months at the beginning of the year, we were told: 'The Ministry [of Education] hasn't sent one yet.' Those who knew said we'd only get one if the headmaster rang the Ministry insistently, every day. Nobody expects the minister to do a fair job or a good one without pressure or individual involvement, so there is a continuous attempt to make things personal. It is indicative of the politicians' appreciation of this approach that there is no minister who lacks an office dealing specifically with personal favours.

We passed into an antechamber, where some smiling secretaries waved us through into Yerasimos's room. The scene was one of benign chaos, like so many other political offices:

overflowing ashtrays, cups of cold, half-drunk coffee, icons, people drifting in and out, and a large television, which showed some priests organizing soup kitchens for the poor of Athens. Yerasimos was attempting to speak on two telephones at once. He had the pale complexion and quick eyes of someone who works too much. A pretty woman who had just been elected as a PASOK local councillor offered a box of chocolates around in celebration of her victory. A colourful parakeet sat chirping in a cage. At one point the Minister came quietly into the throng, and having greeted us all cheerfully, wandered back out to his office.

'Sofka wants to know about the *rousfeti*,' said Vassilis bluntly to Yerasimos. 'Can you tell her about it?' Without blinking, Yerasimos picked out a substantial dictionary from a bookshelf and read out:

'*Rousfeti*, from the Turkish for bribe – *rusvet*. It says here that it means giving something (but not money) in exchange for something else from the governing power. It's a hangover from Ottoman times, where the politician helps "his" person in exchange for political support. For most of the twentieth century it was basically a right-wing phenomenon, because they were the people in power. Then when PASOK got elected in 1981, it became a necessary evil. One of their first moves was to make all the civil servants without proper contracts "permanent", with jobs for life.'

'Wasn't that just like one giant *rousfeti*?' I asked, without receiving a reply.

I'd always been struck by the fixation of the average Greek with acquiring a 'permanent position' for himself and his offspring in the great state leviathan. It goes without saying that hiring (and, to a lesser extent, firing) can still be based on whim and insider contacts rather than merit. This is nothing new. In central Athens there is even a 'Laments' Square (Plateia

Klafthmonos), named in the nineteenth century after the distraught bureaucrats who had been sacked, and stood outside the Interior Ministry, protesting and crying for their jobs. Greece's middle class is unlike any other in Europe, in its extreme dependence on the state. There being no other upper class or aristocracy, it was the state-educated civil servants who became a serious component in the country's elite. Naturally, acquiring the requisite qualifications involved favours too.

Yerasimos admitted that PASOK had not managed to do away with the clumsy bureaucracy or with favours. The way I saw it, rather than political favouritism and patronage being removed, they were institutionalized. These days you were either 'one of ours' or no one at all. And it wasn't just the top dogs who were giving favours. Lowly officials in public offices frequently require small bribes just to process regular papers, and the ordinary person is made to suffer as much as possible. It is not uncommon to discover that employees who appear to be too busy at their computers to attend to the public are actually playing games or placing bets on Internet gambling sites.

I get annoyed when Greece lives up to its stereotype as an unreliable, dishonest place, but there is no escaping the recently published statistics; it is one of the EU's most corrupt countries. It is true that there is now much more denunciation and even prosecution of bribery and dishonesty; since recent legislation, even Athenians with influence are annoyed to find that they can't just 'write off' their speeding fines as before. However, it is still easy enough to encounter corruption.

Many people assume that to obtain the services of a state sector doctor, they must give a *fakelaki* or 'envelope' containing money. Not a few doctors brazenly announce the cost of their 'envelope' to patients, and it is widely believed that you only get the best treatment if you've paid something extra.

There's no way you'll get planning permission to build a house without large handouts – architects have to oil at every level, and it is common knowledge that tax officials take money for turning a blind eye. And who can be expected to pay their taxes properly when the state appears to be so untrustworthy and capricious?

While people bribe to avoid laws in every country, Greeks must often pay or utilize 'connections' merely to benefit from the law. It is one of the worst, most lingering characteristics of 'Mangy Betty,' which no politician has had the temerity to confront head-on. And how do you tackle something which can affect the most minor transaction as well as big business, not to mention most intervening levels? Some commentators have even asked what would be left of Greece if the system did improve. As a friend put it, 'Can Greece become European without losing her soul?'

According to Yerasimos, though, the laws *had* changed over the last decade. 'Now, politicians can only do a *rousfetaki* [little favour]. I help people with these little favours because I'm close to power and I believe it's my social duty. If people want to discuss personal problems, I tell them that it's only after six p.m. on Tuesdays and Thursdays at the "other office" – I refuse to do it here in the Ministry.' I asked Yerasimos if I could come to witness a bit of what is called 'rousfetology' in action, and to my surprise, he agreed.

* * *

The next few days were filled with wonderful storms. Warm southerly winds blew enormous, grey rollers up onto the shore below our house, and I watched waves breaking over the small islands nearby, sending great sprays of water up into the air. By six o'clock the following Thursday, the freezing weather and storms had given way to warm, spring-like conditions.

'It's the halcyon days,' announced Effi authoritatively that morning. I'd always thought this was a nostalgic expression for the golden, carefree, good old days, but it turns out that in Greece you get them for real every year. The balmy, blue days which crop up regularly in January and February have been known since ancient times, and are surrounded with legends and traditions. There's even a myth about the halcyon or kingfisher, which is supposedly so graceful that when it lays its eggs in midwinter, stormy seas turn calm until they are hatched.

'You can tell what the summer will be like from how many halcyon days we have,' said Effi. 'And it's the best time for picnics.'

Yerasimos's 'other office' turned out to be a slightly neglected, converted apartment, in a steep back-street on the slopes of Lycabettus. A secretary showed me into the hallway, where I waited for a few minutes, looking at blown-up photographs of the Minister in younger days, flanking an energetic-looking Andreas Papandreou, and walking with the glamorous former PASOK Minister of Culture (and actress) Melina Mercouri and her enormous smile. I could hear Yerasimos shouting on the phone from an inner room.

'No, I can't help you with your loans. If you owe money to four banks you need to go to the banks, not to me. Goodbye.' He went straight on to another call. 'Yes? Hello. Tell me what you want. Your daughter has a nursing degree? She wants to go to Haidari? Does she have the right papers? Well then, tell her to call me and give me the details and we'll let you know.'

After I'd been shown in, Yerasimos said conspiratorially: 'Come and sit here by the desk, and we'll say you're a colleague.' The next petitioner was shown into the room. *Kyria* Katina looked anxious. She had bronze streaks in her short hair, an awkward, thick, grey suit, and was holding her handbag on her lap with a sheaf of papers. She looked across at Yerasimos as though he alone could help her.

'It's about my son,' she said in a clear, quiet voice. 'He's teaching at the University of Ioannina, but he wants to do a Ph.D. in Piraeus. He's twenty-eight, and I must tell you, he's an active PASOK member. I'd like you, if you can, to make some contact with the University in Piraeus.' *Kyria* Katina then turned to me to explain her predicament, perhaps sensing that I didn't really belong there. 'All the professors have their own clientele, and unless you have some inside influence you can't do anything. Unfortunately there's no meritocracy here in Greece, and you have to knock on the politicians' doors. We have no choice.'

'As it happens, I've a friend who's a professor at Piraeus,' said Yerasimos, picking up his phone to ring him straight away. 'Listen,' he explained to the professor, 'I've got this kid who has all the right papers, and he wants to do a Ph.D. with you. Can you see him? Yes. OK. Thanks in advance.' *Kyria* Katina rose, beaming, and shaking our hands.

'I'll be at your service whenever you need me. I'll be in your debt.'

'Aren't you just continuing the system of the *rousfeti*, even if what you are doing is the legal sort?' I asked Yerasimos.

'I'm helping them because they ask me to,' he replied, ignoring the implication. 'But in fact, it's only because I have the information, and I can put them in contact with people. I can't actually give them the appointment. Anyway, over the last ten years they've changed the laws, so that now nobody can actually hand out a public sector job if the applicant doesn't have the right qualifications.' I recalled a friend who depicted the whole state administration as being organized according to 'a kind of Darwinism in reverse': the worst specimens survive and reproduce to make sure that no one of value is ever given a chance.

'So many different people turn up to see me,' continued Yerasimos, 'from the big businessmen to priests. Often they come with tragic problems – old people who can't afford their medical bills, people without work who can't send their children to university. Of course, some people ask me for a silly *rousfeti*; help with finding a husband for their daughters . . . they tend to be from the lower social classes. It can be soul-destroying seeing all these people, but I'm a Christian and I believe in what I'm doing. I don't see people or help them if I think they are cheating.'

I was intrigued at this Christian interpretation of an old Muslim institution (the Ottoman Pasha awarded loyalty, gifts or favours with string-pulling or favouritism of his own). It reminded me of the Orthodox custom of making deals with the saints. During times of crisis or illness, you make your request to your preferred saint (or often the *Panayia*) and promise a *tama* – a sacrifice, a precious gift, a pilgrimage or a donation in return. In some cases, you can hang your jewel or watch on the appropriate icon, or place a *tama* – the small tin votive offering, imprinted with a picture symbolizing your concern (a baby, a leg, an eye, a house or a soldier). Then, the priest acts as 'civil servant', writing down the sacrosanct transaction, and you wait for the saint to keep his or her side of the bargain. As with the worldly version, success brings loyalty for life.

The ancient Greeks, too, kept the gods happy with appropriate sacrifices, in a sort of religious contract.

'Don't forget,' a friend told me, 'that when Iphigeneia was sacrificed, it was to prompt Aeolus, the god of the winds, to help the wind-bound Greek fleet to leave Aulis for Troy. It's the same principle as the *tama*.'

'And what do people do for you in return for the favour?' I asked Yerasimos.

'I don't ask for anything from them,' he replied simply. 'Though it's true that some people do. A politician might draw in the favour later, but he'll never know quite what he'll get; he's like a fisherman casting his nets and pulling them in. He might ask them to bring supporters to a political meeting, or if someone is a doctor or dentist, the politician might even ask for free treatment. The *rousfeti* ties them together.'

As we spoke, an old crone dressed in a bright green Chanel jacket and wet, muddy gym shoes strode into the room. She looked like the witch in 'Sleeping Beauty', with warts on her face, a substantial beard and only two strangely protruding teeth. She walked unhesitatingly over to Yerasimos's desk, and began shouting and banging her fist.

'I want you to send away all the Albanians, get rid of drugs and close down the brothels!' she shouted. 'All the people are cursing you politicians, and if you don't give me a loan, I'll sue you. You must get me a lawyer so I can get back my fields from my brothers. And tell the Prime Minister to get me into hospital.'

'Theodora, calm down,' said Yerasimos. 'Didn't I drive you to hospital when you needed it? Didn't I get you your medicines? Here, take this,' he said, pressing a ten-euro note into her hand. 'And now leave us, because we've got work to do.' It took another fifteen minutes to get rid of this well-known Athenian beggar. Although illiterate, she regularly sent dictated letters of garbled complaints to all the government ministers. Before leaving, she handed Yerasimos a fresh batch of envelopes for him to pass on: 'Dear Minister, I've already sent 500 letters and you don't help me,' they began. In Greece even crazy homeless women believe in the powers of ministers. Before leaving, she gave me one of the least welcome, most whiskery kisses I've ever received.

'Yerasimos, do you think you could help me with a *rousfeti*?'

I asked, only half joking, as I got up to go. 'I'm trying to become a Greek, but it's very difficult. They want so many papers, and you have to pay 1,500 euros, get your fingerprints done, bring witnesses, and that's just to register. I've heard of people waiting years without success.' Favours may be morally questionable, but if I didn't learn to work the system like everyone else, I'd never get anywhere.

'When you've managed to make the application, just get in touch if you have any problems,' replied Yerasimos with a vaguely world-weary manner. 'Then I'll see what I can do,' he added charitably, seeing me out into the dark stairwell.

CHAPTER 10

SACRED IMAGES

For the world is a tree, and we are its fruit
And Charos, who is the vintager, gathers its fruit.
Modern Greek couplet

One freezing day, I found myself walking by Athens's Cathedral. It was so bitingly cold that the pigeons had fluffed up their feathers and were weaving about looking dazed, while the Athenians were dressed like reluctant Norwegians in thick coats and scarves. The air smelled of chestnuts, which were being roasted by a sad-looking man with purple lips. A long and impressively orderly queue filled the large square outside the Cathedral, and I went over to find out what was going on.

'We've come from Mytiline to see the icon of the Virgin from Jerusalem,' explained a well-padded woman who was standing with her husband and a few relations towards the front of the line. 'We travelled all night on the boat, and we've already been waiting four hours. But it's worth it.' I'd heard about this miracle-working icon, which had attracted hundreds of thousands of the faithful from all over the country during its visit to Greece, and was amazed at the sight of so many determined people prepared to brave the inclement weather.

The icy air took me back to the shock of my first Greek winter in the 1980s, after the sweet autumn days had given way to real cold. In my flat, I huddled over an electric heater – a strange contraption consisting of an upended aluminium bowl fitted with a little stand and a small coil of wire. It was quite pretty, but utterly ineffective. I rued the day that I'd rented a place with no heating, and always respected Greek winters after that.

I was on my way to the main registry office over the road, hoping to acquire a copy of my marriage certificate. I walked up the stairs past an office with a handwritten sign 'new babies only', to the second floor where deaths shared a room with marriages.

'You'll have to go to Hydra where you got married if you want the document,' said an irritating man at the desk. When I tried to pursue the point he became unpleasant.

'Let's keep things nice, Madam,' he hissed. My ongoing application for Greek citizenship was beginning to look increasingly like a wild-goose chase, with unhelpful civil servants blocking my progress gleefully at every possible stage. It wasn't enough even to have the required document; they often had to have obscure stamps, seals and verifications of authenticity from solicitors or ministries.

Nurturing murderous feelings towards the 'marriages' man and wondering what to do next, I drifted over to the 'deaths' section on the other side of the room. Here, a cheery, fat man was attending to several old women dressed in black.

'Last April was it that he died?' he asked helpfully, pulling out a large, ancient-looking brown book from the shelves (the ledgers on the marriages side were black). The old woman sat down to browse, and I saw that the pages were filled with the Greek equivalent of Dickensian copperplate handwriting, listing every Athenian death in a delicate, light blue ink. There were no computers; life's major events were still recorded as they always had been. The large window gave onto a picture-book view of the wintry, pale Acropolis. The writer Vassilis Vassilikos described the 'skeleton of the Parthenon – imperishable symbol of Greek civilization', and that day its columns looked just like a rib-cage.

Outside, I passed again into the Cathedral Square, and hesitated, wondering if there was any chance that I too could see the holy icon. It may be my Russian blood which made me think that it's usually worth joining a queue (in my Moscow days, I knew Russians who regularly joined a line without knowing what it was for, on the assumption that there must be *something* worth waiting for). It was certainly my British upbringing which made me assume I should go to the end of the queue and wait my turn. However, it was my Greek experience which told me there must be another way of approaching the problem, and I sauntered slowly over to the exit door, where cameramen, important-looking men in suits and invalids were being let through the back way by police guards.

A young policeman refused to believe my claims to being a journalist.

'No papers, no entry,' he said officiously. But I'd learned to recognize a no with hope.

'Please,' I wheedled, watching a group of people with learning difficulties being shepherded through. 'I want to write about the icon.' After several refusals, the policeman looked into my eyes and then said in a loud, public voice:

'Are you pregnant?'

I barely hesitated, before understanding his drift.

'Yes,' I lied.

'Well, through you go, then,' he smiled, ushering me towards the large door.

My sneaking in the back and the policeman's favouritism may have been wrong, and was certainly unmerited, but among the dark throng of the pilgrims, silent but for the buzz of murmured prayers, and the light of hundreds of slender, honey-coloured tapers, it felt more like a blessing. I moved over towards the substantial, gold-encrusted icon, with its rosy-cheeked mother and child. Both had the enigmatic, distant look in their eyes which is so characteristic of icons. The *Panayia* (the 'All Holy' Mother of God) and infant Christ are never the living, breathing young women and wriggling, greedy babies who represent the Madonna and child in Italian renaissance paintings. The images in the icon are always still, stylized references to the sacred characters themselves; a direct link to the original saintliness, and to God. They are painted by people who are Christian believers, and according to certain rules. Thus the backgrounds are often filled not with realistic landscapes (the rolling Tuscan hills of so many Madonnas), but with gold, shining like heavenly light. Icons are holiness made visual.

As people in the queue drew closer to the icon, the tension grew almost palpable. Several people were sobbing, and a beautiful young woman stood gazing at the *Panayia* from afar, tears rolling down her motionless face. Many of the pilgrims brought bunches of flowers, which they laid by the icon, and some clutched photographs of family or babies' clothes to touch up against the glass. Inside the icon's frame, a string was hung with personal gifts – sparkling rings, gold watches and little silver votive offerings, all evidence of the prayers of former visitors making a *tama* or vow.

'Hurry along now,' shouted a grouchy priest, grasping the praying grandmothers by the shoulders, and shunting them along as they tried to plant some final kisses on the holy picture. Behind the old women came someone crawling elaborately along the floor. She looked like a rock chick, with her tousled, waist-length hair, high-heeled black boots and hippy skirt, but when she stood up I saw that she was one of the many gypsies who had waited their turn in the line.

These outpourings of religious passion were sometimes spectacular. I'd seen films of the extraordinary scenes which take place every August on the island of Tinos. On the *Panayia*'s feast day the whole island fills with vast numbers of pilgrims, many of whom walk barefoot or crawl their way up the long flight of steps to the church. Miracles are said to occur; sick people are cured, cripples stand up and walk, and there is much partying into the bargain.

There is a practical, everyday quality, though, to the way Greek Orthodoxy is practised, so that its influence is every-where, but it is fitted into ordinary life. A young man listening to the radio in his car crosses himself as he passes a church, or a mother lights the lamp by the household's icons as part of doing the chores. I've even seen a nun talking on a mobile phone as she tidied up a church, taking it with her to the hidden area behind the icon screen where ordinary women are not allowed.

Whatever Greece's turbulent history, its people are extraordinarily homogeneous as far as religion goes. It is taken for granted that almost everyone is Orthodox. Over ninety-five per cent of Greeks declare themselves to be so, and there is a widespread belief that 'religion is the only thing keeping us

Greek'. So although far fewer young people are regular churchgoers, and things are changing due to the levels of immigration, there is a general enthusiasm for hanging on to the trappings of Greek Orthodoxy. Until very recently, only Christian Orthodox teachers were allowed to teach religious classes in Greek primary schools.

The Church of Greece may officiate at almost everyone's baptisms, marriages and funerals, but there is a sense that it is going through the motions rather than peering into individuals' souls. So long as you perform the rituals, nobody tends to worry about dogma and whether you really believe. Unlike Catholicism, there is little preoccupation with sin and guilt. I've never spoken with a Greek who was worried about his or her morals from a religious point of view. Nobody minds if people whisper in church services or wander outside for a cigarette. It is enough that the sacred words are being said and the rituals observed in the correct way.

It is perhaps this very flexibility and ability to be 'ordinary' which gives the Church its strength. People are comfortable with religious paraphernalia; icons are evident in every home and office, and street markets sell the little lamps, oil and wicks for the household icons and family graves in the same stalls as toilet paper, bleach and dried oregano. Like bread, water, wine or oil, the provisions become holy through their use. People also bring an easygoing, homely attitude to church. You see shoppers popping into a church while out on their errands in Athens. They put down their shopping bags in a corner of the dark, incense-filled church, and, with casual efficiency, light a candle and make a quick tour of all the main icons, which are given due respect with a kiss and a sign of the cross. Finally, they may write out the names of some loved ones who are ill and in need of prayer on the little slips of paper which are left ready, and will be read out by the priest at the next liturgy. Within a few minutes they have picked up their bags and head out onto the street again.

As I made for the Cathedral's exit, a pair of extremely pregnant, shy young women came in, bellies first, and headed towards the icon.

'Two women up the duff coming through,' called out a policeman coarsely. There was a general tittering throughout the gathered ranks of women up from the provinces, who were resting on chairs and watching the procession.

'Pregnant, please, not up the duff,' retorted the sullen priest, to increased laughter, as the blushing objects of their attention made their way modestly to the image of the *Panayia*.

On my way out, I stopped to say thank you and goodbye to the young policeman.

'Is that all?' he complained as I made to go. 'Just goodbye?' I was puzzled. He surely wasn't asking for money in front of all these people.

'What do you want, a kiss?' I asked a little sarcastically.

'That would be better,' he countered without missing a beat, as I flounced off smiling.

The next day, the papers were full of a controversy which had blown up about the icon.

'The Church of Greece is exploiting the paganism and sick faith of certain of its members by staging tours of icons and religious relics,' raged a Bishop from northern Greece. 'When believers identify themselves with an icon it becomes idolatry.' The Archbishop of Athens countered with the insult that these comments smacked of Protestant doctrine, which is in itself heresy. Journalists were not slow to realize that this quarrel was strongly reminiscent of the dispute over iconoclasm twelve centuries previously, which had split the Byzantine Empire during the eighth century. It was an impressive indication of how little things change in this Church.

'I know about that, we did it in history,' said Anna when she heard me talking about the subject with Vassilis at home. 'Iconoclasts and iconodules,' she said in Greek, turning on the characteristically plaintive, sing-song voice which children reserve for their 'parrot learning'. 'The iconoclasts tried to smash up all the icons and they put people in prison for having them. Then the iconodules saved the icons and brought them back. And we've had them ever since.'

* * *

In February, Carnival began. We took Anna and Lara to the Zappeio Gardens in central Athens, one chilly Sunday morning. The park was filled with parents trailing along behind little princesses, Zorros, witches, cowboys, gypsies and Spidermen, who were spraying white foam at each other out of cans and whining for the cheap, plastic toys on sale at the stalls.

I'd always loved this time of year; so many of Greece's inherent contradictions emerge and it's a great time for parties. The love of excess is combined with the desire for purification, and Dionysian revelry is the preparation for Christian fasting. Nobody needs Freud's theory on libidinal energy and the death instinct to notice that the three-week period includes not only the glorification of the phallus and a permission of the freedoms brought by wine and masks, but *Psychosavato* or 'Soul Saturday' (the day for commemorating the dead). It's sex and death – *Eros* and *Thanatos*, with as much fun as possible. In general, the Church wisely takes a back seat during the three weeks of wild masquerading, music and feasting (different foods take precedence, and one week is 'meat week,' another 'cheese week'). It allows the people their pagan intemperance, knowing that Lent will soon bring fasting and abstinence and that by Easter, the flock is back in the fold.

On the final Carnival Sunday, television news reports showed fires being lit all over the country and decorum put aside. Men dressed up as women, while tipsy, middle-aged housewives and giggling young mothers waved giant penises made from bread, chocolate or plastic. People wearing masks with noses shaped as male genitals danced around cauldrons of bright green nettle and spinach soup. Someone suggested that these carnival penises somehow represent the souls of the departed, but the dancers looked as though they had other things on their mind. Groups of men sang rowdy songs, which are not normally deemed appropriate for the children and grandparents who were gathered around:

> *My proud cock asks my balls 'what do you say balls?'*
> *Shall we go and fuck . . .*
> *. . . let's go and get the married women, the fiancées and*
>   *the widows . . .*

The next day, 'Clean Monday', was the first day of Lent, but, as if unable to let go of the carnival, and faced with forty days in the uninviting wilderness of restraint and even deprivation, people keep going for one last day of merrymaking. In the afternoon, Vassilis and I took the children for a walk down to one of the local beaches. This is the day when you take the family in search of fresh air, eat a picnic and fly a kite (we'd flown ours on the hill that morning, and ripped it). As we arrived, it looked as though all of Athens had come to Vouliagmeni.

Families had parked their cars, and were sitting on rugs or at little tables with folding chairs, eating the customary fasting foods: *lagana*, an unleavened, oval bread with sesame seeds, always eaten on Clean Monday; sticky, oily chunks of halva;

prawns, octopus and calamari (only bloodless seafood is permitted); stuffed vine leaves, lettuce and creamy, off-white taramosalata. You could tell the taramosalata was home-made, as Greek shops normally supply only the stodgy, tasteless, candy-pink variety. The salty tastes of the sea and sweet, earthy sesame were being washed down with yellow retsina or ouzo in plastic cups, and men who had drunk too much sat slumped in cars listening to the radio. Mothers comforted crying babies, children lit fires, and couples lingered by the water's edge kissing. At one of the beach tavernas, some young men were sitting with their girlfriends, playing guitar and violin and singing. They'd all come for a look at the sea, for a farewell to carnival and festivities.

The sky was filled with colourful paper kites (known as 'paper eagles') bought especially for the day from roadside vendors or carnival shops. I could see them all along the coast towards Piraeus, their long, frilly tails fluttering above us.

'He who never flew a kite didn't look high enough,' quoted Vassilis, putting his arm around me and sounding impressively like Confucius. We strolled contentedly along the sea path, and I pictured us, as if from afar; a Greek family. Gradually, parts of the fantasy were coming true. All around there were crashed kites and tangled strings caught in almost every tree and twisted in electricity wires.

On the way home, we walked across the open hillside which is preserved as common land. The air smelled of honey, and the ground was sprouting with new grass and tiny spring flowers: Lilliputian marigolds, as neat as orange buttons; glistening white stars of Bethlehem; and sprinklings of pink and yellow floral confetti. Swaying slightly in the cool breeze were the tall asphodels, awkwardly beautiful, with their brownish-pink blooms. Scholars believe that their seeds and roots were a staple food in Greece before the introduction of corn, but they are also associated with death. The grim purgatory of the Asphodel Meadows was at the entrance to the underworld, where the souls of fallen heroes and lesser beings lived as shades. Ghosts who were not wicked enough for the punishment-field of Tartarus or good enough for the Elysium orchards were sent here. Seferis mentions these flowers in his poems as emblems of death:

> There are no asphodels, violets, or hyacinths;
> How then can you talk with the dead?
> The dead know the language of flowers only;
> So they keep silent . . .

This time of year always held sadness for Vassilis, and for me. His father, Kostas, had been killed in a car crash at Carnival time, four years previously. I remembered the strange numbness of the evening after the funeral, when we'd returned to Athens from the village. We stayed in a small hotel in Plaka at the foot of the Acropolis, and the area was filled with revellers. Groups of rowdy young men were roaming the streets, hitting people over the head with gaudy, plastic clubs sold specially for that purpose, and squirting canned foam into the crowd. At one point, we saw a gang take on a threatening, Bacchic wildness, beating mercilessly on a car whose hapless driver was trying to steer through the throng. Later, in the dark side streets, we came across a small male choir, accompanied by an orchestra of mandolins, guitars and bouzoukis. They were wandering along slowly, singing an old romantic song about February's flowering almond trees.

The day before, Vassilis's parents had been driving along the main road near the village where they still lived for much of the year. Someone veered over onto the wrong side of the road,

ploughing into the driver's side; his father was killed outright
and his mother injured. We flew into Greece later the same day
after receiving the news, and went to visit my mother-in-law in
the nearby town hospital, finding her in a daze but not in
danger. It was evening by the time we arrived at the village, and
the front door of the house was open. We were greeted by the
chilling sight of a coffin lid propped up by the entrance – a sign
of the dreadful news for anyone passing. Upstairs, Kostas lay
in an open coffin in the middle of the sitting room. He had
been to stay with us only a couple of weeks earlier, and I
couldn't believe that he was lying as solid as stone, in a dark suit,
surrounded by a dainty frill of white lace. Only a plaster over a
wound on his temple, and his pallor, indicated that he was not
sleeping.

We joined Vassilis's four siblings and a collection of about
twenty close friends and relatives to begin the long vigil. The
funeral had already been arranged for the next morning. We sat
on chairs around the edge of the room, and every so often
someone would arrive, and come around the room greeting us
individually, repeating the ritualistic word for 'condolences'. Some
accepted a small glass of brandy. There were no children there;
we'd left ours behind and Vassilis's sisters had not been able to face
telling their young sons about their adored grandfather. The walls,
however, were covered with family photographs: our children;
our weddings; Vassilis's parents as a newly engaged couple,
slightly awkward but smiling, standing in a meadow.

Kostas had not only been a particularly beloved and trusted
man, but a wonderful teacher all his working life. As news of his
death spread, more and more of his ex-pupils and their families
arrived. The village teacher is as revered and archetypal a public
figure as that of the priest; he or she is the route to 'letters'; a
symbol of advancement and enlightenment. Many stopped by

the coffin, weeping and talking to my dead father-in-law, expressing words of grief and disbelief.

'Teacher, teacher,' howled a plump woman who had been taught at primary school by him. 'Don't leave us. You can't leave us.' Her words were an echo of the timeless death laments which have been sung by women since Homeric times; beautiful, expressive, often improvised songs. The singers tailor the verses to the character of the deceased and the circumstances of his or her passing. As in ordinary conversation, these *mirologia* still refer to Charos, the bearer of death, who wrestles his prospective victims on the marble threshing floor in so many traditional poems. Charos is a direct descendant of Charon, the gloomy, miserly ferryman of ancient mythology, who rowed the newly arrived dead across the river Styx.

The next morning, the church was so packed with people that the dark-clothed, white-faced crowd overflowed onto the street. The funeral took place in the strange limbo of anguish and numbness that follows terrible shock. Nobody in the family had slept that night or eaten for twenty-four hours. There was none of the restraint of northern European funerals, which give the mourners up to a week to prepare. In Greece you are expected to be overcome by grief; it is normal to collapse from the weight of emotion.

I had previously believed that the clearly defined death rituals and customs of the Orthodox Church were somehow a comfort, that alongside the misery there was at least the knowledge of what had to be done; a practical order imposed on the emotional disorder. Living through it for the first time as a participant rather than an observer, I wasn't sure. The pain and bewilderment is probably always the same; every culture merely provides its own way of coping. Even at that point we all realized that we had lost the man who held the family together, and gave us all encouragement with the difficult, everyday business of bringing up our children. At the end of the service, we filed past his open coffin to say goodbye for the last time before it was sealed. Vassilis stroked his father's hair and murmured something close to his ear. The air smelled of incense and candles.

As we walked from the church along the road to the cemetery, Vassilis looked pale and taut.

'This is going to be the worst bit for me,' he whispered. We weaved our way between the crowded tombstones, to the raw, rocky earth of the open grave. The coffin was lowered jerkily into the ground. Everyone was crying. Someone fainted. I looked across the valley to the mountains which still had snow left on their summits. When Vassilis was a child, his father told him stories about these places, and explained the mythology. Straight opposite was Mount Oiti, where Achilles was born and Hercules died, and far in the distance was Mount Parnassos. Beyond that was Delphi, the most sacred centre of the classical world, and home to the Delphic Oracle. These were his connections as a modern Greek with the ancient world, Vassilis had once told me. It was nothing to do with race or ancestry; it was that he had grown up looking at the same rivers and mountains, and maybe even walking the same paths as Greeks had 2,500 years before. Now, burying his father in the same soil, he was only confirming the connection.

Afterwards, we all gathered at a *kafeneio* in the square. It was over. Exhausted, we drank small glasses of brandy and Greek coffee, and ate *paximadia* – hard, sweet, aniseed-flavoured rusks.

* * *

After my father-in-law died, there had been various memorials: after three days, nine days, forty days, and then each year. On the first anniversary, Vassilis and I came to Greece with the children. By that time, only Vassilis's mother was still dressed in black; his sisters had kept going for six months, but it had made them more miserable, they said. Stella helped her mother make *kolyva*, the 'food for the soul', which is eaten on *Psychosavato* (the 'Soul Saturday' of the dead) and at memorials. Boiled wheat, pomegranate seeds, ground almonds and walnuts, sugar and a touch of parsley are moulded onto a large tray, and decorated with silver balls and sugared almonds. Stella marked out her father's initials – a big KP for Konstantinos Papadimitriou. During the ceremony, the plate sat on a table in the middle of the church by a large, framed photo of Kostas. Afterwards, everyone was given a little paper bag filled with *kolyva* and a plastic spoon.

Kolyva is thought to have continued directly from the ancient Athenian festivals for the dead. Odysseus too, sprinkles white barley, honey, milk and sweet wine as libations to the departed. The ingredients are symbolic as well as tasty. The grains of wheat are interred in the ground (like dead bodies), but they rise up into new life (like souls). And the red, jewel-like seeds of the pomegranate have been associated with the dead since Persephone made her fateful decision to eat some of the seeds offered by her abductor Hades, thus condemning herself to living in the gloomy underworld for part of every year. Darkness and light, death and fertility, grief and hope.

Now, four years after the accident, there was talk of putting up a roadside shrine for Vassilis's father. My mother-in-law wanted to mark the place where she'd lost her partner of forty-six years, and I could understand her motives. The small light shines out at night as a living, burning memory in the darkness. I liked these memorials, with their mix of doll's house informality and workaday quaintness. The iron structure tends to consist of a glass-fronted box topped with a cross, standing on four spindly legs. Inside is a collection of icons, matches, incense, wicks, plastic flowers, and as often as not, an old lemonade bottle containing oil for the lamp (nobody stands on ceremony with the ingredients; the actions are enough in themselves).

I remembered our drive back to Athens in the afternoon after the funeral. We had a morning flight the next day to get home for the children. The entire stretch from the village to the National Road, the main highway to the capital, was lined with 'little churches' (as the shrines are sometimes called). We passed the point where the crash had happened, and there were several shrines nearby. Some of these memorials mark near misses, and are put up as thanks to the 'All Holy' *Panayia* or a saint, but they are a grim reminder of how dangerous Greece's roads are.

We were being driven by a family friend who went at a terrifying speed along the lethal stretch of winding, coastal road south of Lamia, where many people are killed every year.

'Could you ask him to go slower,' I whispered to Vassilis, 'I'm frightened.'

'I always drive fast,' the man replied in explanation. 'That way I spend less time on the roads, and I run less risk of having an accident.' His logic might have made me laugh at another time.

Although some people think that the shrines act as a safety warning, there are sometimes so many of them that the reminders of mortality become merely distracting. Vassilis was vehemently against the idea of setting up a memorial for his father.

'The whole of Greece is going to turn into a continuous line of shrines at this rate,' he said at a family gathering. 'The place for the dead is in the cemeteries, and we've already put up a nice marble stone there.'

'Anyway,' added his sister Stella, 'there's no point if you're not living nearby, because you need to tend to it and light the lamp every day, and our mother's in Athens now.' Eventually, Vassilis's mother was appeased on learning that there was already a shrine in place at exactly the same site; someone else had also been killed there (or survived, we didn't know which). She agreed that this would do just as well for carrying out the rituals, and offering a prayer. The matter was dropped.

Around Athens's edges I noticed new, smarter shrines springing up by the roadside. In addition to the old, rusting variety, people had taken to erecting stone edifices at the sites of car crashes, after the initial improvised memorial with flowers, icons and candles. On the main road in Vouliagmeni, a miniature mausoleum of white marble went up next to the blackened tree stump where an accident had occurred. I stopped one day to take a look. 'To the memory of our Children' read the inscription, giving the names and pitifully brief dates of a young man and woman. I imagined, mawkishly perhaps, that they were lovers, and after that I noticed it every time I drove home, instinctively slowing down slightly. The little flame was constantly alight and fresh bouquets of flowers were always in place.

This luxury shrine was almost a scale model of the grand mausoleums which rich Athenians sometimes build for their loved ones in city graveyards. There are some in our local burial ground, but the best examples are in the exclusive First Cemetery where all the significant contributors to Athenian public life end up. Unlike the traditional graves with a headstone and a bed-shaped space marked out in marble, these structures resemble miniature houses, each with their own, idiosyncratic architecture. Like many contemporary Athenian homes, they have expanses of gleaming marble, and sometimes a glass-fronted door revealing the bunk-bed shelves for the coffins; often a broom and cleaning materials stand in a corner. They are both homely and a little grotesque; I'd rather be buried in the earth than left on a shelf.

I liked walking through the First Cemetery, with its dark cypress trees, shady paths and beautiful monuments. Many of the sculptures depict sleeping maidens, reflecting the idea that sleep is a close relation of death; it's behind the term *koimitirio* or 'sleeping place', which gives us the word cemetery. Greeks don't tend to appreciate graveyards for their aesthetics as people do in Britain, but this one is an exception. It retains the atmosphere of the smart, late nineteenth-century Athens, with its sentimental angels and gentle, neoclassical pomposity. It is extremely hard to acquire a plot here, and I'd heard rumours of nouveaux riches families offering fortunes to impecunious owners of these sites.

Near the main entrance, Melina Mercouri's tomb is always covered with flowers and mementoes. Well-wishers have left pots of basil, painted stones and even a hand-inscribed marble slab. When Mercouri died of lung cancer in 1993 I watched the funeral cortège on Greek satellite television in England, as a crowd of 300,000 friends, colleagues and admirers followed her coffin to the First Cemetery. I'd been to her house to interview Mercouri a few months before she died. She had stalked around the room like a lion, before curling up on the sofa, her long, slim, bare feet tucked up beneath her as she lit one cigarette after another. She was ill and in her sixties, but looked fantastic; still as tall, feisty and blonde as she'd been acting the neighbourhood whore in *Never on Sunday*.

'I will never reconcile myself with death,' she said. 'I reconcile myself only with a bullet from a firing squad, not with illness.'

Now, the Acropolis Metro station is dedicated to her memory. There are ancient funerary gifts (which were excavated there) exhibited in glass cases, reproductions of the Parthenon frieze set in the walls and a blown-up photograph of Melina (as she was always known), standing in front of the Parthenon. She's smiling her gigantic, toothy smile, holding a bunch of bright, spring flowers, and waving goodbye. I'm not sure you could exactly call it an icon, and electric ceiling lights take the place of an oil lamp, but in many ways this is her underground, 'roadside' shrine – halfway down to Hades.

CHAPTER 11

FOREIGN BODIES

ZHIGALOV (a minor civil servant): *Tell me, are there tigers in Greece?*

DYMBA (a Greek confectioner): *. . . in Greece is everything!*

Anton Chekhov, *The Wedding*

On the first day of March, Lara came back from school with a twisted red and white thread around her wrist.

'It's a *Marti* [a March-thread],' she explained. 'My friends made it for good luck. We have to wear them until Easter.' Just as I was saying 'How lovely,' and 'did you know that the custom is so old that it goes back to ancient times, to the Eleusinian mysteries?' I noticed something crawling along Lara's eyebrow. I picked it up, and a small, brown insect waved its arms at me. Oddly perhaps, I'd never seen a louse before, but we quickly determined that that was what it was. An exploration of her head revealed a well-developed colony, and an impressive quantity of lice eggs. Predictably enough, Anna had them too. Both Vassilis and I felt sympathetic itching, although examinations revealed nothing.

'It's all these foreigners we've got these days; they don't live in very hygienic circumstances,' commented a woman in the chemist's, who overheard my request for louse killer.

'You know lice prefer clean hair,' announced the pharmacist, handing over some powerful chemicals to combat the infestation.

'Of course. That's why they jumped off onto your girls,' confirmed the customer to me.

This clean hair–dirty hair conundrum was something I was to puzzle over during the next weeks as I sat in the evenings with Anna and Lara on my bed. Like a mother ape with my young ones, I picked out what were revealed to be a new, indestructible super-breed of lice from their scalps. Gradually, we gave up on the poisonous sprays and potions, resorting to fine-combing with a traditional vinegar solution. This was just as ineffective; the tiny, camouflaged eggs mysteriously reappeared every few days.

One by-product of our new grooming routine was that we watched a lot of television. The entire nation was gripped by a reality show called *The Farm*, in which a cross section of urban Greeks played at being subsistence peasants on an artificially constructed set in the countryside. Only a generation or so ago, these fake, small-screen dilemmas were real, daily predicaments for many Greeks; now many would only learn about them on TV. It appeared that soon, like Western Europeans, Greeks would romanticize and idealize their image of rural life, which until recently was widely associated by many with backward villages, relentless hard work and the lack of progress.

We also became particularly well acquainted with the early evening soap operas and sitcoms. Lara's favourite was an over-the-top comedy about two neighbouring couples having affairs with each other's spouses – all clandestine meetings by moonlight and histrionic jealousy. Mine was about an Albanian gardener who had an affair with his Greek boss's wife. There was no holding back on the melodrama and passion in spite of the time of the show. There is no cut-off point for children; the fact that many go to bed late is indicated by the advertisements for toys and sugary cereals shown as late as midnight.

While the soaps were mildly unsuitable, the news programmes were more so, and required not only a strong constitution, but a prurient curiosity about Greeks' private lives. 'Sperm and blood. That's all they're interested in,' said Vassilis one evening, restlessly flicking channels. 'I wonder how those newsreaders can face saying these things on air,' he added. 'I'm surprised they're not too ashamed.' Favourite subjects include close-ups of bodies and blood on the roads following car crashes, interviews with distraught relations in hospitals, live takes of hysterical villagers in the middle of violent family tragedies, and any disruption or aggression at obscure provincial law courts. Murdered mothers-in-law, vengeful husbands and outraged sons and daughters are all given their fifteen minutes of fame, normally accompanied by manic orchestral music sounding like the soundtrack from *Jaws*.

Known as 'the channels', most of the numerous private TV companies are owned by business moguls, who spread their influence by buying up newspapers, magazines and football teams too. Everyone knows that there is a close collaboration between politicians and 'the channels', which are used as propaganda tools. In recent local elections there was only limited objection to the fact that an extreme right-wing candidate not only set up his own party, but had his own TV channel on which to air his anti-Semitic, racist views. Viewers of this channel were 'good Christians', pronounced the Archbishop of Athens, showing a cynically politicized approach to his job.

The Albanian in the soap opera I liked was extremely handsome and spoke Greek with barely a trace of accent, although he was a real Albanian, as were many of the minor characters. The drama was considered quite daring, being the first to focus on the daily problems of Albanian immigrants who make up about sixty-five per cent of over a million migrants who had entered the country over the previous decade. It had produced Greece's first Albanian TV star, something which until then would have been an oxymoron.

Albanians have become the archetypal 'foreigners' to whom Greeks refer when they speak of social problems, whether it's the illegal work market or lice. While there has long been an implicit suspicion of people who are different, it is only recently that there have been significant numbers of other races in Greece. And the changes happened terribly quickly. There is little of the organized or extremely violent racism that is found in Britain and America – there aren't racist thugs who kill people of a different colour – but racism is widespread and tolerated. Anna and Lara reported that several of their school friends declared that they felt 'revolted' by blacks and Albanians. Greeks have not yet adapted to the reality of a multicultural society, and political correctness is still virtually unknown.

Like most Athenian state schools, our children's has its share of Albanian pupils, and some of the Greek parents were worried. Lara's class of twenty children had four Albanians, which statistically, is about the national average; two out of every ten primary school pupils are now foreign-born, though in some Athenian neighbourhoods the number reaches over seventy-five per cent.

'Won't the foreign children keep ours behind?' the Greek parents asked at a meeting with the teacher. 'They barely speak Greek.' The word they used for the young Albanians was the formal word *allodapos* – a cold, bureaucratic, unwelcoming word, which is closer to 'alien' than the commoner *xenos* or 'foreigner.' My sister-in-law Stella told me that when she had visited a politician friend and mentioned my application for citizenship, she tried to express my worthiness by saying that I was 'not just some *allodapi* [female alien]; not some Yugoslav or whatever.' In her affection for me, she had not thought that *allodapi* is exactly what I am. Naturally, this subjective way of categorizing strangers is not just Greek. When my mother came to visit, some months after our move, I overheard her asking Anna and Lara whether they'd now 'turned into foreigners.'

Local anxieties are not limited to education either. When I rang up the paediatrician to ask his advice on whether the children should have the vaccination for TB, he prevaricated, admitting that his daughter hadn't.

'It depends where your children go to school,' he said. 'The alien communities have a problem with TB, and it can spread easily. My daughter goes to a private school. If yours go to the state school they should have it.' Newspapers described an epidemic of hepatitis among immigrant populations in western Attica; many live in dreadful conditions.

The immigrants often arrive with nothing but false papers. Kurds and Pakistanis come clinging on to dinghies and fishing boats from Turkey, and Albanians climb over freezing mountains. There are regular horror stories of bodies washed up on beaches and frozen corpses on snowy passes. Those who survive the journey sleep in stations, parks or migrant holding stations, until something better comes along.

'There's not room for even one more immigrant,' said

worried politicians. There had been amnesties with legalization documents, but obtaining the right residence and work permits had become a nightmare for most incomers. My struggles with bureaucracy looked utterly trivial in comparison.

'Do you play with the Albanian children at school?' I asked Anna during one of our nit-picking sessions.

'No,' she replied, 'they usually play amongst themselves. And the other children tease them. I saw one of the older boys from the secondary school writing "Albanian wankers go home" in the playground.'

'But do they treat you like that?' I asked, worried that my little 'aliens' might be having a hard time.

'Oh no. They're nice to us,' she answered. Some aliens were evidently more alien than others. But she was looking thoughtful.

'Mum, can I ask you something? Is it true that the English were the worst conquerors?'

'Well, they did have lots of colonies,' I answered cautiously.

'My teacher said that the English tortured the Greeks in Cyprus, and that they sold out to the Turks. The other children were calling me "conqueror".'

'It's true, they did torture people,' I replied, feeling surprisingly awkward about this painful episode in Anglo-Hellenic relations.

My father had spent six months working as a government geologist in Cyprus in 1960, when Greek rebels were branded as 'terrorists' by the colonizing British, before being granted independence in 1961. My father got on well with the Greek Cypriots, but did that stop him being a colonial and them being terrorists? Now, only months after 11 September, these definitions were more complicated than ever. I wondered how my daughters would reconcile the two opposed world views of their two heritages: the British former colonizer and the Greek natural rebel.

I tried to give Anna a balanced history lesson, but criticizing your countrymen as occupiers and torturers is strangely harder to stomach away from home. Even at home it is difficult. Vassilis regularly veered between patriotism and frustration with his country. I'd begun by laughing, when I once witnessed him stop the car on a country road by some giant billboards, which reared grotesquely from beautiful, virgin hillsides. He was determined to do something, and actually rang up the advertising company which had erected them, threatening legal action. It was then that I realized he felt personally wounded by this rape of the landscape. Like so much in Greece, the advertisements were illegal, but the authorities did nothing about them. Needless to say, complaining was a thankless task.

If Greeks traditionally identified with the underdog, they were now in the novel position of being the bosses. Even small villages employ Albanians to work in the fields and do the lowly jobs, and almost every building site and taverna kitchen in the country is manned by Albanians. Everyone has 'their Albanian' these days. They say: 'Bring an Albanian to fix it.' In the past, only wealthier Athenians had domestic help, although during the 1980s they took on so many Filipino servants that 'Filipino' became a generic term (I once overheard a child remark: 'Maria's Filipino is Romanian').

While the recent wave of immigrants has helped the Greek economy, racists, populists and the less scrupulous TV channels neglect to mention this aspect of it. Crime rates have risen, and though this is due to numerous factors, the Albanians (but not other immigrants) have become easy scapegoats.

'They don't have any culture; they're a wild people,' said the girl washing my hair in the local hairdresser's. 'We used to leave our doors open, but now we have to lock them. People are slaughtered in their beds.'

Fortunately, many people hate these attitudes. One day, as I collected the children from their after-school Greek dance class, I stopped to talk with Panayiotis, their teacher. It was two-thirty, and he had somehow procured a plastic cup of raki and was smoking a roll-up in the sunny playground.

'Do the Albanian kids do Greek dancing?' I asked.

'Only very few,' he replied, taking a sip of the firewater. 'But it's mostly because of money. It's hard for the parents to pay for the lessons, though I've taught a couple of them for free. Sometimes I'm disgusted with being Greek and how they treat the Albanians. Nobody mentions the importance of Albanian culture in Greek history or that many of the heroes of the Greek revolution were Albanian – Botsaris, Bouboulina . . . Even the *foustanella*, the Greek national costume, is Albanian . . .' He trailed off, relighting his roll-up. 'There've been Albanians here for centuries; there are still areas where people speak the old Albanian, *Arvanitika*.

'We Greeks know about exile,' he continued. 'We should understand the Albanians. After all, our grandfathers were refugees from Asia Minor and our fathers were emigrants – they went to America, and to the factories in Germany . . .'

'You know that the Americans used to call them "dirty Greeks" in the 1920s?' I said. 'They classed them along with the blacks then. They suffered just as much as the Albanians do here.'

'Exactly,' said Panayiotis. 'And we have so many songs about the sadness of exile or being far from home. We call it *xenitia*. Those songs from the 1970s about Greeks in Germany now sound as though they could have been written for Albanians here. Do you remember that one by Markopoulos?' Without hesitation, he sang a strongly rhythmic song in a sad, minor key:

Here in the foreign country, it is true sorrow.
I'll go back to the village,
I can't bear it.
I'm searching to find a brother
And they all call me 'foreigner'.

* * *

Lara was determined that she should not miss out on having a name-day celebration like all the other children, and we managed to unearth St Larissa's day on 26 March. She made lists of presents, party food and guests. Number one was a scooter. Lara didn't want one of the huge parties which took place regularly in fast food outlets, so invitations went out to eight of her favourite classmates, who included an Albanian boy called Elvis and Alexandros, the local Mayor's son.

The day of the party seemed to mark the end of winter; spring was here. The children ran out of the garden gate to play on the hill, where fresh, bright green grass was sprouting. The spring flowers made hectic, uncoordinated splurges of colour: shocking, canary-yellow giant daisies; mustard-coloured Jerusalem sage with velvety, grey leaves; palest duck-egg-blue love-in-a-mist; striated mauve mallow; and lime-green tuffets of euphorbia. The children shrieked, and somewhere, dogs were barking.

'I love his name,' I said to Elvis's mother, Alma, as she arrived with her son. 'Is he named after Elvis Presley?' She looked blank, as though she'd never heard of 'The King', and said something about her brother having encountered the name in Switzerland.

Alma was a small, pretty woman in her early thirties, with delicate features, quick eyes and an air of quiet confidence and submerged anger. We sat down together and I asked her about where she was from. It emerged that she was a 'Northern Epirote'.

191

'But I just say I'm Albanian; it doesn't make any difference,' she said defiantly. The distinction is one which created a double standard in Greece. The so-called Northern Epirotes are an Orthodox, Greek-speaking minority, originally from the northern Greek region of Epirus. They found themselves part of southern Albania when the country's national borders were established in 1913. While their successes (such as the famous Olympic weightlifter Piros Dimas) are classed by Greeks as 'Greek', their failures (especially criminal elements) are labelled as 'Albanian'. It is yet another example of the complex Balkan mess; ethnic groups split across state boundaries, suspicion of minorities and inept impositions of national identity.

'Elvis says that he's Greek now,' said Alma. 'What can I tell him? I'd go back to Albania if I could . . . If I had the money.' She smiled. 'It's beautiful in Avlona where my family are, and the people are nicer. I've been in Greece for five years, but my kids don't have a future here. I won't be able to pay for them to study. They won't even let my youngest son in the nursery because they say he doesn't speak Greek. And Elvis says: "Mama, why is our flat so small and horrible?"'

I liked Alma; I thought that perhaps, like Chekhov's Russian characters in *The Wedding*, we'd had our own fantasies about what Greece had to offer. I also imagined that maybe I could empathize with some of her problems as an alien. But she quickly put me right.

'I earn thirty euros for an eight-hour day, working in the café at the bottom of the hill, and my husband's unemployed now. You can't possibly understand what it's like if you haven't lived it,' she said, fixing me in her gaze. I felt ashamed.

Alma left for work, and the children played timeless party games: musical chairs, musical statues, and made secret plots under the large pine tree on the hill. In the early evening, the parents came to collect their offspring. The last remaining guest was Alexandros, the son of the mayor; a handsome boy with gilded curls, and the mischievous glance of a Caravaggio cherub.

'Alexandros must have a very nice house,' Lara had remarked to me once. 'His father's the president.' She wasn't so far wrong. Grigoris Kasidokostas had been mayor of Vouliagmeni for almost twenty years, and was probably the nearest thing the neighbourhood would ever have to a president.

The bell went, and I heard a husky voice through the intercom.

'Hey guys, you mean I have to climb up all those steps?' It was the Mayor. I'd often seen him at parades and school events (his shaggy, platinum white hair was visible from afar), but I'd never spoken to him. Everyone had a story to tell about the Mayor. Beloved among locals for keeping the area clean and uniquely green, he was also a controversial figure. Some spoke of undercover deals and of his cosy relationship with the highly influential, super-rich minority who had villas along the coast of the exclusive Kavouri ('Crab') peninsula. I'd once been told his whole life story by a taxi driver who'd been at school with him in the early 1950s. In those days, Vouliagmeni was a village of 300 people; the end of the road; only a dirt track led towards Athens.

'He had about ten brothers and they went all barefoot,' said the driver. 'Grigoris was always laughing and creating havoc. He left school at fourteen, but he became national swimming champion for butterfly stroke, and set up his own waterski school in Vouliagmeni in the 1960s. That was how he met Marianna Latsis. You know, the daughter of the great shipowner.'

In walked the Mayor; our local Dick Whittington, puffing slightly after the steep climb. He had sharp, blue eyes, the tanned, lined face of a fisherman or an ageing playboy, and the compact body of a former athlete. Passing through onto the terrace, he surveyed his princedom, spread out before him.

'It's quite a view you've got,' he remarked, and began to talk with Vassilis and me about all the problems he'd had with the Church, which was still the major landowner in the area (as it is throughout Greece).

'They sell up and rent to unscrupulous developers, and make plans to put up hotels. I brought the Archbishop down here and told him: "Don't build a hotel. Look out at the sea here. You should build a lovely villa, where you can bring visitors, but not a big hotel. Sitting quietly, looking out to sea; that's where you'll see God."'

The Mayor was evidently in reflective mood, and he spoke about his life, and in particular about his relationship with the famous shipping families, who started building villas in Vouliagmeni at the time when his waterski school was getting going.

'I had all the shipowners' kids here with me at weekends,' he said. 'Onassis, Goulandris, Latsis ...' The pretty, blonde Marianna Latsis had been only sixteen when she fell in love with Kasidokostas while on holiday in Vouliagmeni. He was well over twice her age, but photographs from the early 1980s show the unlikely couple looking ecstatic. The teenager, who was as stubborn as her devoted father, defied all attempts to dissuade her, and married him.

The couple had a son together, but eventually divorced; both had now remarried with two more children each. There were those who said that Latsis and his cronies had given Kasidokostas a leg up to the mayorship, but no one was quite sure how to interpret the maverick character. Those on the Left called him a mafioso, and those on the Right didn't know where he stood; he was very thick with Andreas Papandreou when the latter was the socialist Prime Minister.

'I used to take him on my boat,' said the Mayor. 'When he was first with Mimi, they came on a cruise with me. The whole affair was still secret, and I told them we shouldn't land anywhere, but she insisted on getting out at an island and going to a taverna. Before we knew it, they'd sent a helicopter over to get photographs. We tried to make it appear that she was my girlfriend – I put my arm around her, but it didn't work. I never really liked her, with her huge tits . . . but it just shows what a woman can do to a man.' Briefly, he looked slightly rueful.

The Mayor may have separated from the Latsis family, but his son, Paris, was still grandson of one of the world's richest men, with a mother who has three jets and two helicopters just for her private use.

'Paris is nineteen and he lives in London now. He prefers it because he doesn't get chased by paparazzi; he can be anonymous. And when he comes to Greece in the summer he sleeps on his yacht. I understand him – I'd do the same.' We looked the across the water to the marina, crammed with the extravagant, white, pointed-nosed pleasure boats of Vouliagmeni's elite, still shut up for the winter.

Greece's super-rich shipowners are distant from day-to-day Greek life. They are at the opposite end of society from the immigrants and Albanians, but both categories are outsiders. The shipping magnates buy up football teams, open museums, and build palatial villas, but most of them don't live in Greece, preferring Geneva, London and New York. Their money and manners bring them into the highest society, but they keep their names and customs, marry into each other's families. While some belong to dynasties dating back to Ottoman times, others joined the milieu more recently; Yiannis Latsis was the fourteenth of a poor, Peloponnesian fisherman's fifteen children, and worked his way up from deck hand to captain. From our terrace we quite often spotted Latsis's yacht moored across the bay – a floating palace which had been provided for the holidays of Prince Charles, the former President Bush and Marlon Brando, amongst others. I imagined it had the opulence which had become de rigueur with Aristotle Onassis – another of the richest, and certainly most famous twentieth-century Greeks.

'Latsis is a vegetable now,' said the Mayor. 'He's had loads of strokes and he's ninety-two. They've managed to keep him alive, but he won't last long.' It was dark now and the air was chilly, but we were still standing outside. Lara and Alexandros were taking turns to speed around the smooth marble terrace on the new scooter, skimming past us, just missing, as we talked. Kasidokostas was nothing if not passionate about Vouliagmeni, and after all the rumours, I'd taken to him, with his straight-talking enthusiasm and boyish quickness. Calling his son, the Mayor took his hand and we waved them off as they walked down the steps into the night.

* * *

If the immigrants and the shipowners are two ends of a spectrum, there is another category of outsiders, which has fallen off the end. They came from Bavaria and Denmark, and though they sat at the top of Greek society for over a century and a half, the royal family never overcame their image as foreigners who had been imposed on the Greeks. Being the monarchs of the Hellenes was always going to be difficult; their subjects knew only too well the oppression of being ruled by outsiders, and the political situation was unstable from the start. The troubled saga finally ended in 1974 when Greeks determined that their country should become a republic, but recently, the monarchy had come back into the news again. The ex-King Constantine was suing the Greek state for compensation over confiscated royal estates. Yet again, old wounds were being opened.

It's hard for Greeks to forget that 'the Ex' (as the former King Constantine is known) supported the Colonels' dictatorship, and that he legitimized their regime by swearing them in. It was only when he realized that the Junta was not supporting *him* that he changed tack and tried to organize a counter-coup. But it was too little, too late. He went into exile in London, and when democracy was restored, sixty-nine per cent of Greeks voted in a referendum that he should not return.

'So why does the Ex refuse to become a Greek citizen?' journalists asked persistently. 'Why won't he take an ordinary name and renounce his claims to the throne? He can be Mr Glucksburg [the royals' Danish family name] and then he'll be allowed to come to Greece as much as he likes.'

One of the properties at the centre of the row with 'the Ex' was Tatoi. I had long been curious to see the former royal estate outside Athens, which had been abandoned for decades, and was said to be rotting away. One Sunday we packed the scooter, dog and children into the car, and drove to the north-western suburbs, eventually arriving at a small country road on the slopes of a beautiful, wooded valley.

At one point, the road was blocked by a locked gate, and we proceeded on foot through the green forest full of horse chestnuts, oaks, walnuts and pine trees. Eventually, we emerged in a bucolic scene which could have been Denmark, Holland or even England, but didn't seem anything like Greece. There were some elegant, nineteenth-century stone farm buildings and a steep-gabled farmhouse set by lush, green water meadows filled with bright yellow buttercups. A chubby, blue tractor sat rusting by an old petrol pump, and a sleek cockerel paced around the outside of a collapsed wooden shed, crowing from time to time. Further up the road, the somewhat dour, northern-looking royal residence itself was boarded up and surrounded by a tall mesh fence. Two angry dogs circled the stone building barking at us.

The 40,000 acres of the Tatoi estate were bought by King George I in 1872, a few years after Greece's Protecting Powers brought him over from Denmark. His Bavarian predecessor, Otto, the first King of the Hellenes, had been deposed. The youthful Otto started off his reign without so much as a palace. He'd been lent a modest but comfortable town house in Klafthmonos Square, which is now a museum; his ornate, silk-covered furniture and Queen Amalia's dainty sitting room can still be seen. King George had a real palace, and the shady Royal Gardens (now National Gardens) had already been designed by Queen Amalia with palms and pathways. But he wanted a country house too. Tatoi was built as a little corner of Denmark, where he and his family could feel at home, and all the buildings were designed in the Danish style; even the livestock were imported from his country of origin. It was a strong hint that he didn't embrace his adopted kingdom wholeheartedly.

Beyond the palace was a sturdy stone building. Above some weed-covered steps, its front door gaped. It was too tempting not to take a look into the dark interior, which had been closed up when King Constantine took his Danish wife Anna Maria and their children to London in 1967. We walked gingerly through rooms which smelled of undisturbed damp and woodland decay. Upstairs, some bats flitted from the broken rafters, surprised by the unfamiliar noise. Soggy mattresses lay collapsed like corpses on the bedroom floors, their intestines spilling out. The rusting iron bedsteads and functional wardrobes had evidently been for employees rather than royal occupants.

Downstairs, a large room was filled with smashed cupboards, old-fashioned electric fires, broken typewriters and, everywhere, piles of crumbling, yellowed papers. Vassilis stooped to pick some up.

'Look at this,' he said, pointing to one with the blue imprint of a crown and 'House of the Deputy King' (whatever that was). 'He was an official,' explained Vassilis. 'And look here. It's a royal command.' He held out a complicated-looking form with dotted lines for dates, signatures, title, and details of the order.

'That's why it never worked with the monarchy,' said Vassilis, blowing off some of the dust. 'They were always trying to run the country, to overrule the strong politicians; from Venizelos to Karamanlis and George Papandreou, they were all at loggerheads with the kings. The royal family couldn't stop meddling in politics. That's what destroyed them. Ever since the beginning there've been abdications and exiles, and most Greeks never really accepted them. They were nothing like the royals in Britain.' I took the mouldering pieces of paper from him and put them in my pocket as souvenirs.

'Can we take that table too?' asked Anna, pointing at a serviceable if dirty wooden desk.

On our way back, we paused by the large, empty swimming pool. With its marble balustrades and urns, it was easy to imagine the last royal family having elegant summer drinks parties here in the dappled sunlight. Politicians and visiting dignitaries were invited for visits, and Tatoi's cool, green shade was always a refuge from the dry, burning Athenian summers. The last King Constantine had been a young man of twenty-four when his father died in 1964, and his mother, Queen Frederika, was not ready to let go of her influence. A German princess by birth, she was a Nazi sympathizer, and was widely seen as dangerously manipulative and domineering. Even following her husband's death, she continued to hold sway and it seems likely that (along with the CIA) she gave her son bad advice after the Junta's coup; she was long a figure of hate for the Left. When she finally died in 1981, 'the Ex' was allowed into the country for the day to attend her funeral in the graveyard at Tatoi.

I'd seen 'the Ex' being interviewed on television recently. With the sly eyes and pugnacious air of a minor civil servant, he claimed that he wanted nothing more than to live in a little house in Greece and to be able to visit his ancestors' tombs. But he didn't look trustworthy to me. He still had a limited support network of extreme conservatives and reactionaries in Greece, especially in the traditionally right-wing Peloponnese.

Greece's unhappy experiment with a monarchy had been over for decades, but there was still unfinished business. Now though, with the compensation for confiscated properties about to be finalized, these issues would soon be closed. Mr Glucksberg or Constantine De Grecia, or whatever he wanted to call himself, would be able to come and buy his 'little house', and the Greeks would be able to use the former palaces for other purposes.

'When this court case is over we'll be able to go and have picnics at Tatoi, we'll roast a few lambs there; it'll belong to the Greek people,' said a radio journalist optimistically.

Walking back through the buttercup meadow, we passed a large, colourful group of people who were already doing exactly that. Men were carrying baskets of food, women were holding dishes covered with linen cloths, grandmothers were pushing infants in strollers, and children were riding bikes. They chatted as they moved unhurriedly along the track in search of a picnic spot. It was a wonderful picture of life after all the neglect and decay we'd seen. The sense of unlovable royal ghosts lurking in the green woods was already evaporating.

CHAPTER 12

RADIANT, BRILLIANT, GLORIOUS

O my sweet spring, my most beloved Child,
Whither has thy beauty fled?

Easter Lament

One morning, Eurydice Street was covered with a strange, yellow dust. It was everywhere. Our terrace was a nasty, sulphurous colour, cars had a pale, bilious tinge, and leaves were covered in what looked like the aftermath of a chemical attack. On the way to school, Anna slipped on a slimy patch, where it had gathered in slicks on the pavements and in the gutters. As I picked her up, *Kyria* Panayiota, the tiny, ancient woman who cleans one of the buildings across the road, came over. Her worn clothing and traditional greetings were wonderfully out of place in this modern suburb.

'Good progress, go and learn letters!' she'd call noisily to the children in the mornings. And when I passed again on the way back she was usually bent double over a bucket, but she'd straighten up to give me little lectures and pep talks.

'I don't know reading and writing, but I know that the woman has to be strong, to love her children and her husband, and that's all that matters.'

'Do you know what this yellow stuff is?' I asked her.

'Of course. It's pollen from the pine trees,' she answered, wiping her large, red hands on her apron. Her faded headscarf was so threadbare it could have dated back to her youth during the Second World War.

'It comes every year in April. Look, you can see it falling.' We looked across to some pine trees, and sure enough, with each breeze, a puff of powdery yellow seed wafted out into the air. Relieved at the innocent explanation, I dusted Anna down, and we continued on our way. The air was scented with the nearly overwhelming, miraculous smell of the white blossom covering the bitter orange trees.

Spring had arrived with an extraordinary urgency. The earth erupted with flowers and grasses. You could almost see them growing, reaching out to tangle into one another. It was as if they had to live their lives and quickly reproduce before the overpowering, desiccating heat arrived. In Greek, the word for spring means 'opening', and it did indeed look as though everything was unfurling. Windows were flung open for the morning sunshine, and people brought tables and chairs out onto their balconies where they drank coffee, made phone calls, read the papers and kept an eye on neighbours and passers-by. We put away our winter clothes, rolled up the rugs and bought pots of bright red and pink geraniums for the terrace.

Along with the darting swallows, lovers were suddenly everywhere; lingering in parks and on street corners, kissing, whispering and walking slowly, arm-in-arm, utterly absorbed in each other.

'Love spot!' called Lara, pointing indiscreetly, remembering the expression from the previous year. All the girls in Anna's class were in love, and the most popular boy lived around the corner from us in Orpheus Street. When he sent Anna a love note ('My little one, I adore you . . .'), it was, for a while, a huge excitement, and a major triumph in the school yard.

The long, tense build-up to Easter was nearing its climax during Holy Week, coinciding with the unapologetically luxuriant and fertile arrival of spring. The excitement and joy associated with the festivities are such that a British person would have to roll Christmas, Easter, May Day (the old sort, with maypoles and dancing), and the August bank holiday all into one, to begin to appreciate the impact. The schools shut, and Athens was emptying for the holidays, as families returned to their islands and villages. By the weekend, one million people, a quarter of the capital's population, had left.

When I got up on Good Friday, I could hear the slow toll of a funeral bell, which kept on periodically throughout the day. The anniversary of the crucifixion is played out with real sorrow, as if marking a recent death. Flags are hung at half-mast, and celebrations are inappropriate throughout the week. Radio stations which normally play popular music were broadcasting Bible readings and Orthodox chants. Fashionable singers had released recordings of the hauntingly sad Byzantine hymn 'O My Sweet Spring'. The Virgin Mary's mourning for her dead son is all the more poignant for being set against the beauty and life of springtime.

> O Light of my eyes, my beloved Boy, how are You now hidden in the grave?

Out on the streets, people dusted down their old spits, and prepared for the great feast; entrepreneurial types were selling wire, charcoal and grills by the roadside. All across the country, many thousands of lambs were slaughtered. I remembered seeing a village road stained with blood at Easter; a reminder that the sacrifice of the paschal lamb clearly parallels that of Christ himself. Greece is more usually represented by blue: the deep marine shades of the sea, the vivid skies ranging from turquoise to mauve, and the national flag striped with white. Easter, however, is the season of reds. On Maundy Thursday, people hung red ribbons or cloths on doors to bring luck and protection, and we dyed hardboiled eggs a deep vermilion, rubbing them with oil to make them shiny. Red communion wine was drunk in church as the re-enactment of the Last Supper, and the irrepressible life force of spring was signalled by the poppies, which waved like papery scarlet flags (or according to some, drops of Christ's blood) by the edge of the road.

One of Vassilis's sisters and her husband went to a mountain farmer to collect our family's designated animal, which had been specially reared organically. Unusually, we were all going to celebrate Easter in Athens this year, but they were determined to 'do it properly'. This involved buying a motorized spit on a stand and making *kokoretsi*, a dish in which the lamb's intestines and chopped pieces of offal are tightly wrapped around a long skewer and cooked over charcoal. This traditional delicacy had recently been banned by the EU in the fallout from mad cows, but that had only increased its desirability.

The atmosphere throughout the country is one of almost explosive tension: sadness is combined with excitement, hunger with anticipation of feasting, and grief with the inherent optimism of spring and the Resurrection. It's probably now a minority who keep to the rules of fasting for all forty days of Lent, but most people mark 'Great Week' by some kind of abstinence, even if it's only for the last day or so. The whole period is not unlike the initial period of mourning; a dark time of asceticism, when people avoid meat, parties and weddings.

'I haven't eaten *anything* all week!' said Effi with a glimmer of pride. This turned out to mean that she had given up meat, oil and dairy products, but that's hard enough; it's all dreary, unadorned, boiled vegetables and bread. 'I can't wait for the lamb on Sunday,' she said. 'We'll burst from eating so much meat.'

In the late afternoon of Good Friday, we went on a 'church crawl' around Plaka, and it turned out that many Athenians who hadn't left town were doing the same. Walking through the quiet streets of neoclassical houses in the shadow of the Acropolis, we dipped into every church we came across. Each one was hung with sepulchral purple rosettes and ribbons, and had its own *epitaphios* – a canopied funeral bier. Years before, I'd sat up late with women in Nafplio on the night of Maundy Thursday, helping them decorate the bier with flowers for the Good Friday service. There was a peaceful atmosphere, which mixed the sadness of a vigil with a companionable, female creativity. Women are excluded from the central roles in most Orthodox rituals, and are not allowed in the sanctuary behind the icon screen, but they are the guardians of death. Whether it is that of Christ or their loved ones, they hold sway over these informal but deeply significant rites. The women had brought roses and arum lilies from their gardens, and there were buckets full of clove-scented carnations to cover the canopy and its slender columns.

Plaka's more popular churches were already crowded with worshippers and lines of people were waiting to pay their respects. We joined the queues, waiting until it was our turn to bend down and kiss the small gilded cloth embroidered with Christ's dead body, which is laid out on the *epitaphios* as a corpse in a coffin. It was scattered with rose petals and lemon leaves. Lara liked doing it so much (evidently pleased that she now knew how to cross herself efficiently) that she lined up to do the whole thing again on her own, unaware that she was acting out exactly what you would do at a funeral.

'If my mother could see me now,' said Vassilis smiling. 'It's the first time I've done that since I was ten!' He looked astonished and not displeased to have found himself observing the old rituals again, with a foreign wife and two half-foreign children leading the way. We stood together at the back of the church.

'Do you think you should go and stand on that side?' asked Vassilis, uncertain whether we should behave correctly and follow the practice which places females on the left and males on the right in church. It didn't look as though many people had adhered to the custom, and in the end we stayed together, listening to the sad chanting. Some young boys dressed as acolytes wandered past us, and people drifted in and out, lighting candles, kissing their chosen icons and quietening children. But there was also a tense hush. Nearby, a large wooden cross was hung with a crown of real, painfully spiny thorns; the depiction of Christ which is normally there had been taken down and wrapped in a white shroud. Some people drink vinegar or eat salt to recall the pain of Christ on the cross, and many cry on this darkest day in the Christian calendar. Everyone remembers their own dead, whose souls are thought to be all around. The suffering is specific and universal. My eyes kept pricking.

Outside each church, beggars held out their hands for alms, and gypsy children were selling caramel-coloured candles of unbleached wax in different sizes – smaller ones for lighting in the church and larger ones for the procession, with plastic cups to catch the drips. We walked past Plaka's popular tourist tavernas, which had sprung into life in the last couple of weeks. The lethargic, quiet winter had ended; there was a smell of fresh paint, and pots of colourful flowers had been hurriedly planted to give a bit of atmosphere. The only people eating were tourists, who stared inquisitively at the purposeful families and groups of locals carrying candles through the streets.

'All the fasting foods here,' a waiter called to us, not very hopefully. We didn't look like tourists, but we didn't look entirely Greek either.

As the sun went down, we walked up into the narrow steps and winding alleys of Anafiotika, on the slopes of the Acropolis, below the eastern cliff face. It was built by stonemasons from the island of Anafi, who came to help construct the new Greek capital in the mid-nineteenth century. Some said that previously, the Ottomans' Ethiopian slaves lived there. The pretty, ramshackle houses are perhaps too small to be gentrified, and the steep, whitewashed steps make it too out-of-the-way for shops and cafés. The result is a quiet neighbourhood of neglected beauty which still resembles a Cycladic village. Apricot-coloured cats were sprawled on walls, which had turned a dusky orange colour in the evening light. A few sweethearts and tourists ambled along the uneven pathways, which had snapdragons forcing their way up between stones along the edges, and were shaded by eucalyptus, pines and cypresses.

From certain points, we could see right across the city to the mountains of Hymettus and Pendeli, and down to the West, where the sun had left purple streaks in the sky. It had gone down beyond Elefsina, a place whose very name summons up fantasies of the extraordinary ancient Eleusinian mysteries, although little of the secret cult remains. The Sacred Way still runs along the route of the illustrious annual processions, but it is now a grimy thoroughfare, and many of Elefsina's ancient ruins are stinking industrial expanses covered with oil refineries.

Directly above us we could see a large Greek flag, waving from its pole on the edge of the cliff. Anna had been on a school trip to the Acropolis recently.

'I hated it,' she said. 'It was really boring.' But she remembered one story. 'Mum, do you know about the man who threw himself off with the flag?' she asked.

'I know about Manolis Glezos and another young man who climbed up in the night to take down the swastika and put up the Greek flag instead,' I replied.

'No, this was when the Germans ordered a Greek soldier to put up their flag. He took down the Greek flag, wrapped it around him and jumped off the edge.' This story was never actually proved (though it was published in the *Daily Express* at the time), but it said much more to children than the abstract-sounding dates and facts of the 'golden age of Pericles' 2,500 years ago.

Anna had been made to learn various ancient history chapters by heart: we'd been through the midsummer Panathenaic festival in honour of Athena, the details of Pheidias' carvings, and we'd seen an unashamedly kitsch reconstruction of how people imagine his massive, twelve-metre-high, ivory and gold statue of Athena, which stood inside the Parthenon temple. In the end, though, it is the anecdotes about the more recent heroes which grab the imagination, and show Greek children the significance of the Acropolis. They can all understand that when the Greek flag was put up again after the Nazis' departure, it echoed the time when it was raised at the same point in 1833, after 375 years of Turkish rule. These ruins on a hill are not just interesting historical and archaeological sites; they are a matter of life and death.

We'd visited the 'Sacred Rock' recently, on a cloudy, windy Sunday, before the first floods of tourists spill in at Easter. What used to be a chokingly polluted, busy road around the base of the Acropolis has now been pedestrianized, becoming one of the loveliest walks in Athens. Families strolling sedately, children with balls, small dogs, an old man pushing a traditional *laterna* or barrel organ; it is like going back eighty years. Outside the extraordinary Herodes Atticus Theatre, some boys were skateboarding on the temptingly smooth, ancient marble paving slabs. It was still closed for the winter, but throughout the summer, this spectacularly beautiful, Roman-era amphitheatre is regularly packed with spectators watching plays, concerts and dance performances on warm evenings. It is one of the Athenians' great, inspirational successes, in managing to incorporate the ancient world into living, creative, contemporary culture.

We were among the last people to enter what is described in a small understated notice as 'World heritage site 1987'. The public employees who work the Acropolis ticket office depart at two p.m., and one of the most famous tourist destinations in the world is left closed for much of the day because that's when civil servants finish their day's work.

As you climb up the worn marble steps you can't help thinking of who might have walked there before. The curious visitors are nothing new; even in its early days it was filled with people and processions. At the top, we wandered about somewhat aimlessly on the slippery rock surface. A carefree, handsome street dog was nosing around (ignorant of a sign forbidding singing, loud noises, food and animals), and sauntered along a narrow ledge at the bottom of the small Erechtheum temple. He lay down lazily below the line of serious, sturdy-necked caryatids whose worn, leprous heads support the roof to what has been in its time a shrine to a pagan cult, an early Christian church and a Turkish harem. I tried to explain to the children about the perfect proportions of the Parthenon's honey-coloured Doric columns, which were partially hidden behind tastefully beige-coloured cranes. These are part of an enormous restoration project, which will eventually put back every existing block as it was meant to be. Apparently, we've been seeing things 'wrong' for generations: stones back-to-front to hide the damage, cemented into the wrong place or merely scattered indifferently around the area.

Standing on the summit, I felt strangely frustrated. The site is almost too much up close. It is better glimpsed from afar or admired with sidelong glances. Every Athenian finds his or her own meaning in the Acropolis. It's a personal, almost intimate relationship, based on something which is solidly visible every day, but it is also remade according to each generation's ideals. It exists in the mind just as much as in reality. Several writers and film-makers have explored the metaphor of the Acropolis as a female body which is violated, venerated and exploited. It is picked over by scholars, trampled over by tourists, and reproduced as gaudy plaster mementoes and as tacky ouzo bottles. As a symbol, this hill can be a saint and a goddess, a virgin and a whore, a mother and a daughter. It is used as a backdrop by romantics and cynics, by revolutionaries and dictators, and by men of the Church and visiting film stars.

The poet Kostis Palamas claimed that 'The Parthenon takes its colour from all our thoughts and all our dreams.' First-time visitors have been known to burst into tears from the emotion, while others like Sigmund Freud are disoriented:

'So it really does exist, just as we learned at school,' he wrote, bemused. Some people have been disappointed after the exaggerated build-up of expectations and the overdone enthusiasm of others:

'However, I am at least quit of Athens, with its stupid classic Acropolis and smashed pillars,' wrote George Bernard Shaw following his visit.

In Anafiotika it was getting darker, but the evening was balmy and the air scented with warm pine resin and the powdery, sweet smell of wild flowers and grasses. We passed a large group of middle-aged German couples, all dressed in beige slacks, pastel shirts and sensible shoes. They were pointing up at the huge stones of the Cyclopean walls below the flag. For all I knew, it could have been their fathers who raised the swastika up there sixty years before. Not that I should feel complacent; the British committed other crimes. Anna had already learned at school about the wicked Lord who, almost 200 years ago, stole the 'Parthenon Marbles' (you mustn't call them after a thief in their homeland). Lord Elgin's name is blackened by what is seen as an act of vandalism: he hacked down the extraordinary sculptures, bribed the occupying Ottoman oppressor, and carried off a part of Greece's greatest treasure and national symbol.

'That's where they're going to build the Acropolis Museum, just down there,' said Vassilis, pointing. 'There's going to be a whole room left empty, waiting for the marbles. One day the English will have to give them back.' The marbles' exile is viewed as a desecration; very few Greeks believe that the sculptures should remain in the British Museum. More would probably agree with Kazantzakis's florid impression that 'in her sooty vitals London stores these marble monuments of the gods, just as some unsmiling Puritan might store in the depths of his memory some past erotic moment.'

Vassilis believes that the Parthenon Marbles should come back. It is a point of honour and justice after the brutal and arrogant way in which they were removed. But he hates *progonoplixia* or 'ancestor-obsession'. This boasting about ancient glories sometimes fills a modern vacuum, and helps the 'ancestor-bore' prop up his own insecurities with his fixation.

'Do you remember that deputy minister a few years ago?' Vassilis asked. 'He was caught mishandling EU funds, and his response to the Europeans was a classic case of *progonoplixia*. He said: "When we were building the Parthenon, you were eating acorns," as if the modern Greeks were superior because of their heritage, and that excused his crimes.' The Colonels encouraged this form of vain ancestor worship, and their regime was characterized by kitsch parades and gaudy shows with handsome youths and maidens in pure white robes, holding flaming torches. They wanted people to feel good about the past so they'd forget about the awful present.

People have used every sort of argument in the stale and unhelpful debate about how contemporary Greeks are related to the ancients. One approach traces its logic back to the nineteenth-century racial theories of Jacob Philipp Fallmereyer, who denied modern Greeks any connection with their brilliant, pure, ancient 'ancestors'. He claimed that their blood had been sullied by too many invasions and population movements. Greeks were stocky, swarthy Slavs and Turks, not the uncontaminated, marble-white Adonises we could see in the sculptures which were left from earlier millennia. The counter-attack became just as wearisome. Greek folklorists, archaeologists and historians strained to prove the existence of 'continuities' from the classical era. Dances, customs, foods, expressions . . . anything would do to confirm the relationship.

The arguments over the marbles have also become ritual

choruses, traded back and forth. The details in the debates are often petty; it isn't a subject for logic and calculations. It doesn't matter whether the British are worthier custodians of ancient Greek civilization, whether the British Museum scrubbed off the ancient patina with cleaning bleach, whether Lord Elgin really had the *firman* (the Sultan's permission document) or bribed the Ottoman rulers, or whether or not the 'irresponsible' Greeks and their polluted city 'deserve' the treasures.

I think that the beautiful statues should return to Greece as it would help close a chapter. Once they were back, a wrong would be righted and passions could calm down. Perhaps it would help Greeks emerge from their old role as victims, always controlled and wounded by stronger powers. It could allow them, instead, to become the benevolent champions of culture; the marbles could even be swapped from time to time, with a perfect copy to fill the gap as a symbol of Anglo-Hellenic friendship. And who would know the difference anyway? The last time I visited the British Museum, there was a reproduction of a horse's head from one of the Parthenon's pediments in the gift shop. It was thrilling to see the flaring nostrils, wild eyes and straining veins, and to be so intimately close to its open mouth, which is permanently fixed in a nervous whinny (in its original position high in the temple you would only get a rough idea of its beauty). Though it sat amongst the silk scarves, tasteful mugs and postcards, and bore a price tag of £1,000, I was even more moved by it than I had been by the real thing.

We arrived back down in Plaka just as the biers were being carried out of the churches. Single bells were slowly tolling, and people had now lit their candles. Each flower-covered *epitaphios* was carried by several strong men, as carefully as a coffin on its way to the cemetery. The processions making their way through the parishes were quiet and respectful, and there was a sense of being part of something terribly old. Perhaps Easter had not been so different from this in the sixth century, when the Parthenon was transformed from a temple honouring the goddess Athena into a Christian church honouring the Holy Virgin. The virginal daughter of Zeus (born from his head, as the legend goes) was banished, and the ancient, pagan spring ceremonies underwent a metamorphosis into celebrations for a much more recent son of God, born of a virgin.

We walked up into Philhellenes Street, past St Paul's, the Anglican church. An incongruous little corner of England, this solid, stone building has stood here since the 1840s, and there are dedications to the philhellenic Britons who lived and died in Athens when it was still a two-horse capital. We paused at the Russian Orthodox church. Normally, Philhellenes Street is a heavily polluted, noisy road, packed with traffic, but it had been closed off. The only sound was a Russian women's choir singing heart-rendingly sad harmonies as the congregation circled the building.

'That's my church,' I said to Anna and Lara, feeling a little fraudulent for claiming my baptismal Church, which had actually been less a part of my life than the Anglican hymns and prayers I'd learned at school.

We continued on into Constitution Square, where the *epitaphios* from the Cathedral was just arriving. This was the grand, metropolitan version of what is normally a modest, parish affair. Several military bands played funeral dirges, and there was an intriguing collection of uniforms: some mismatched girl guides; all sorts of military types and Church VIPs; a dozen Catholic nuns in short dresses, white gloves and rather high heels; and a group of slightly miserable-looking Greek Catholic priests. Like their Orthodox compatriots, Greek Catholics keep the old Gregorian calendar, but these clean-shaven priests looked somehow denuded and incongruous.

Some way down was a short, massively broad, shimmering figure in stiff, gold-embroidered robes. He was wearing a dazzlingly bejewelled, round-topped mitre and was regally waving a hefty gold cross. The archbishop of Athens looked as I imagine a Byzantine emperor. He seemed to radiate a luxurious, gilded light in the dim, candle-lit procession, as he made his way past the television cameras positioned on ladders outside McDonald's.

* * *

The next day was bright and sunny with a stiff breeze. The heavy, mournful atmosphere had lifted. People had reached a spiritual rock bottom on Good Friday and could now prepare themselves for the most important celebration of the year. I went out for a walk with Lily, our dog. Vouliagmeni's beach had the first tourists on it; a pale family of redheads had spread out towels on the sand, but they looked awkward and chilly in the wind. Some middle-aged, mahogany-coloured diehards in minuscule, black bathing briefs were playing beach ball.

Heading up the hill, I made for my favourite area of hillside, known after the herb that grows all over it – Faskomilia (Sage). It was covered with a million coloured flowers, lush grasses and delicate wild garlic in bloom. Lily chased plump, brown partridges, making them flap up into the air, squawking and chirruping noisily with irritation. I paused for a moment, by some eucalyptus trees, and looked across at the hazy hills of the coastline towards the south, past Lagonisi (Hare's Island) to Cape Sounion. The view and the eucalyptus's scaly, peeling bark and papery leaves reminded me of Edward Lear's marvellous, sweeping watercolours of Greek landscapes. In spite of awful illnesses, injuries and the torments of mosquitoes on his travels, he often painted their elegant, feathery cascades of faded, grey-green and pinkish foliage.

I was standing at a point with no sight of any houses. Here, it was possible to imagine that little had changed since the mid-nineteenth century, when Lear wrote that 'owls, the bird of Minerva are extremely common, and come and sit near me while I draw'. This region had been a remote, brigand-infested hinterland, far from the small town of Athens, but philhellenes, classicists, painters and adventurers made their way along the horse tracks, usually en route to the temple at Sounion.

British and other European travellers like Lear had been visiting Greece since the sixteenth century. These proto-tourists were fascinated by classical culture and its civilizing influence throughout Europe; the ancient Greeks were viewed not only as ancestors of the modern inhabitants of this land, but as ancestors of all Europeans. 'We are all Greeks,' Shelley famously wrote at the height of romantic philhellenism in the early nineteenth century. 'Our laws, our literature, our religion, our arts have their root in Greece.'

The fine gentlemen (and occasional lady) arrived with their horses, trunks, valets, cooks, and draughtsmen for recording the landscapes and ruins. They frequently saw the contemporary Hellenes as poor, wretched slaves of the Turks, who had lost all of their ancestors' former glory. Not all early travellers were enamoured with the Greeks (in Elizabethan England, a 'Greek' was a cheat, crook and liar), but opinions gradually changed. By the seventeenth and eighteenth centuries, the countries were drawn together both by Greek heritage and by their common enemies. British suspicion of the Muslim Ottomans brought them closer to their Christian Greek brothers, while both the Protestant English and the Orthodox Greeks despised the Catholics. It was said that when in 1685 the Venetians conquered the Morea, or Peloponnese, they behaved far worse to the subject Greeks (as 'heretics') than the Ottomans had done (to the 'infidels'). The old adage that your enemy's enemy is your friend helped produce many a British (and other European) philhellene, who wished to see the Greeks reclaim their 'rightful inheritance'.

I never learned ancient Greek or studied the classics, and I dislike it when Greece's present is swamped by the distant past. When non-Greeks assume that 'Athens' or 'Greece' means ancient, it seems unjust. Nevertheless, I can sometimes sympathize with these idiosyncratic travellers who came to Greece before modern travel made it accessible to everyone. Some may have been arrogant, pompous and prejudiced, but many were inspired and changed by their adventures. They came with ideas gleaned in libraries, but found new meaning reading the ancient philosophers and poets *in situ*.

I'd felt this kind of revelation one summer in Greece, when reading an English translation of Homer's Odyssey. The physical reality of the landscapes was so recognizable: the 'fragrant cypresses' and 'thriving garden vines'; the 'cloudless limpid air with a white radiance playing over all'; how the night *is* 'ambrosial'; and how Dawn *does* appear 'on her golden throne'. Odysseus' love of talk (his words fell 'like snowflakes') and his wily cunning are still characteristics Greeks claim as their own. There are the same little domestic details: the guest welcomed with sweet wines; the feasting on roasted meats; and how, as Odysseus said, 'the gods made music and banquets to go together'.

I had visited the temple of Poseidon at Sounion one winter morning a few months earlier, before the coaches of sightseers got there from Athens. Arriving alone was a breathtaking (and rare) way to see this spectacular ruin, which stands on the rocks above the sea at the southernmost tip of Attica. Experts say that its position in relation to the Parthenon and the magnificent temple of Aphaia on the nearby island of Aegina makes a perfect equilateral triangle, but nobody knows how the ancients could have measured it to within a metre.

The whole place was bathed in the golden light which often looks like wishful thinking (reveries of a golden era) when you see it in romantic paintings. I spent some time searching for Lord Byron's signature, which was said to be there somewhere. Eventually, having ducked under the rope cordon, and circled the sacred temple twice, I found it: 'Byron' in a bold, rounded, slightly childish script, etched deeply into the marble. I was ludicrously pleased; it was a link both to his times and to the much older mysteries which had captivated him. This long-lasting graffiti was a popular if mild form of vandalism among visitors until quite recently, but at least Byron didn't cart off the antiquities like so many of his compatriots. He was a romantic in his calls for emancipation for the downtrodden descendants of Pericles and Socrates ('I dream'd that Greece might yet be free'), but his verses and vision contributed substantially to support for the burgeoning revolutionary spirit (both in Greece and abroad). However, Byron wasn't above a teasing dig at the fanatical classicists' reverence for the ancient world. On seeing the Parthenon one day, he commented sardonically that it was 'very like the Mansion House' in London.

Byron's party closely escaped being attacked by pirates camping in caves at Sounion, but he still memorialized the place in verse:

> *Place me on Sunium's marbled steep,*
> *Where nothing, save the waves and I,*
> *May hear our mutual murmurs sweep.*

It was still possible in Greece to enter into the spirit of Europeans on their grand tours, but only for brief periods. As I continued on my Easter Saturday walk, I came around the corner to see the white apartment blocks of Varkiza, and the windsurfers speeding across the bay. Stretching out over the wide plain to the east of Mount Hymettus was one of the most industrialized regions in the country, filled with factories, quarries, stinking rubbish dumps and ugly, sprawling townships. It was criss-crossed with half-completed highways, jagged metal pylons, and the tarmac expanses of the flashy new airport. As far as I could see, it was only going to get worse.

When Osbert Lancaster was the British Press Attaché in Athens in the 1930s, he waxed lyrical about this area being one of the loveliest in Greece; it had been famous for its wines, olive oil and pistachios since ancient times. You still see the remnants of struggling vineyards and pistachio groves, though they are now dusty and polluted from the speeding juggernauts. The occasional donkey leans over the road barrier, accustomed to the roar of traffic, and scabrous, malnourished dogs lurk amongst the piles of litter. The once pretty villages are now swamped with advertising hoardings and tasteless new developments, and bereft of civic amenities or pride. The latest mock villas and flashy apartments are harmonized only in the latest trend for painting them the salmon pink of old women's bloomers, and as a nod to 'tradition' the concrete roofs are decorated with a few useless terracotta tiles.

When I see this new, semi-urbanized Greece, I hate it. It combines all the country's worst traits: making a quick buck, corruption, disrespect for the environment, and a rejection of both traditional values and the potential of modern architecture. The overwhelming ugliness which has swamped some parts of Greece is alienating and dislocating. It makes me realize that I arrived too late to see the raw innocence and still untouched, elemental beauty that was written about so eloquently by the wonderful mid-twentieth century British and American writers who loved Greece: Patrick Leigh Fermor, Henry Miller, Lawrence Durrell, Peter Levi and Kevin Andrews. They not only saw a different place, but they had heroic adventures, which are improbable in the comfortable, wealthy, urbanized Greece I live in. They walked incredible distances across dangerous mountains, often during times of war, and encountered epic levels of hospitality and *joie de vivre* in their Greek hosts.

But there was something about the way in which these modern philhellenes cast off their own personal and cultural baggage which was entirely familiar to me. Even though I came to know Greece in the era of mass tourism, satellite TV and urban sprawl, my initial fascination with the place followed a well-worn path, trodden first by the Grand Tourists, and later by their twentieth-century descendants. My children, of course, would know none of this; Greece would be familiar not exotic, home not abroad, and they would be the welcoming hosts not the fêted guests.

* * *

That Saturday night we went to midnight mass near our house. St George's is set among pine trees on a hillock and looks like a simple island church, with its shady courtyard, freshly white-washed walls and simple, barrel-vaulted roof. Lara and Anna met up with some friends from school and ran off to play. Everyone held tall, white candles, the children's specially decorated with ribbons, flowers and small toys, and given to them by their godparents.

Vassilis and I went into the small church, which was already almost full. The male chanters were singing ancient Byzantine hymns, unchanged for centuries; the human voice is the only instrument used in the Orthodox Church. The modal music is as unfamiliar to the newcomer as its Arabic-like symbols, which bear little relation to ordinary musical notation; there are even fractions of tones which you don't find on a piano. More and more people with expectant expressions pressed into the church, squeezing up against us amicably. I thought of the generations upon generations who have lived through this hour of transformation and regeneration. The church's interior smelled of hot wax, hairspray, incense and aftershave. Everyone was dressed in their best, and the array of impressive, blow-dried hairdos now made it obvious why the hairdressers had stayed open until later than usual. Church is always a place where you go to show off yourself and your family, or to find a wife or husband, and Easter is the prime time.

Just before midnight, the lights went off in the packed church. Only three small oil lamps were left burning, along with the tiny, flashing red sensor of the burglar alarm. The priests, now dressed in the white robes of hope (the day before they'd been in mournful black), emerged from the darkness behind the iconostasis bearing a large burning candle. The flame had travelled a long way. A special Olympic Airways flight had brought it from its source in the Holy Sepulchre in Jerusalem that afternoon. Every year, the Greek Orthodox Patriarch of Jerusalem and his Armenian counterpart have an awkward scuffle down in the depths of Christ's tomb, as there is much heated debate as to who should be the first to take the flame. The holy fire, which some say lights itself spontaneously, is received with special ceremonies at Athens airport, taken by motorcade to a church in Plaka, and then distributed among many of Greece's churches. Other planes are laid on to take the symbol of resurrection around Greece, and a helicopter transports it to the holy centres on distant islands without airports.

We all lit our candles from one another and streamed out of the church, as hundreds of people pressed in towards the flame for this moment. Nobody misses 'the Resurrection' if they can help it, and you see old and young, believers and atheists, Communists and Fascists united on this night. It's a pivotal point, not only in the year, but in the very idea of what it means to be Greek. Only the infirm and dedicated outsiders are absent. The priest began a short sermon but before he could finish, the bells for midnight began to peal noisily. Immediately, dozens of firecrackers exploded deafeningly, making us jump and draw breath in fear each time. In the distance, fireworks flashed in the sky and ships sounded their horns.

It's an overwhelming moment of joy and relief; a huge ecstatic shout. In comparison with the quiet, joyful miracle of Jesus's birth, as it is celebrated in Britain, Greek Easter is a holy festival of extremes, with black and white emotions. For Orthodox Christians, it is Christ's resurrection, his defeat of death, and his existence as God that counts. The 'opening' of spring's annual rebirth is complete, and the dark, quiet, deathly sadness of the previous days and even weeks are cancelled out with light, noise and exuberance. It is no coincidence that Easter is also known as *Lambri* – Radiant, Brilliant or Glorious. The world is taut and closed as you look into the abyss of death, and then everything opens up, reaching up to the skies, like going from winter to summer in an instant.

Anna and Lara came running up laughing, holding their lighted candles. They'd been hiding around the back of the church with their friends, avoiding the squibs. Their faces were shining and animated as we kissed them. The priest was still speaking into the microphone, but nobody was taking any notice. Everyone was kissing their families and shaking hands with acquaintances.

Christos anesti! 'Christ is risen!' you say.

Alithos anesti! 'He is risen indeed!' comes the reply.

Some were already making their way off for the customary midnight meal; only a tiny, pious minority would go back inside the church with the priests to continue the service. People want to celebrate, to go home and eat *mayiritsa* – soup made from the paschal lamb's intestines – and knock the red eggs with each other in a game where the last intact egg wins. I recognized faces in the departing crowd: children from school dressed in unfamiliarly pristine clothes; their parents smart and smiling; and people from the local shops and restaurants.

After the late night, many would be up early to prepare the charcoal fire for the spit. All across the country, families roast their lamb (usually somewhat younger than a yearling) in gardens, terraces, courtyards, on hillsides and by beaches. Stretched out on the skewer over the charcoal, its long, muscular hind legs are extended rather like a large, racing greyhound. Its lean stomach is sewn up and bound with wire, and its teeth are clenched in a permanent grin.

'It's as sweet and tender as Turkish delight,' people say, eating little pieces with their fingers.

Easter is always beautiful in Greece, but this was the first time I had not felt like a tourist or an observer. I was so happy and peaceful I didn't want to leave. Even after the crowds had departed, we stayed, sitting on a bench under the pine trees, listening to the bang of firecrackers going off all around Athens.

CHAPTER 13

TURKISH SEEDS

Do not present . . . Turks as dark skinned and Greeks as
disorganized; it pays back generously to show Turks with
blue eyes and Greeks punctual and reserved.

Hercules Millas,
Dos and Don'ts for better Greek Turkish Relations

One day, Effi came in for work a couple of hours late. It was
a perfect, breezy, young summer morning, but she was in
a bad mood. Her face had a greyish tinge and she complained of
tiredness.

'It's 29 May today,' she announced by way of explanation.
'It's the "Cursed Day". You know why, don't you? Today's the
day the Turks took over Constantinople – a black day for all
Greeks. I just feel like going to sleep. I'm not up to working at
all.' I thought of offering her a 'Turkish coffee', but I realized it
was the wrong day for a jest; only 'Greek' would do today. Effi

got out the copper *briki* and stirred in the powdery coffee, sugar and water over a low heat.

'There you are, just right, with *kaimaki* [the Turkish word for froth],' she said, handing me a cup.

She spoke gloomily about the awful anniversary.

'It was in '53,' said Effi. '1453,' she qualified. Everyone still knows about how the handsome twenty-one-year-old Sultan Mehmet II rode into the capital of Byzantium on a white horse, with his shining scimitar and plumed turban. Constantine the Great had founded his city on the Bosphorus in the fourth century, and it survived attacks by Goths, Huns, Slavs, Arabs, and Catholic Crusaders from Western Europe. But after more than 1,000 years, this Queen of Cities, the jewel of eastern Christianity was finally conquered by the Muslims. It's true that throughout Christendom, people spoke of 'the darkest day in the history of the world'. But that was a very long time ago for Effi to be taking it this seriously.

'I've been to "The City,"' said Effi, using the familiar term for the place that Greeks have mourned and yearned for ever since they lost it. 'To the City', *Eis tin Polin* as it was known then in Greek, became Istanbul for the Turks.

'I went with a group, and we saw all the sights. I visited the [Greek Orthodox] Patriarchate and Saint Sophia's cathedral. Of course.' Effi blew over the steaming cup of coffee, took a sip, and then lit a cigarette, exhaling the smoke out of the kitchen window so it wouldn't bother me.

'And it made me so sad, seeing those minarets,' she added. The mother church of Eastern Christendom was quickly turned into a mosque by the Ottoman Emperor, and the extraordinary city became the centre of his empire for almost half a millennium. The building is now a museum, but the sense of bitterness never left the Greeks. On the Sunday nearest to 29

May there is an annual service held in Athens Cathedral as a memorial to the tragic event. Worshippers call out 'Immortal', *'Athanatos,'* in reference to Constantine Palaeologus, the last and 'immortal' emperor.

'The Fall', the great tragedy for Greeks, was of course, a huge triumph for the Turks, who hold a celebration each year on 29 May. This opposition holds true throughout their shared history: the Greeks' War of Independence in 1821 is what Turks call 'the Greek rebellion'; and each expansion of Free Greece was at the expense of the Turks – the Greeks' 'liberation' of Thessaloniki in 1912 was the Turks' loss. What Greeks call the 'invasion' of Cyprus, the Turks call 'a peace operation'. What is good for Greece had to be bad for Turkey, and vice versa.

When one of the great Greek football teams, Panathinaikos (All Athenian), went to play Fenerbahçe of Istanbul that winter, Vassilis had gone with ministers, diplomats and journalists to 'The City' to witness the historic moment. It was part of a daring new peace initiative between the two countries, begun by George Papandreou, the Foreign Minister for whom Vassilis was working. There were now joint business ventures and collaboration over tourism and environmental issues, but until now, sport had been considered too risky. In spite of all the preparation, things didn't go according to plan. On the evening of the match, Vassilis called me from the stands on his mobile.

'Can you hear the chaos?' he shouted over the uproar. 'The Greek fans have been winding up the Turks all evening. You should turn on the television.' I did, and it was shocking to see how old prejudices and ugly aggression had erupted uncontrollably in the midst of a modern, media-age PR event. The Greeks were yelling: 'Turks, Turks, you're giving a blow-job!' (which rhymes conveniently in Greek), and had thrown yogurt, coins and even chairs at the passing (both Greek and

Turkish) dignitaries. The Turkish supporters unfurled a twenty-metre banner with a picture of the fifteenth-century Mehmet on his horse. Underneath, written in English, was the patriotic taunt: 'Istanbul since 1453.'

Greeks and Turks may still annoy each other, but it's a complex relationship; it's not just conquerors, wars and politics that link the two peoples, it's music, food and language – among the most intimate aspects of life. Even the Greeks' sex life is said to be influenced by the Ottomans' inclinations; 'Ottoman law' is a reference to sodomy. Hundreds of demotic Greek words for everyday objects are Turkish in origin, including expressions for kitchen utensils, curtains, rugs, gardens, fences, alleyways, neighbourhoods, and so are a large variety of exclamations and insults. Numerous Turkish place names in Greece have actually been erased in the attempt to cover up history; the Turkish Harbour (Tourkolimano) in Piraeus has now become Small Harbour (Mikrolimano), though many know it by its original name.

My conversation with Effi about the 'Cursed Day' turned to food. I was interested in the edible Ottoman legacies which have retained their Turkish names and we started listing them. We began with mixed appetizers or *mezedhes*, worked through the different meatballs (*keftedhes*, *soutzoukakia*), and ended up with the syrupy pastries such as *baklava* and *kadaifi*, and the sesame-based halva. My children's favourite food was *yiros* from the *souvlaki* (kebab) shop: wafer-thin shavings of meat trimmed from the massive, glistening, slow-turning, fat-dripping column constructed from slices of pork. It is Greece's and Turkey's original street food, and remains one of Europe's few cheap and delicious fast foods.

'One *pita*, with *yiros* and everything,' says Anna fluently at our local *souvlakia* place, and a thick, greasy circle of char-grilled pitta bread is wrapped tightly around the slivers of meat, along with salad, garlicky tzatziki, and the odd potato chip.

'And one *pita*, *yiros*, plain,' chimes in Lara categorically.

'And what about *imam bayildi*?' I asked Effi, remembering the exquisitely rich dish of roasted aubergines with onions and tomatoes. 'Doesn't it mean "the Imam or priest fainted," because it was so delicious?'

'Either that, or because his wife used so much oil in it, he was shocked. But you know the Ottomans copied many recipes from the Byzantines,' she answered, pulling back a few patriotic points for Christianity. Effi had brought in her *Tselementes* – the cookery book whose author became so widely respected by Athens's rising middle classes after the 1920s that his name became the generic term for a recipe book. Hers was a battered old copy which had belonged to her grandmother and was written in the formal, 'cleaned up' *katharevousa*.

Like his language, Tselementes tried to clean up Greek cuisine of anything suspiciously oriental; herbs, spices and Turkish elements were not welcome in his kitchen. Having trained in France and America, Tselementes introduced a blander, more international style which used unfamiliar products such as butter. He also promoted sauces which had always been viewed as suspect and somehow dishonest in Greece; to an extent they still are; 'adding sauce' to a conversation implies hiding or exaggerating the truth. The tasteless moussaka with its four-centimetre stratum of gluey béchamel (which you find in every lousy tourist taverna, with chips) must owe some thanks to Tselementes.

Fortunately, Effi was not a dedicated fan of Tselementes. She only needed it to check up on measurements for the odd recipe, she said, and anyway, she planned to throw her copy away; it was too tattered to use now.

'I'm traditional,' she said. 'I believe in eating pulses. Bean soup, chickpeas, lentils, "giant beans"; that's what keeps us healthy. They stop you getting you-know-what,' and she mouthed the word 'cancer'.

'*Ftou ftou!*' she said, making the sound of a mock spit to ward off the evil eye. 'And touch wood!' she added, tapping the wooden table. 'I don't know why, but God loves me . . .'

It's not only Tselemendes's fault, of course, that you can find poor quality food in Greece. There was never a tradition of restaurants or chefs. Haute cuisine couldn't exist in a land which had long been poverty-stricken and regularly threatened by invasions and oppressors. There were just home kitchens, and the taverna was always a male drinking place with songs and snacks rather than a place in which to fill one's belly. The foodies of the Ottoman Empire lived in Istanbul or Smyrna, where Turks, Greeks and Armenians shared a sophisticated cuisine, drawing on Mediterranean, Middle Eastern and central Asian traditions. It's only recently that Greeks in Greece have had the money and inclination to appreciate dining out, and restaurateurs have begun to produce quality Greek cooking, which eschews both the rough taverna approach and the smart international style.

* * *

That evening the air was balmy and scented with jasmine and the mysterious, mushroom-like odour of gardenias. I picked a lemon leaf from our tree and crushed it in my hand, inhaling its miraculous, green, citrus smell. Vassilis's sister Stella had come over with good news about my application for Greek citizenship. An influential friend of hers was hurrying my papers through distant, unknown offices, which had backlogs of two years. Soon the police would be investigating me to make sure I'd never been expelled from Greece, they'd check for a criminal record in Britain and then I might be in luck.

'I don't know what you want it for,' she added.

We were sitting on our terrace, drinking a pungent, dark pink wine which Effi had brought in an unlabelled plastic bottle (organic, barrelled rosé). It reminded Vassilis and Stella of the strong, home-made stuff their uncle used to produce. It was a fierce, slightly vinegary, woody wine, but it went well with the mad, clotting pinks and crushed-strawberry crimsons in the sky. The sun looked so fiery that I imagined it touching the sea, and letting out a bubbling hiss of molten rock entering water. In the calmer, violet twilight, the island of Aegina became a shadowy, sleeping dinosaur, with the dark orange sea lapping at its underbelly.

Inside, the girls were dancing to the famous Greek pop singer, Despina Vandi, with their friend Nefeli from next door. They'd done their best to imitate the Siren's get-up with what they'd gleaned from television shows: cherry-red Lolita lips, smudged black-rimmed eyes, and they'd rolled up their T-shirts to reveal pale, soft-skinned tummies.

'You light up fires, and burn everything,' they sang, dancing a bastardized version of the tsifteteli, an eastern (and Turkish) belly-dance which adapts itself easily to the gyrations of the disco. They were gradually turning up the volume to a deafening pitch. It was one of those awful moments of realization when I heard myself shout: 'Turn it down a bit.' Surely that was something other people's parents did? It marked the uncomfortable crossing of a new boundary as my children grew up. Strange though, that this was happening to the skittering, slithering tones of a harem courtesan's dance.

Vassilis had pooh-poohed Effi's overdone reaction to the 'Cursed Day'.

'You can't assume that the loony opinions of a royalist-Junta supporter are representative,' he said caustically. I asked Stella what she thought about the subject.

'A Turk is the same for me as a Spaniard or an English person,' she replied. 'We don't have anything against them.' She and Vassilis were so easygoing about the subject that I began to feel I'd got the whole thing wrong. If there's one thing outsiders think they know about Greeks and Turks it's that they are enemies. But it's obviously a complicated relationship. There had always been Greeks, since the Fall of Constantinople, who were pro-Turkish, deeming the religious tolerance of Ottoman masters preferable to Catholic intolerance. 'Better the Turkish turban than the Catholics' mitre,' warned Grand Duke Loukas Notaras. And there are the contemporary, usually left-wing Greeks who prefer an eastern orientation to the overwhelming domination of Americanized globalization.

In the past I'd grown tired of hearing the refrain: 'We were 400 years under Turkish occupation.' These centuries became an excuse, a convenient coverall: for unreliability, lateness, corruption, too many 'eastern elements', too much Americanization, the lack of progress, too much progress. The weighty Turkish yoke gives a comfortable explanation for the chink of inferiority in the armour of Greek pride and patriotism. And the skewed history lessons begin young. Anna's school history book clearly showed that the Turks were still the 'baddies' in the eyes of the nation's educators; everything was skewed towards a patriotic promotion of Greece. The Fall of Constantinople was described in melodramatic prose: 'Slavery began to cover Hellenism.' Anna had doodled pink flowers around a traditional folk song cursing the Sultan:

> *Be damned, O Emperor, be thrice damned*
> *For the evil you have done and the evil you do . . .*

And every child learns the nursery rhyme 'My Bright Little

Moon', sung to the tune of 'Twinkle, twinkle, little star', which refers to the secret schools. These were supposedly the only opportunity for Greek culture to be handed on to children and operated at night in churches and monasteries during Ottoman rule.

'The hidden schools are all a myth, you know,' said Vassilis. 'Now we're starting to admit that there were perfectly good Greek schools under the Ottomans. And it's only now, that we talk about the Greek atrocities committed against Turkish women and children during the War of Independence.'

Naturally, Greeks aren't the only ones with clichés and myths about Turkey; the West has a long history of stereotyping them too. They have been depicted as cruel warriors (Bluebeard's scimitar, the Armenian genocide and the horrendous prisons of *Midnight Express* come to mind), and oriental sensualists (with their courtesans, harems, rose-scented Turkish delight and priceless spiky-tipped tulips). Greeks may say: 'I became a Turk,' when they are beside themselves with anger, but children all over Europe have been threatened with 'The Turk will come and get you!' at various times in history.

Some things are evidently changing in Greece. In spite of protests from the Orthodox Church, permission has been granted for a mosque and large Islamic centre to be built in Athens. Admittedly it is in a peripheral suburb, and some locals are unhappy about the possibility of an influx of Muslims, but nevertheless, it is a sign that Greeks are overcoming their antipathy towards crescent moons and minarets. Just as Turks dislike crosses and bell towers, the sight of a minaret is still considered too negative an image for Athenians to stomach in the centre of town (all the historic mosques have been closed down or transformed into something else). Whether it was fear of shame at the prospect of a mosque-less Olympics or genuine respect for minority religions, the project finally looks likely to go ahead. It will be the first mosque to function in the capital since Ottoman rule.

It was dark now, and the children had stopped dancing. Some cicadas struck up their sawing background trill. The heady wine was definitely getting better. In ancient Greece, wine was so strong it needed watering down, and it crossed my mind that maybe this was something similar. Even the giant Cyclops was knocked out when Odysseus gave him undiluted wine. The Muslim Ottomans didn't drink wine themselves, and put huge taxes on what was the marker of both feasting and religious libation for Greeks (it had passed easily from Dionysian rituals to the Orthodox liturgy). For the centuries of Turkish rule, drinking wine marked a Greek as Greek.

I grilled some fish I'd bought at the little port, along the coast in Varkiza. You can watch the fishing boats come in, and buy the fish still twitching on the stone jetty. It seemed a miracle to have this as part of a basically urban existence.

'Go to the man at the end of the stalls,' warned Effi. 'All the others are cheats. They'd sell you stale fish if you don't know the difference.' I'd checked for shiny eyes and plump flesh, and went home with my silvery prizes. Now we divided them up, and the children came to join us at the table.

'We had earthquake practice at school today,' said Anna.

'They made us hide under our desks,' added Lara, laughing. 'And they told us not to hang heavy pictures on the wall near our beds. And then we had to line up in the yard without running.'

Stella shuddered, remembering Athens's last big earthquake, four years earlier.

'I was out in the street and there was complete panic,' she said. 'Glass windows fell out all around me; people were screaming. My heart was banging and I was terrified because I'd left the children and their cousin at home on the fifth floor. I tried to ring from a café – it was before I had a mobile phone – but the lines were down. It was dreadful. It felt like the end of the world.' She picked nervously at her fingernails and looked strained. 'In the end everything was fine. Dimitris (who was fourteen then) had shown the younger two how to hide under the table like he'd been taught at school. Later, I found them playing in the park. But we didn't dare go home in case of aftershocks. We slept in the car that night.'

'You know it took something as shocking as the earthquakes to help bring the Turks and the Greeks together,' said Vassilis. 'When Turkey had that catastrophic earthquake in 1999, thousands were killed. It was hard to think that something positive could come from it, but when Greeks went to help with the rescue operation it was as though decades of hatred and suspicion crumbled along with the buildings. When Athens was hit the following month, the Turks helped us too. They saved a little boy – pulling him out of the rubble. Since then, it's been much easier for the politicians to be friendly; they call it "earthquake diplomacy".'

* * *

I'd always been interested in the areas of Athens which had been settled by Greek refugees who left Turkey in the 'Catastrophe' of 1922: New Smyrna, New Ionia, New Chalcedon, New Philadelphia, to name a few. Although some are now smart suburbs, others have retained something of the atmosphere of refugee neighbourhoods. The street names in these districts still refer to places in Asia Minor: Smyrna Street, Constantinople Street, Trebizond Street, Byzantium Street, Bosphorus Street . . . After a friend took me to lunch in one of Kaisariani's many tavernas, I went back again to explore the narrow lanes which are reminiscent of an island village. Tiny, two-room houses built from mud bricks have remained from the 1920s, still immaculately painted, with Lilliputian front yards. The metre or so appropriated from the pavement is just enough for a few upright chairs, a canary in a cage, and a row of old oil cans planted with colourful geraniums, carnations, jasmine, lemon trees and vines.

In the whitewashed alleys, children were playing ball and old people sat out on the pavement, drinking coffee, preparing vegetables and sewing. Smells of bleach and frying meatballs wafted out from what in many cases are glorified hovels. The oldest inhabitants are the last living refugees who actually remember Smyrna and the 'Catastrophe' which turned so many lives upside down and affected all of Greece. But even those who don't remember grew up with the stories, the tears, the songs, the food and the prayers.

Some of the minuscule houses had coffee shops and tavernas squeezed into them. They made me think of Karaghiozis's tiny shack; the run-down dwelling of the famously cunning, lazy, ever-hungry shadow puppet, which sits scruffily next to the pasha's seraglio. These days you are more likely to hear: 'Hey, what are you doing, Karaghiozis?' as an insult traded between angry drivers on the road than in a live show. But even with the inroads made by cinema and television, the Balkan equivalent of Punch hasn't quite died out as often predicted. It is no longer performed in Turkish (as it was until the 1880s), and the old masters have been replaced by young newcomers, but it was always an adaptable satire, and you can still find family shows at weekends which keep the tradition going.

Many of Kaisariani's new buildings are comical slivers (rather than blocks) of flats. Some are four or five storeys high, but only one room across; the width of a refugee's house. Sticking up ridiculously next to their neighbours' tiny dwellings, they look like concrete beanstalks which sprang up next to Jack's house. It is a case of Athens's individualistic part-exchange system taken to the extreme of its own logic.

I stopped to look at a particularly pretty house. A pair of sleepy dogs lounged amongst potted plants, and I heard music through the open front door. I felt like a character in a fairy story (curious Goldilocks, perhaps) as I peered into the darkness. A smiling woman in her fifties, with hennaed hair twisted into a loose bun, came out to see what I wanted. I complimented her on her house.

'I was born here,' she said. 'My mother brought up eleven children in one room, and I'm the youngest. My children have left now, but I've stayed on. I love it here. I'd never leave.' Seeing my indiscreet glance towards the interior she invited me in.

'This second room was added on later, and made into a kitchen,' she explained. 'In the beginning it was the stable for our horse.' I followed her into a cosy room about the size of a spacious horsebox, where food was cooking on the stove, and a television set was broadcasting some regional traditional dance group. Through an open door I saw the cramped living room where *Kyria* Irini (as she turned out to be called) and her ten siblings were born and brought up. They must have slept in shifts to have fitted there. And what about the parents?

'My mother was twelve when she arrived,' said *Kyria* Irini, getting out a jar of home-made 'spoon sweets' and putting some thick, yellow rolls of citron peel in sugary syrup onto a saucer. She placed it carefully on a tray with a glass of water and a napkin. 'My grandparents were rich in Smyrna – they had servants. And my mother went to the French school. When they left in 1922 they came with nothing, just their clothes. It was a huge shock.'

The exodus from Smyrna is another of those historical moments, like the Fall of 'The City,' which will probably be remembered by Greeks for centuries. The trauma (and ultimately the survival) generated its own mythology, poetry, novels, films, music, academic studies and even political movements. Photographs of Smyrna Greeks in the first two decades of the twentieth century show handsome young men in blazers on the seaside promenade, rich merchants with fur coats, fez and worry beads, and ladies with parasols, dressed in Parisian fashions, in leafy boulevards. The young girls with floppy bows in their hair and white muslin dresses have the same clever expressions and dark-eyed beauty as my Russian grandmother in her youth. With the easy logic of hindsight, they appear to have a doomed innocence.

Greeks made up over half of Smyrna's 700,000 citizens. They had their own refined schools and clubs, exclusive shops and cafés, lively concert halls and philanthropic associations, and well-kept churches. These Asia Minor Greeks had lived side by side with the Turks (and Armenians, Jews, British, Germans, Italians and French) for centuries. Their city was far richer than Athens, and they were far more sophisticated and cosmopolitan than their Athenian counterparts. Then the Greek army invaded Turkey, having been first encouraged, then let down by the Great Powers. They'd been pursuing their nagging, dangerous dream, known as the 'Great Idea', whereby they hoped to recapture 'The City', and make Constantine's capital the centre of Greek Orthodoxy again.

The Greek army's occupation of Smyrna is rarely mentioned in Greek descriptions of the disaster. Neither is its foolhardy advance towards Ankara, which enraged the Turks, who joined Kemal Atatürk's liberation movement in droves. What *is* well known is that after their subsequent defeat, there was widespread bloodshed during the burning of Smyrna. Hundreds of thousands of refugees poured into Greece from all over Asia Minor within weeks, and the subsequent Treaty of Lausanne agreed an ambitious exchange of populations. Well over a million 'Greeks' were sent 'home' by the Turks and almost half a million Turks living in Greece were 'repatriated'. Some of the refugees arriving in Greece spoke only Turkish but were Christians, others leaving the country were Greek-speaking Muslims; there was no time for fine-tuning definitions of ethnic identity.

I'd seen a television documentary interview with an old man who told of his experiences in 1922. He'd been six at the time, and his face was trembling like a brave child's – struggling not to cry before the camera.

'It can't be described what happened,' he said, searching for words. 'In Smyrna there were fifteen days of rape, murder, fire . . . we managed to get onto a boat, but people were falling in the water, drowning. And when others swam out and tried to climb onto the American and Italian boats, they chopped their hands off to prevent them. I held on tight to my father's jacket, and said, "Where's Mum?" He answered, "I don't know. She's lost." Then we came to Greece . . .' He couldn't go on. Even after eighty years it was too much to bear. About 120,000 people were killed (and mutilated, blinded and hanged) by the rampaging Turkish army, and the city was practically razed to the ground, to be rebuilt later as Izmir.

Three thousand years of Greek culture in Asia Minor ended abruptly. The environment which had produced Greek poets and scientists, from Sappho to Hippocrates, and which always retained its orientation to Constantinople rather than Athens, vanished. The poet George Seferis was from Smyrna. He left as a teenager, before the Second World War, but many of his poems

are about displacement, homelessness, and ships with tired
travellers searching for something.

> What are they after, our souls, travelling
> on the decks of decayed ships
> crowded in with sallow women and crying babies
> unable to forget themselves either with the flying fish
> or with the stars that the masts point out at their tips?

Kyria Irini didn't live through the horrors, but she knew all the
stories.

'Lots of people died on the way over, and they had to go
wherever they were sent – mountains, swamps, up to northern
Greece . . . In the beginning, they camped. Some people stayed
in cinemas, schools or stations. My mother lived in a tent for a
year or so when Kaisariani was still just open hillside. But
everyone helped each other. Neighbours were called "Auntie."
They'd give you food and you'd help them with jobs. And
everyone was very proud; we believed in principles, in keeping
your word, in being good householders. Even in the communal
refugee houses they always had separate toilets for men and
women; they kept everything clean, and they planted flowers.'

Not that it was easy. The floods of Asia Minor refugees
swelled the Greek population from four million to five and a
half. Suddenly, Turkish was heard in the streets again, something
which was hard for people to accept (the nearest equivalent in
England would be the post-war association of the German
language with the Nazis). The refugees were not always
welcomed by a population which had suffered recent wars,
unemployment and widespread poverty.

'We might have come from better, more educated families
than many Athenians,' said *Kyria* Irini, 'but it was difficult to find

work and we had nothing. They looked down on us. We were the "baptized-with-yogurt-ones" [at a time when yogurt was still associated with Turkish cuisine]. They called us "Turkish seeds".' She didn't add, however, that many of the refugees looked down on the mainland Greeks. They believed them to be simple and unsophisticated, and often called them 'stupid shepherds' and 'peasants' in return.

When they arrived, the refugees were almost all liberals – supporters of Eleftherios Venizelos, the great anti-royalist politician, now commemorated on road signs all over Athens ('El. Venizelos' is the new, oddly Mexican-sounding airport). Finding themselves on the periphery, however, they became increasingly dissatisfied with the state, and later, during the Second World War, many turned to Communism and joined the resistance. The opposition in Kaisariani was so strong that the Germans were afraid to enter. You still see walls pockmarked with sixty-year-old bullet holes, and the Café Proletariat indicates that some have kept their political ideals.

Their transformation was not unlike that of my Russian grandmother, who left St Petersburg as a privileged young princess, and came to England in 1919 with nothing. By the 1930s she was a Communist herself – much to the horror of most anti-Bolshevik Russian émigrés. Hers was another, parallel story of searching for home, for meaning after upheaval and for justice. Like the White Russians, the Asia Minor refugees nurtured dreams of going back; it was hard to let go. Our friend Stelios told me how his grandmother had left a box of gold sovereigns in Smyrna with her French neighbour.

'Look after it for me and I'll be back to collect it,' she'd said, in the terrifying rush to escape. She survived, arriving newly widowed and pregnant in Greece, and getting by as a dressmaker for Athens's middle classes. But she always fantasized about going back to get her box.

I thanked *Kyria* Irini, who invited me back to meet some of her friends.

'We all get together on Sundays and talk about the old days,' she said. 'We sing Smyrna songs – you'd like it.'

* * *

When I got home, Lara and Anna wanted to go swimming, and Vassilis and I took them to Vouliagmeni's famous thermal lake. The girls liked capturing the small, slimy black fish that gather disconcertingly around the steps to suck your toes as you're getting in, and Vassilis liked reading the newspapers and drinking coffee there. We sat at a table under a large white umbrella, and watched the dark, sleek-bodied swallows with their sickle wings speeding through the air. Mouse-coloured ring doves cooed and swooped around the vast cliff running down the side of the lake. The whole verdant, watery crater is what remains of an ancient, collapsed cave, and there are labyrinthine tunnels and potholes which lead through to the sea. The slightly saline water stays permanently at around twenty-two degrees and is said to have therapeutic qualities. A couple was helping a frail teenage son to the water's edge. He wore bright orange water wings and his white, skinny legs were as unsteady as those of a newborn colt's.

There was always a scattering of golden-limbed youths who smoked languidly, gazing into the distance, and well-preserved ladies in high-heeled, glittery sandals, talking loudly on their mobiles and leaving large tips for the barman. Nearby, a gaggle of the old, dark-tanned, wrinkly regulars were chatting in the water. They were the dominant habitués, and I'd labelled them the white-hatted wallowers, as they floated happily for hours on end. Swimming past them, I'd catch snippets of conversation as

I came up for air ('. . . terrible haemorrhaging . . .' '. . . he's a person with courage . . .' 'Glory to God . . .').

'Welcome to Antonis, my *palikari* [brave young fellow]!' one man shouted across to his elderly friend, who was pausing at the water's edge in his sagging, baggy bathing trunks.

I left Vassilis with his coffee and the children catching the black fish in a plastic bottle, and swam off towards the distant end of the lake. The water smelled bewilderingly like the muddy, English rivers I remembered from my youth, mixed with iodine, sea salt and sudden whiffs of something like honeysuckle and the evocative scent of Ambre Solaire (though all such creams are strictly forbidden there). The lake has both a sense of cosy municipality (the man in the little white rowing boat scooping out weed and the tinkle of teaspoons on coffee cups) and dark danger (jagged rocks and murky, unseen depths). As you swim, the odd turquoise kingfisher skims along the water's surface and jewelled dragonflies hum past your ears. A pretty young woman sat on a rock, half-submerged in the water. Her dark hair was slicked down her wet back. She could have been a mermaid.

All this couldn't be further from the conventional image of Athens; from concrete, traffic, crowds, refugees, migrants, politics and from settling old scores. Swimming in Vouliagmeni's lake may seem very un-Athenian, but it is also one of Athens's great pleasures. The sense of timelessness passes by the idea of the ancient Greeks, the Byzantines and the Ottomans. It's more like entering a prehistoric or geological era, where time passing is measured not in centuries or millennia, but in millions of years.

CHAPTER 14

UNMASKING A MYTH

Dispatch and drive away all diabolical force, every Satanic incursion, every hostility, evil suspicion and injury . . .
Greek Orthodox prayer

By June, the long grass and flowers on the hillside by our house had dried into pale, scratchy straw and the red earth was baked hard as terracotta. All sorts of insects appeared in the house: a giant, pink, stinging centipede, which nested in our bed; green and gold beetles good enough for earrings; and a curious yellow-striped cross between a daddy-long-legs and a hornet, which was unnaturally interested in the colourful books in the bookshelves. In the evening, the cicadas trilled, and eerily translucent, flesh-coloured geckos edged jerkily around the terrace, flipping behind the warm flowerpots like escaped embryos. Later, the ominous whine of distant bomber planes revealed mosquitoes coming in for night raids.

As the days got hotter, school wound down and even the dreaded hours of homework evaporated. A weighty carapace of heat settled on the middle of the day, and any activity became an effort. The only thing which appealed was a rest in a darkened room. This midday abyss is officially a time for halting activity, when shops close and it's too hot to be outside. 'The hours of public quiet' (during which even phone calls are apologized for) last until about five-thirty when the raging sun begins to ease. You emerge again refreshed, with the pleasurable prospect of the second part of the day – the long, mellowing afternoon which, by Greek thinking, lasts until it gets dark at about nine.

School finished in the second week of June and a new ban on the annual ritual of burning schoolbooks was announced in the papers.

'Oh please, Mum, just my geography book – that's my worst lesson,' pleaded Anna. 'I've already agreed with Aphrodite to burn ours together.'

The last day of term was a short but nerve-racking business. Instead of lessons, parents had to queue up to receive their children's grades. Even at eight-thirty a.m. it was terribly hot, and an unseasonably early and fiery *meltemi* wind was buffeting everybody into a state of tension.

'It's earthquake weather,' warned some pessimists, and sure enough, some small tremors had been reported around the country. Lara's class of first-years were considered too young for formal marks, but were duly given their end-of-year diplomas and kissed by the teacher. The parents of Anna's fourth-year class waited for the moment of judgement like souls in purgatory. Hanging about in the stuffy, chalky corridor, we tried to read the expression on each parent's face when they emerged from seeing the teacher. They all clutched a folded yellow card with a stark list of Alphas, Betas or Gammas (no 'could do better', 'improving', or 'a friendly, sociable child' here). Some were beaming irrepressibly, unable to prevent announcing to a friend:

'All As . . . Well, he's always been excellent.' Others kept quiet and hurried off.

In the end I was just as bad as the boastful parents. When I emerged with Anna's column of straight As, I was so pleased I almost cried. They were certainly the grades of an encouraging teacher, but they were also a sign of the amazing progress Anna had made in one year.

'She'll have to climb a mountain,' the teacher had said when Anna could barely write in Greek at the beginning of the year. Now it seemed that she had.

'Have a good summer! Happy holidays!' we all wished each other, and walked across the blistering asphalt school yard with three hot months of freedom ahead of us.

That evening, we celebrated with a trip to our local open-air cinema. We made ourselves at home in the fading dusk, setting our drinks and popcorn down on one of the many strategically placed iron café tables, and leaning back in the directors' chairs. Lara and Anna eyed up the other children and the entwined young couples:

'Quick, look over there! A love spot,' they hissed. To the children's delight, we had taken them to a film which we only realized was a '15' when the opening credits came up; the age-rating isn't advertised and the box offices rarely refuse young children entry into 'unsuitable' films. Each curse and naked breast was all the more intriguing for being forbidden, and they begged to be taken to more 'grown-up films'.

White plumes of cigarette smoke floated up into the indigo sky, as it filled with stars, and the evocative smell of outdoor tobacco mingled with the scent from a mass of flowering honeysuckle, which encircled the entire cinema. I could see into the apartments of a couple of neighbouring buildings; some people drifted onto the balconies, catching the film for free. The little details of their lives became a parallel story to the film, as women cooked, children and cats wandered in and out, phones rang and visitors arrived.

Over the next weeks, we developed a passion for the summer cinemas which have become fashionable in Athens again, following their heyday in the 1950s and 1960s, and their seedy decline in the 1980s. Over the hill from us was the Varkiza, which stands like a surreal neon hallucination among the olive groves, an imitation of a 1950s American cinema with pink lights, clipped lawns and tidy rose bushes. We also visited the more urban screens like the old Dexameni (Reservoir) on the slopes of Lycabettus, and the breezy roof terraces, such as the Vox in Exarcheia and the Cine Paris in Plaka. Some of them, like the deluxe, revamped Aigli (Glory) in the Zappeio Gardens, have become so smart they even serve cocktails and dinner.

That weekend, we went to the nearby beach at Varkiza. The last time I'd been swimming there had been the previous September and October. On still, limpid mornings, I had dropped the children at school, then driven to the large bay with its stretch of sand, and swum the length of it. The sea had been smooth as pale blue glass, and the only disturbances were a few seagulls or the odd barking dog. This hot, summer Sunday presented another picture. We had gone to the non-paying section of the beach, which was packed with large quantities of Attica's youth, coachloads of elderly pensioners, and immigrant families having picnics. There was barely room to park the car, let alone find a comfortable place on the beach. Eventually, we found a small gap in the seething mass of humanity under some pine trees, and I tried to pacify Vassilis, who was appalled and wanted to go straight home.

Nearby, a deeply tanned woman of a certain age was dressed

entirely in leopard and snakeskin patterns, with towels and beach bed to match. Several pale, overweight mothers in high heels and white stretch trousers tottered past, clutching overheated, crying babies. A bony, mange-ridden puppy was nuzzling up to Anna and Lara, much to their delight. Ignoring the hellish situation, I marked out a limited beach territory with our mats, towels and bags. Immediately, a large group of teenagers came and sat down right next to us. Handsome youths strutted about in pirate-like headscarves, bearing small tattoos and interestingly shaped lines and sprouts of beard, and smooth-skinned girls in new, bright bikinis with pierced belly buttons shrieked and flirted. They all wore heavy, unlaced athletic shoes and smoked. Someone somewhere had put on a tape of very loud popular songs. The sand was full of cigarette butts.

I went for a long swim. Unlike the shore, the sea was clean and uncrowded and I soon forgot that anyone else existed. Shoals of minute silver fish wafted like clouds of glistening needles, and evil-looking black sea urchins with menacing spines lay on the rocks, their delicious, bright orange roe a hidden secret. I returned to the beach in a better mood. Lying wet on my towel and relishing the strong, purifying heat of the sun on my salty back, I felt myself tumbling into the familiar sense of well-being that comes with the Greek summer. It is the realm of the senses, of a seductive laziness and a simpler, more direct ease with the body.

I looked through half-closed eyes, past the crook of my elbow at the teenagers next to us. I now felt more forgiving of the throng who'd come in search of the same pleasures as us. The slim-hipped teenage boys with their tightly muscular, newly grown limbs reminded me of the figures on ancient vases; reckless Icarus about to fly too close to the sun, and tumble forever down into the Aegean. For a brief moment, silhouetted against the sunlight, the noisy, unabashed party hinted at beautiful images from another time and realm. It was one of those fleeting flashes of myth which are too fragile to hold on to, but which are implicit in Greece's sometimes elusive appeal. They slip away before they can be grasped, like the shards of ancient pottery which rise up through the earth in Athenian parks after the rain, and then disappear again back into the dust.

After we returned from the beach that Sunday, Anna fell off the scooter and hurt her wrist badly enough for us to go to hospital for X-rays and for her to wear a sling for a week.

'Bring in a priest and do a blessing,' advised Vassilis's sister Stella. 'The curse has obviously spread to your house now. You know that Petros [her son] broke his finger this week and then Kostas [her husband] broke his arm.' We laughed at the idea of exorcizing our house. The next day, Lara cut her head quite badly on a stone wall at a school friend's party. We waited until midnight at the Children's Hospital, among blood-spattered toddlers, howling infants and shocked, wan-faced parents. In the end, a kindly if overworked medic shaved off a patch of Lara's long hair, and stitched up the gash with spidery black threads.

Two days later, Vassilis had a minor (admittedly scheduled) operation on his elbow to remove a cyst, and appeared at home with impressive bandaging all over his arm.

'It's your turn next,' they all called to me, laughing. And sure enough, that afternoon I fell and banged my knee. By the evening it had ballooned up to twice its normal size and I couldn't walk for three days.

'Buy some little glass eyes. Pin them on the children. It can't do any harm,' said a writer friend who was as broad-minded and educated as anyone I knew. 'And hang one over the doorway.'

'Write all your names on a paper and the priest will read them out in the church,' said one of Vassilis's colleagues. 'I've got a friendly bishop you could see.'

'It's obvious that you've been "eyed",' said Eleni, a friendly mother at school. 'It happened to me when I was pregnant. I saw a woman looking up and down at my belly as she greeted me, and within ten minutes I was in terrible pain. They don't know they're doing it – it's from envy and jealousy. It just takes one look. Headaches, listlessness and exhaustion are sure signs. They say blue-eyed people are the most dangerous.' When Eleni offered to get me 'de-eyed', I felt ready to try anything.

'I didn't believe in it before either,' she said, 'but I know this woman who's really good. I'll phone her; I just have to tell her your name.'

Later, Eleni rang me at home.

'My friend says she's surprised you could even sleep at night. She did it twice – dropping the oil into the glass of water, and using burnt cloves – and it showed that you were very badly "eyed".'

'Thank you very much,' I said, unable to prevent myself laughing a little. Scepticism is a lingering vice.

'Never say thank you for undoing the evil eye,' replied Eleni seriously.

Although the 'de-eyeing' spells contain Christian elements, belief in the evil eye is not an official part of Orthodox doctrine; the Church disapproves of pagan spells. Nevertheless, when priests bless a household, they too use water (holy in their case) to purify, and their prayers refer to 'the eyes of evil working'.

The next day I bought four little glass 'eyes' at a jewellery shop – the characteristic simple, round, blue beads ringed in brass with a black 'pupil'. The girls and I wore ours on chains around our necks, but Vassilis looked slightly embarrassed at all the fuss.

'Soon you'll believe in this,' he said teasingly. But he didn't mind pinning his on a safety pin (as they do with babies), albeit hidden inside his shirt pocket.

* * *

A few days later, our friends Thalia and Alexis gave a party to celebrate their baby daughter's baptism. It was held in Politeia, a smart, green suburb north of Athens, and was bursting with movers and shakers in politics and the media, plus a sprinkling of intellectuals and business people. Everyone seemed to be talking about terrorism; there were rumours that the police were getting closer to the leader of 17 November; at least one well-known writer had been mentioned. Stelios was at the party, and over glasses of champagne, he and Vassilis speculated wryly about whether 17 November's founding father could even be mingling here among the guests. Such was the impact of the terrorists that everyone had their own fantasy about the person lurking in the darkness behind the killers.

'The Greek police are just incompetent,' said Stelios. 'That's why they can't catch them. You know that British detectives now use examples from the Greek police as training tips on what not to do.' Lighting a cigar, he went on. 'Of course, there's no tradition of good detectives here. We never had much crime in Greece – no serial killers, and hardly any burglaries. So there was no Greek Sherlock Holmes or police fiction either. Anyway, the anti-terrorism branch was always the cushiest job in the police force. Everyone wanted a position there; good pay, no uniform, no office hours, little trips to Washington . . . and with a job like that, no incentive to find the terrorists.'

Our host was more optimistic than Stelios that the end of the story was within sight. Alexis had played a significant role in making the Greek public aware of the reality of 17 November's crimes in his articles and television programmes. In fact, he had already uncovered so much about what was really going on that he'd been given a police guard on a motorbike. It was handy for nipping around town and beating the traffic, but it was an unpleasant daily reminder that terrorism was still a threat in Athens.

According to Alexis, the Scotland Yard detectives who arrived in Greece after Brigadier Saunders's murder were working purposefully and discreetly.

'The English police are giving the Greeks a system,' he said. 'And they've promised to remain here until they find the killers. They've started the investigation completely from scratch, going right back to the beginning of the story. Unlike the Americans, who've behaved like cowboys. They paid Greek police for exclusive tips, listed Greece's left-wing journalists as most-wanted suspects, and they've even accused the government of being involved. They keep on stirring up the antagonism which has always been part of American dealings with Greece over the terrorists.

'It's a wonderful irony though,' he went on. 'The aim of 17 November was to get rid of all the elements of American Imperialism, NATO and globalization and to keep Greece Greek. But in the end they've succeeded in filling the country with the very people they wanted to keep out – the FBI, Scotland Yard and all the rest of them.'

Soon after the party, we went out to dinner with a large group of friends and acquaintances in a built-up district called Ambelokipoi (meaning 'Vine-gardens'); the area was once green slopes covered in vineyards. The evening was hot and we met at Balthazar, a restaurant in the garden of an old neoclassical house. I remembered the place from the 1980s as one of the new wave of fashionable bars I visited on trips to the capital from provincial Nafplio. At that time, bars were the latest craze. Young Greeks were enthusiastically abandoning the drinking habits of their fathers and grandfathers; a glass of ouzo with food was being replaced by quantities of vodka, cocktails and whisky, not to mention the odd snort of cocaine. The place had now become more slick and stylish, and we drank smart, new Greek wine in bottles with elegant labels and ate self-consciously genuine, 'Mediterranean' food.

I was introduced to a tall, kind-faced man called Yiorgos Momferratos. His glasses and slightly shy, intelligent gaze gave him the air of an academic, though he worked as an investment banker. I wasn't surprised when we got around to talking about the terrorist group 17 November. It was exactly two years since Saunders had been murdered and there had just been a much-publicized memorial service for him and other victims of terrorism in Greece. Yiorgos told me about it; he'd been there, he said. He added quietly that his father had been murdered by the 17 November group too. He looked calm and spoke fluently, but admitted that he had spent most of the last seventeen years frozen and speechless on the subject.

'The families of Greece's terrorist victims always felt terrible shame as well as grief,' he explained. It was a disgrace to be associated with one of the people 'executed' by 17 November, and it's only now that the suffering and pain is coming out into the open.

'There was the attitude that my father deserved what he got in some way,' said Yiorgos. 'That unlike the so-called "innocent victims" – the drivers or passers-by – he was guilty, and being "punished" for his wrongdoings.' A part of society always sided with the murderers, who in turn exploited the Left's frustrations to justify their violence.

It was in 1985, just at the time when Greek youth were discovering the pleasures of late-night sessions in the disco-bar, when Yiorgos's father and his driver were shot. Nikos

Momferratos was the editor of the best-selling, right-wing newspaper *Apoyevmatini*, and 17 November justified their 'punishment' on the grounds that Momferratos was responsible for the press campaign of 'misinformation and systematic distortion of the truth' against the Greek people. When Yiorgos heard his father had been killed, he was twenty-three.

'I was doing military service in the Navy,' he said. 'Normally, people were given a week of compassionate leave, but they only gave me three days. It was never explained why. I had my own personal differences with my father, but I was made to feel as though he was a pariah.'

Yiorgos admitted that he barely even spoke to his wife about the subject until about a year before, although 'three years of psychoanalysis had woken me up to my anger about the situation'. The turning point was when Saunders's widow spoke out.

'She gave a human dimension to the murders,' said Yiorgos. Now, he had helped found a protest group against terrorism in Greece called No More. He was even giving press conferences.

'I've finally spoken to my children,' he added softly. 'For the first time, I was able to tell them positive things about their grandfather – to let them be proud of him.'

* * *

Two weeks later, all of Athens was in uproar. A man had been badly injured by his own bomb, when it exploded accidentally in the port of Piraeus. Near him were some grenades and a gun, which turned out to have been used in several 17 November killings. He was taken to the central Evangelismos hospital, and was in a critical condition on life support. Police had already released his picture and named him as Savvas Xiros. It was a momentous time, when twenty-seven years of dark fantasies were suddenly flooded with light. It seemed unbelievable that the menacing threat, which had remained invisible for so long, had been unmasked.

The careless bomber turned out to be an icon painter and the son of a priest. One of ten children, Xiros was originally from Icaria, an island which was once a place of exile for left-wingers. Its people are known for their anarchic and eccentric ways; even local shopkeepers change their opening hours on a whim, some preferring the middle of the night. Aged forty, Xiros now lived in Athens, but he had spent several years in the isolated monasteries of Mount Athos in northern Greece, where he learned his trade and shared the monks' ascetic life.

We all scrutinized the photographs, searching for marks of evil, or some indication of Xiros's guilt, but he looked disappointingly ordinary. In fact, his face was rather attractive, with a shock of dark, curly hair and slightly chubby cheeks. One photograph showed him younger, with a beard and long hair, throwing back his head in laughter. Could he really be one of the untouchable terrorists? Was this one of the men whose threat was so great that the Americans called them (somewhat exaggeratedly, given the thousands dead in Northern Ireland) 'Europe's most lethal terrorists'? Everyone we knew was phoning one another in shock, unable to take in that this was actually happening. Television reports showed a dignified old priest with a long grey beard arriving at the hospital, accompanied by a plump elderly woman with strong worker's arms and a black hairnet. They were Xiros's parents. The priest spoke to the gathered press who were so excited they could barely control their cameras:

'It's a set-up. My son is a good person.'

Within an hour of the explosion, the police had arrived at a flat belonging to the terrorists. There had been a key in Xiros's pocket, but there were signs that the police were prepared. Neighbours recognized Xiros from the television, and said they'd thought the place was used for illicit trysts; they'd noticed mysterious comings and goings. When the police went in, they found anti-tank rockets, guns, grenades, wigs and the group's red flag with its five-pointed star. There were boxes full of papers, which turned out to be carefully recorded minutes of meetings and plans. The discovery of a typewriter and computer was an emotional moment, as it was at first believed that they had been used to write their proclamations, which were published in the Greek press after each attack. As weapons, words had probably been just as powerful as the revolvers and automatics. Soon, other safe houses and weapons caches were opened up. It was an incredible relief, like the bursting of a boil.

The next days were a time of complete obsession with Xiros. Everyone became an expert on terrorism. We all felt a buzz of adrenaline, knowing we were witnessing history, but nobody was quite sure what to believe. Conspiracy theories abounded; surely it couldn't be as simple as it seemed?

'What if the police planted the bag with the gun?'

'If they did, was it the British, the Americans or the Greeks?'

'Was Xiros sacrificed for some purpose by his terrorist colleagues?'

'What if he dies?'

The media were so frenzied that journalists were improvising wildly. They were like a pack of hounds let off the leash, and didn't know where to turn first. As usual, there was little respect for truth or ethics; anybody willing to talk was described as an expert, and extraordinary theories and 'revelations' were aired throughout the day and night. Friends, neighbours and acquaintances of the terrorist were unearthed. They described him as 'a quiet kid' and a 'good person' who never discussed politics. Xiros turned out to be divorced; he was supposed to be getting married that summer to his pretty, Spanish girlfriend

Alicia, who was a make-up artist. She became a daily feature in news reports, shouting 'Vultures!' at the reporters every time they harassed her outside the hospital.

Commentators of every kind were trotted out. Within a day of Xiros's arrest, even monks on the 'Holy Mountain' of Athos were showing the cameramen around the monastery chapels to view his wall paintings and icons. They helpfully pointed out the Byzantine script of his signature.

After a few days, Xiros woke up from his coma. It seemed he wasn't going to die. He had no idea of the mayhem he'd created, as he hadn't been allowed visitors. There were bomb scares near his hospital, and police were rumoured to have rounded up other suspects, but little was being given away. All of a sudden, the police had become careful, circumspect, and professional, and were said to be methodically trawling for forensic evidence. We glimpsed them on television in bullet-proof vests, sinister black balaclavas and dark glasses, jumping in and out of jeeps. The Greek public had changed too, and was now fanatically anti-terrorist. We'd all forgotten that just a few months ago, polls showed that about one in four Greeks 'agreed with the terrorists' positions'.

I called Yiorgos Momferratos, who said that the victims' relations had been thrown into emotional turmoil.

'We are excited, depressed, and hopeful – it's a very different experience for each person. Now we are actually seeing who held the pistol, it's quite a shock. It's weird when a myth gets a face.'

As the police started to arrest Xiros's fellow assassins, the story only became more unlikely; it was turning into a family tragedy. Among the assortment of ordinary-looking killers were two of Xiros's brothers, and another group consisting of some cousins and their *koumbaros*. Greek families are nothing if not loyal. The Xiros paterfamilias couldn't believe it:

'They grew up with Christ,' he repeated like a mantra. One brother was the plump, shifty-eyed Christodoulos, who made traditional musical instruments. The forty-four-year-old had been visiting his brother in hospital and chatting confidently with the reporters about the 'mistake'.

'They'll be arresting me next,' he had joked confidently. The younger brother, Vassilis, filled police in on the group's slang.

'We called money "lettuces," guns "pens," bombs "baskets," rockets "pipes," and when we spoke of a person's murder we said we'd "do something for him".'

According to the press, there was little ideology in the terrorists' lives; they'd carried out numerous violent robberies, and had houses all over the place. Other commentators said they had their ideology all right (after all, so did Hitler and Stalin), but that it was tragically flawed to link any ideals with murder. Historians compared them to the bandits who had plagued Greece in the nineteenth and early twentieth centuries. When Greek brigands kidnapped and ultimately killed a group of aristocratic British travellers in 1854, the extent of revulsion and anti-Greek feeling in Britain was just as strong as that which followed Saunders's murder. There had also been political pressure on Greece to wipe out the scourge of bandits, who, like their twentieth-century terrorist counterparts, maintained a somewhat romantic public image in spite of their vicious ways. As recently as the 1920s, the members of an infamous gang consisted of several sons of a priest. They killed, kidnapped and robbed their way to notoriety and eventual execution.

That the face under the terrorists' mask was an Orthodox Christian one seemed at first bizarre. It gave a particularly Greek twist to the tragedy, though there were links between religion and terrorism in other countries too; the Italian Red Brigades had connections with the Catholic Church, and Ulrike Meinhoff (of the German Bader-Meinhoff terrorists) was a priest's daughter. The Xiros brothers' father suggested in public that his sons should pray, and Savvas, the hapless bomber, asked to confess to a priest and to be allowed to live a Christian life, painting his icons. It is generally accepted that an icon painter should be a believer; he should take Holy Communion before he paints a picture, which will become a holy object, imbued with the Spirit. It was truly shocking that such a person should also be plotting murders. Another of the detainees had a theologian father, and there were rumours that some of the stolen money had been donated to the Church.

It seemed inappropriate, to say the least, that Marxist terrorists should have such a direct link with the Church, but then historically, the Orthodox clergy often played a fundamental role in supporting an independent and even rebellious spirit among Greeks. When Greeks began their revolutionary movement in 1821, much of the Orthodox clergy (if not the leadership) was a staunch and powerful ally. Contemporary pictures show priests standing proudly with the massed ranks of rebels: *klephtes* (literally 'thieves', but referring to the bandits who became guerrilla fighters); rich captains from the islands; and the dispersed Greeks and philhellenes from around the Balkans and Europe who supported the cause.

The clergy were never separate from the Greek people; their concerns were the same. During the Greek Civil War, priests were to be found on the side of the Communists (who were not opposed to the Church in Greece) as well as with the right-wing government forces. They experienced the same deprivations and violence as the rest of the population. A similar divide occurred during the Junta too, and while the Colonels used the Church to justify their regime, they also treated left-wing priests badly. The

Xiros brothers' father brought up his ten children with a severe, austere spirituality based on the extreme, apocalyptic version of Orthodoxy preached by the notoriously right-wing Bishop Kantiotis. Living in dire poverty on a priest's measly salary, they often went hungry.

The jubilation at finally finding the terrorists was mixed with a curious disappointment; the ghostly killers (the 'phantoms' as they were called in the press) were being revealed as depressingly ordinary. Now that the myth was crumbling into sordid reality, people were muttering: 'What happened to the guerrillas with a sacred cause?' Above all, people wanted to know who the leader was. These people might be the hit men, but where was the intellectual who wrote the announcements? Where was the spirit behind these decades of fear?

Following up on leads gleaned at the icon-painter's hospital bedside, Athens's police primed a local policeman on Lipsi, a remote island near the Turkish coast. The young man (who became known only by his first name, Socrates) was to call his seniors in Athens if there was any sign of an Athenian known as Michalis. Socrates must have been shocked, however, at the reaction when he rang them to say that a certain Michalis was just leaving his holiday house to catch the 'Flying Dolphin' hydrofoil. Frogmen, plain-clothed detectives, and police boats were dispatched to Lipsi, and the anti-terrorist squad were sent out with the first means available – a bright red fire brigade helicopter.

Socrates was instructed to capture the suspect, and quickly reported back to Athens that he had arrested the fifty-eight-year-old man known as an economics professor, who had been coming to the island for years. He had apparently been intending to escape from a neighbouring island across the few kilometres of sea to the Turkish coast. Greece's most wanted suspect spent the next hour chained to a radiator in Lipsi's little police station. Nobody recorded Socrates' reaction when his prisoner announced high-handedly: 'I don't talk with traitors.' The word he used was *Nenekos*, the name of the infamous Greek who collaborated with the Ottoman overlord, Ibrahim Pasha, and the implication was that the police were the poodles of imperialist powers such as the USA.

Michalis Economou turned out to be a pseudonym for Alexandros Yiotopoulos, and he was not a professor but a translator. Before long, he had been sped across the Aegean back to Athens. Police announced immediately that fingerprints and handwriting linked him with a 17 November safe house, and that there was 'evidence of his involvement with the planning of terrorist attacks'. Photographs showed a rather handsome, tall, white-haired man, with a stubborn face and sympathetic eyes – who, Vassilis pointed out, looked very like my father. Yiotopoulos was born and lived in France, and his father had been a close comrade of Trotsky (ironically ending up a miserable anti-Communist). His long-term partner was a Frenchwoman, and he had been on police wanted lists for three decades.

So many loose ends were being tied up that there was a bit of a tangle. Everyone seemed to know the terrorists, or at least know someone who did. Not everyone denounced them, and there was some criticism about police treatment of the detainees; Savvas Xiros was not given access to a lawyer for two months. As more arrests followed, the terrorists' faces became as familiar as celebrities and we knew them by their first names. By the end of the summer, the first rembetika song about 'Savvas and Alicia' had been written. It was a sign that the musical world had recognized their place in the dark underground realm of doomed romances, illegal activities and prison cells.

It was hard to take in that such pandemonium and terror had been wreaked by people who seemed so run-of-the-mill. They may have had extreme political views, but they were certainly not monsters. They were people we all could easily have known. Greeks had unearthed some demons, but they were also facing the darker side of their own character; it was as though we were all guilty. In the hot, summer sunshine, we were looking into a dark chasm; Orpheus stepping down into the shadows of death in the underworld. It was also unclear what would happen when the ghostly enemy who had haunted a people for so long was finally removed. What would life be like without the threat? It was a bit like the line in Cavafy's famous poem 'Waiting for the Barbarians':

And now, what will become of us without barbarians?

In Athens there was jubilation. Alexis was spending so much time reporting the developments he hardly slept. He was writing a book about the whole saga, and believed that this was the end of 17 November. The Public Order Minister had become the unlikely hero of the moment, and the Greek police had never been so happy and popular. In England, Heather Saunders was reported as being 'elated':

'I'm not going away until all of them have been caught and punished,' the widow said to reporters.

Even the pitiful, gaunt figure of the Xiros brothers' father appeared to be relieved that the truth was out. Father Triandafyllos had publicly asked for Mrs Saunders's forgiveness, for the sins of his sons:

'They made the mistake of turning their back on the Church,' he said. 'Whoever has done wrong must pay. And he will pay. Either here or in the life hereafter. It is better that we pay here.'

CHAPTER 15

GOOD ROOTING

It takes hold from the eyes
And to the lips descends;
And from the lips to the heart,
It roots and never ends.
'How Love Takes Hold',
Greek folk song

'It's time we went to my house in the mountains,' announced Vassilis. 'I've been meaning to go ever since we moved here, and it's July now. We've got to decide what to do.' He had a strange look; a secretive smile with a touch of melancholy. I recalled the long phone conversations he had with his father during the year before his death; wood for the window frames, stone for the fireplace . . . The house had belonged to Vassilis's godfather who migrated to America, and then left it to his favourite godson. By then, Vassilis's family had moved down to the flourishing, busy plain, and the house became run-down and unused. The restoration, which my father-in-law began, was left unfinished and Dikastro, the village, was gradually withering away as the old people who lived there died off. It weighed on Vassilis's mind that he should make his mark on (or at least claim) the only piece of land and building in Greece that actually belonged to him.

Before we left, Stella rang up about my application for citizenship. I'd been hoping to complete the process before everybody left in August, but in spite of her efforts, the news wasn't good.

'I don't think we'll be able to get it completed until at least September,' she said. 'There are still some details to sort out, and nothing happens over the summer.' I still liked the idea of belonging officially in Greece; of being able to say: 'This is how *we* do things in Greece,' and 'What will *we* vote at the next elections?' But I didn't mind about the papers any more. It was now exactly a year since we'd arrived, and I understood how far we had all come in that time. What I'd hoped to confirm with formalities and ID cards was happening anyway; I'd started to love and understand my adopted city, and to find my place in it without any bureaucrat's seal of approval. As in so many circumstances, Cavafy's poem 'Ithaca' was applicable; you should keep your aim – your own Ithaca – in mind, but concentrate on the 'marvellous journey'.

We left Athens on a very hot Friday afternoon. Weather reports warned we were heading for forty degrees. The children were listless, and Vassilis arrived back from work looking crumpled and overheated. It was time to go up to the cool mountains which, after all, was what people did in the old days, before tourists made sun, sand, sea and sex the requisite ingredients for a successful summer. At the traffic lights in Athens, Pakistanis were selling small bottles of frozen water. We put them against our foreheads, feeling the drips run down our necks, taking lip-numbing sips as the ice blocks melted.

'My godfather was my grandfather's brother,' Vassilis reminded me. 'The two of them went to America in the early 1920s when everyone was leaving. People were terribly poor. Whole villages were abandoned, and there were places where there were no young men left at all.' Vassilis had found their names in the Ellis Island register through the Internet, among the hundreds of thousands of men who left their families behind and set off on the difficult sea voyage to the USA in the hope of success, adventure and making some money.

We had some old sepia photographs of Vassilis's grandfather Christos and his brother Yiannis. Christos had been an Evzone – a soldier in the National Guard – before he left. He is solid and tall, staring gravely back at the camera from his pose among studio pot plants. Dressed in a military tunic, leggings and clogs, he had the long, black tassels of his cap draped graciously like hair over one shoulder, and his hand rests on his sword. I felt strangely touched that my daughters should be descended from this straight-gazing, strong-looking Evzone, who looked as though he was from another world. A true *palikari* – the brave young man of so many songs and poems. I framed his picture, and hung him in a collection of family photos on the stairs, next to some pale, wide-eyed children in sailor suits – my Russian grandparents. The pictures had probably been taken within a few years of each other, before they knew that they were all destined to leave their countries.

Today, there are around five million diaspora Greeks (seven million if you count every kind of intermarried descendant) around the world. Melbourne is the third largest Greek city after Athens and Thessaloniki. The Odyssean approach to life suits

Greeks, and though their wanderlust was often exacerbated by deprivation and political upheaval, the impulse was there all along. The ancients were great travellers, and after the Fall of Constantinople in 1453, Greeks became café owners and physicians in London, goldsmiths and shipwrights in Venice, scholars in Milan and icon painters in Moscow. But these wanderers keep their own Ithaca in mind; those who spend a lifetime abroad often come home to die.

Even the most remote village has its returnees, with their money and their foreign ways. Sometimes they despise their own countrymen, who in turn don't know what to make of these hybrid creatures. I realized that Vassilis wanted to avoid this trap. Our expedition to find his place in the land of his forefathers was an attempt to close the circle, to bring a real sense of homecoming and belonging. After his father died, the unused house came to represent a means of continuing his father's work and passing a piece of Greek earth on to his children. As Kazantzakis said, the notion of 'paternal soil' rather than 'fatherland' is 'something deeper, more modest, and it is composed of age-old pulverized bones'.

Christos and Yiannis returned to Dikastro after six years in Ohio, but Yiannis didn't stay.

'The whole point of his house is that it's based on a tragic love story,' said Vassilis. Anna and Lara craned forward on the back seat to listen. 'Before Yiannis left Dikastro he'd been in love with a beautiful girl in the village over the valley. He wanted to marry her, but her family wouldn't agree as he was too poor. "You haven't even got a house," she said to him. Nobody had any money in those villages then, but you needed a home. So Yiannis went off to America with his brother, dreaming of the day he'd return with enough money to claim his bride and build a house. After several years, the two young men made the long ship journey back to Piraeus, took the train to Lamia, and finally, there was the mule ride up into the mountains. Yiannis's first questions after greeting his family were about his sweetheart. That was when he learned that she'd married someone else. He was devastated, and determined to have his own form of revenge.'

Yiannis returned to America, and when he came back to Greece for the second time, some years later, it was with all the trappings of someone who had made money: fancy suits and hats, wonderful presents and fat cigars. Unlike his brother who joined the restaurant business, the refuge of so many Greek emigrants in the USA, Yiannis started as a shoemaker and ended up with his own successful shoemaking business. The first thing he did in Dikastro was to build a house.

'But not just any house,' said Vassilis. 'It was to be the grandest house in the village. And most important, it was to be visible from all around. He wanted his old love, her family and her husband (who was far from rich) to look out of the window and see what had become of the poor boy across the valley.' Yiannis went crazy. He brought in the best stonemasons, carpenters, decorators and craftsmen, and ordered them to make him a three-storey building. On top was an unusual round tower, topped with another smaller dome bearing a spectacular brass bird weathervane. By village standards it was a mansion. No one could have missed it.

The house was also a folly; Yiannis never lived there. He found a Greek bride, took her back to Ohio, and their children, grandchildren and great-grandchildren are still there. But Yiannis came back to Greece from time to time, and it was on one of these visits, when he was already a solid sixty-year-old with an American twang that he was asked to stand as godfather to his infant great-nephew Vassilis. Within a few years the grand *folie d'amour* was to be humbled. An earthquake in 1963 cracked the walls on the tower and the top floor, and they were pulled down. It became just like another solid, two-storey village house. Now, if you didn't know, you couldn't tell about its glamorous past. Vassilis's family went there for summer holidays when he was a child, but no one visited now.

As we progressed further north along the main Athens–Thessaloniki highway, we passed Thermopylae. We stopped the car at a commemorative statue of Leonidas, the Spartan who died there fighting the Persians in 480 BC. There were two coachloads of teenagers on an expedition, taking photographs and shouting. Vassilis told the children about Ephialtes' night-time betrayal of Leonidas to the enemy; his treachery was thought to be so despicable that his name is still used as the word for nightmare. My contribution to the discussion was an Edward Lear limerick:

> *There was an old man of Thermopylae*
> *Who never did anything properly . . .*

We headed away from the sea at Lamia and snaked up into the mountains. The way was full of childhood landmarks for Vassilis.

'That rock up there is where I'd go with my friends and we'd have competitions to see who could pee furthest,' he said. 'And just here is where I once lay down in the middle of the road as a dare, and waited for the bus. The driver was so frightened and furious at having almost killed me that he got out of the bus and chased me down the road so he could spank me.'

After four hours, just as it was getting dark, we finally arrived, and parked in the small village square by the church. Fireflies zipped erratically, and there was an electric trill of cicadas sounding like a chorus of distant alarm clocks. Some old men stared curiously from the coffee shop. Climbing a steep flight of steps and following a winding path, we went to get the key to Vassilis's house from his Uncle Mitsos. He and his wife Marousso had moved back for their retirement in the 1980s after thirty-five years in Piraeus, and they were always pleased to see visitors.

'Welcome! Welcome!' they called. We replied with the formulaic: 'Well found!' as they kissed us all and exclaimed over the children.

'Come in, come in!' insisted Aunt Marousso, a dramatically pear-shaped woman with a still-beautiful face, elegantly plucked eyebrows arching over intelligent blue eyes, and a sculpted wave of grey hair. We were unable to avoid the rituals of hospitality, which are bound with obligations; both sides ignore them at their peril. The worst kind of person is someone who doesn't even offer a glass of water to a visitor, and a guest who doesn't respect his host's generosity is a disrespectful, ungrateful wretch.

We entered the small courtyard of their old stone house, passing piles of logs cut for the brutal winter, workshops with tools, and a dark room filled with barrels, smelling of sour wood and alcohol.

'That's where I make the tsipouro [a clear spirit],' said Uncle Mitsos, showing us around, his lithe, bony ease belying his eighty-three years. 'You must try some.' We sat up on the rickety wooden veranda, looking out across the valley to the lights of the village where the godfather's faithless sweetheart had lived. Her grandchildren were probably middle-aged now, and it was unlikely that they still lived there; these mountain villages had never been easy places. The Ottoman overlords left them well alone and even the Nazis only came once and then retreated; there was no point in controlling the back of beyond. These days, Dikastro is a ghost of its former self; a self-managed old people's home where the aged come back to die. It is unclear what will happen when this elderly generation is gone, within a decade or two.

An assortment of cats slunk across the vine canopy (hung with tiny, unripe grapes) and slithered past our legs. Aunt Marousso brought tall glasses of cool water on a tray and a selection of Turkish delight and biscuits for the children. We tried the tsipouro too, feeling the hot tingling firewater run down the throat and into the stomach. The cool, pine-scented breeze was the greatest luxury after the baked cement heat of Athens.

'Even in the summer you sleep with a blanket here,' said Aunt Marousso – high praise in a country where summer nights can end up as a sweaty, insomniac tussle with an overheated sheet.

Eventually, we left, taking the large key for the godfather's house.

'*Kaloriziko* – good rooting!' called Uncle Mitsos behind us, using the customary wish for a fortunate life in a new house. In Greek, finding your roots is not merely discovering the place of your forebears, but has implications of destiny and life force. Your *riziko* (from the word 'root') is your fate. From Homeric times, the uprooted tree has been a metaphor for death.

We walked in through the small back courtyard which still had its own well (an unaccustomed luxury when it was built), and climbed the outside steps to the heavy, wooden front door. None of us said anything, but there were many unanswered questions in our minds: Would this become our place? Would we restore it? Could it be part of an Athenian life? I waited impatiently, full of anticipation as Vassilis unlocked the heavy front door.

Anna and Lara ran through first, chasing around the two bedrooms, looking under old brass bedsteads, opening trunks full of forgotten clothes, photographs, books and bedclothes. I walked slowly on the dusty floorboards, examining some old family photographs which were framed and hung, haphazardly on the walls: the godfather with American-looking, horn-rimmed glasses and a small moustache; Vassilis's tyrannical grandmother Styliani – looking seductively severe with eagle eyes and a smart fur collar; and his father as a handsome, smiling, teenage soldier with a dark slick of brilliantined hair.

The ceilings were all painted with decorations: swags of vines, stars, country flowers and an assortment of flags including French, German, Russian, Turkish (not British), and above all, the blue stripes and cross of the godfather's native land and the bold stars and stripes of his adopted country.

'My godfather used to send me presents and clothes from America,' said Vassilis, sifting through some photographs in an old suitcase. 'He gave me clothes which were completely different from what children were wearing then in Greece.' He picked out a photo of a round-faced boy of about five, with a crew cut, and dressed in a fancy little jacket and matching shorts, with white ankle socks and sandals. 'I was always well dressed,' he laughed. 'It was like that popular TV series we all watched in the 1970s – *The Uncle from America*.'

A little later, we walked down the path to the square and Dikastro's only surviving grocery-café-occasional taverna. Paper tablecloths were spread on a table outside the shop; Uncle Mitsos had arranged for some food to be made for us. The proprietor and other customers were friendly and interested: 'Aah, so you're Kostas the teacher's son,' they said, shaking Vassilis's hand. We were brought wine in a copper-coloured jug, a platter piled with cold cuts of goat, a big dish of fried potatoes and a salad. That was what the establishment ran to on special occasions. It looked modest, but the tastes were honest and good; the mountain tomatoes were small but startlingly sweet and delicious, the potatoes fresh and home-grown, and the goat was, like a dark, gamy mutton . . . inescapably goaty.

Just as we were polishing off the food, a large group of Vassilis's Athenian relations trooped into the square. By coincidence, all three of his first cousins (Uncle Yiannis and Aunt Xanthe's children) had come to Dikastro that weekend too. The two sons had recently bought a house there, and now organized winter trips from Athens; men-only affairs, where they roasted vast quantities of meat on the fire, drank too much, slept in sleeping bags and went on hikes up to the snowline. This time though, they'd brought their wives and children, and their sister (who hadn't been there for fifteen years) had arrived with her family too. The wives had tight, white, city clothes, manicured nails and gold jewellery, the children had skateboards and Walkmans, and the men were cheery and animated. They had been Vassilis's city cousins in the old days (the brothel-crawling, cinema-heckling ones) but now, they too were staking their claim back in the village. There was a noisy round of greetings and backslapping, and more tables were set up.

Tired from the journey, we climbed up the path to the godfather's house at around midnight, leaving the cousins in the square, drinking wine and telling noisy stories. Lying in one of the brass beds (forcibly pressed up against Vassilis in the lumpy trench which had subsided in the centre), I could hear the voices getting louder. The cousins' children had started skateboarding too, banging the boards with a clatter as they jumped and twisted. The church bell struck each quarter of the hour with a bold, resounding chime. It was suspended in a bell tower a matter of metres away from our bedroom window and at about the same height. At one-thirty I wandered onto the balcony and looked down into the sound bowl of the village square. Quite a party was going on; the guffawing was only increasing. Finally, at some time after the three-fifteen bell, the revellers drifted off, and we eventually fell asleep with pillows over our heads.

At about seven a.m., the church bells began pealing so vigorously that our bed vibrated. I cursed the countryside, the village, bells and the noise that is such a vital and beloved element in Greek life. Why is it, I wondered, that music is blared as loudly as possible, television and radio are natural backgrounds to discussions, street salesmen have vans with booming loudspeakers, and conversations shouted across balconies or yelled for the hell of it are so often preferable to a quiet tête-à-tête?

'Why are you shouting?' Vassilis would ask me. 'You're becoming like a Greek.' Even more often, he'd shout: 'I'm not shouting, I'm just expressing myself.'

That morning it became entirely clear to me why the Turks forbade the Greeks their noisy church bells; they were provocative, unequivocally joyful, proud, boastful things, which hinted at celebration, victory and merriment. During the Ottoman years, Orthodox worshippers beat wooden planks instead, as the call to church, but naturally, after Greek independence, bells were rung with a vengeance. In many cases they are now amplified, which was certainly the case of the service ensuing that morning. Soon an off-key chanting with the booming decibels of a rave was bouncing off the bedroom walls.

'It's for all the old people who can't get to the church,' explained Vassilis, looking haggard, and getting up to make some coffee. 'This way they can hear the service from their homes.'

The morning was a bright, sparkling reproach to sulking, and eventually, the grumpy exhaustion I'd felt at seven evaporated in the almost fizzy, clear mountain air. When the reverberating church service ended several hours later, Lara and Anna went off to play football with some of their newly discovered cousins, and I took a cup of coffee and my book out onto the wooden veranda. It was hung with a rampant vine, which twisted the length of the balcony, hanging from the supports and creating a luscious, lime-green bower.

After a while, I heard voices below in the garden. I peered down through the vine leaves and saw two of Vassilis's cousins with measuring tapes, pacing out the small triangle of land adjacent to our house. They looked fresh and bouncy in spite of the partying, and were evidently full of plans. Uncle Mitsos was there watching them with a non-committal expression.

'The boundary shouldn't be on this side of the cherry tree, it should be at least a metre back on that side,' said one.

'It's divided into three, so that bit must belong to us,' said another. 'The fence should go through the woodshed.' I had only just spent one night in this house, but already I found myself bristling indignantly as I tried to eavesdrop. What on earth were they up to in the small, tangled patch of wasteland abutting 'our' garden? I felt as absurdly and unjustifiably defensive as if my children's home were being threatened by marauders.

Vassilis joined his cousins politely, though his expression was a little icy; the small cherry tree they were quibbling over had been planted by his father. The cousins were jovial and bluff as they put away their measures.

'We're just thinking about our sister,' they explained. 'We've got our own place anyway down the road.' These were delicate matters. Greek inheritance laws are brutally fair, splitting up everything equally between siblings, so pieces of land are divided and subdivided over and again, with cousins taking little slivers of their grandparents' properties. Lawyers spend much of their energy over boundary disputes, and cases of stalemate leave houses unoccupied and land unused over decades. Often, there are distant diaspora cousins whose signatures are never forthcoming; perhaps the Ohio descendants of the godfather could become a case in point.

Leaving the men discussing cesspits and mobile phones, I went off for a stroll. The village was surrounded by chestnuts, walnuts, pines and oaks, and little streams trickled by. I wandered past well-tended gardens with dahlias, roses and chickens, and stopped to admire a vegetable plot. Some old people sitting outside the neighbouring house greeted me curiously, making it clear I should explain my purpose there.

'Aaah, you're Kostas's *nyfi*,' one woman exclaimed when the connections were made. 'Taki,' she called enthusiastically to a man inside, 'it's the teacher's daughter-in-law.' I enjoyed arriving in a new place and finding that my position was already marked out.

On my way home I met Vassilis who'd come in search of me. He seemed to have recovered from the measuring-tape incident and the cousins had parted on good terms. We sat down on a stone wall by an abandoned house, under a fig tree which was emerging miraculously from the stones. The figs were still unripe, but the warm leaves gave off a heady, erotic smell of deep summer.

We meandered down the hill to the main church, and lit a candle for Vassilis's father. The church had been rebuilt on its fifteenth-century site at around the same time as the godfather's house; it looked as though the same decorator had painted some of the decorations, as identical yellow eight-pointed stars were visible on the ceilings. All around were icons and wall paintings of saints, the 'All Holy' (Virgin) and Christ, which had been paid for by villagers; the sponsors' names and the dates of the work were clearly marked in Byzantine script in the lower corner of each section. We found Uncle Mitsos, with his patronymic and surname in full ('Dimitris son-of-Christos Papadimitriou'), Vassilis's father, and a panel listing the godfather and various other Papadimitriou family benefactors.

'Mitsos asked if we'd pay for a section so they can complete the church paintings,' said Vassilis. 'I've given him some money, and they'll put our names: I'll be "Vassilis son-of-Konstantinos Papadimitriou" and they'll put you in as Sophia.' People liked putting their names up in the village; the square has a prominent notice commemorating Vassilis's Athenian Uncle Yiannis, who replaced the dirt track leading up to Dikastro with a proper asphalted road in the late 1970s, when he was General Secretary in the Ministry for Public Works. You don't get to a position like that without doing something for 'your place'.

We left Anna and Lara playing happily with their cousins, and walked out of the village.

'I want to go and find the Great Spring,' said Vassilis. 'I haven't been there since I was a child.' We walked along the road in the sunshine. There was a pleasant, green heat smelling of damp leaves; more reminiscent of Russian summer than the familiar Greek burnout.

'Uncle Mitsos took me to see some other plots of land,' continued Vassilis. 'We've got a share there too. His patch has a cherry tree and sweet corn and vines, and mine has three walnut trees. But Mitsos hates the walnuts; he says they have bitter roots and a heavy shade. The roots prevent other things growing nearby, and if you sleep underneath you wake up groggy. He told me to cut them and plant something better.'

Pausing by a giant evergreen oak, Vassilis explained that it was supposedly over 1,000 years old. 'It's one of the so-called "elevated trees,"' he said. 'They used to put special charms and blessings inside the bark and the tree supposedly protected the villagers from illnesses and harm. There's a ring of these old trees all around the village, and it's always been said that whoever cut even the smallest branch from them would be cursed. That's how they lasted so long.'

We left the road and walked up a small path to a glade where ancient plane trees rose up above great boulders and a gushing spring of cold mountain water emerged from the earth. We sat quietly on one of the rocks, looking down through the wooded slopes.

'I'm going to fix the house,' Vassilis announced decisively. 'Whatever happens, I want it to be there, ready. I want to do it for my father; it's his place here, and I want it to be ours too. Even if it's just somewhere to go when we're old . . .'

At that point, all the superficial distractions evaporated. It didn't matter that we were committing ourselves to a crumbling house, in a dying village in the middle of nowhere, with amplified bells and potential land disputes. Just as you can't choose your parents, you can't choose your village; this wasn't a question of holidays, but something that went much deeper. It was the point where Vassilis embraced his homecoming to Greece, and I confirmed a new connection to the land. Where else would I have my name written in the church, and an old uncle who admiringly called me a 'jackal' for being bright and sprightly?

I went to the mouth of the spring and drank. The enormous plane tree behind Vassilis was like a great beast emerging from the hillside. Its knobbly heavy trunk reared upwards and its snaking roots were as thick as a child's torso. The roots had gradually become revealed as the earth was eroded from around them, and they had grown a scaly bark. Over the decades, if not centuries, they'd become branches. In Dikastro, we too had found some roots. Now the question was what kind of tree we would grow.